Ecclesiological Investigations

Series Editor

Gerard Mannion

Volume: 17

The Crisis of Confidence in the Catholic Church

Other titles in the series:

Further Praise for *The Crisis of Confidence in the Catholic Church*

'This sobering yet hopeful assessment of the challenges facing the Catholic Church at the outset of a new pontificate could not be more timely. Father Helmick situates current travails in the context of a long history of light and shadows, in which the Good News of Jesus Christ was often obscured. In his thought-provoking analysis of where we are now, how we got here, and what needs to be done, he does not shy away from controversial issues. Even those who may differ with his diagnoses are likely to agree with his prescription—that the path to true *aggiornamenti* begins in the Gospels.'

Mary Ann Glendon, *Harvard University, USA*

'Helmick is an engaging writer, a careful researcher, and an incredibly even-handed interpreter of Catholicism today, its problems, and its resources for change. Taking Vatican II as his point of reference, he shows how many faithful and formerly faithful have been scandalized by "official" refusals of the Council's vision, as well as how Catholicism's evolving history may carry the seeds of recovery. Helmick's account is erudite yet captivating, replete with plenty of insider details, poignant or amusing recollections of the Vatican II era, and on-target readings of how various Vatican dicta come across to "people in the pews." The audience most in need of this book is the episcopacy; but the lay readers who no doubt will be more numerous will happily discover it to be a highly readable eye-opener.'

Lisa Sowle Cahill, *Boston College, USA*

'A remarkable survey of the past fifty years of Catholic experience, at once learned and accessible. Helmick issues an impassioned call for reform in the Church, but his analysis is admirably balanced and sensitive to historical context. This is a book that deserves a wide readership.'

Leslie Tentler, *The Catholic University of America, USA*

The Crisis of Confidence in the Catholic Church

Raymond G. Helmick, S.J.

Foreword by Gerard Mannion

BLOOMSBURY

LONDON · NEW DELHI · NEW YORK · SYDNEY

Bloomsbury T&T Clark

An imprint of Bloomsbury Publishing Plc

50 Bedford Square	1385 Broadway
London	New York
WC1B 3DP	NY 10018
UK	USA

www.bloomsbury.com

Bloomsbury is a registered trade mark of Bloomsbury Publishing Plc

First published 2014

© Raymond G. Helmick, S.J., 2014

British Library Cataloguing-in-Publication Data
A catalogue record for this book is available from the British Library.

ISBN: HB: 978-0-5672-2401-9
PB: 978-0-5674-6425-5
ePDF: 978-0-5675-8796-1
ePub: 978-0-5675-6566-2

Library of Congress Cataloging-in-Publication Data
Helmick, S.J., Raymond G.
The Crisis of Confidence in the Catholic Church / Raymond G. Helmick, S.J. p.cm
Includes bibliographical references and index.
ISBN 978-0-5672-2401-9 (hardcover) – ISBN 978-0-5674-6425-5 (pbk.)

Typeset by Deanta Global Publishing Services, Chennai, India
Printed and bound in Great Britain

CONTENTS

ACKNOWLEDGMENTS

9 January 2014

I wish to thank, especially, Jerome Maryon, Esq., who joined me in teaching this material as a course in the Theology Department of Boston College. His many suggestions and extensive editing work have been a major contribution to this book.

Theologian Gerard Mannion has provided me with constant encouragement as I went through this work, including my earlier book, *Living Catholic Faith in a Contentious Age* (Continuum 2010).

The many students who have had this material as a course have responded with keen and regular observations and often helped to shape my own thinking on these matters.

And finally, Anne Turton of Bloomsbury T&T Clark, Caitlin Flynn, Miriam Cantwell, Ken Bruce, and Grishma Fredric have most generously helped as the book has gone through the publishing process.

Raymond G. Helmick, S.J.

FOREWORD

Crisis and beyond: A new dawn for the Catholic Church?

In February 2013, the Roman Catholic Church was suddenly thrown into a state of liminality—a phase of its long existence wherein it was caught between a troubled past all too familiar and a future as yet unknown and so variously anticipated with hope, fear, and even trepidation. Sometimes these emotions were all felt by the same people within the church! Of course, this was not the first time the Church had endured such a state of being. In many ways, the Church was born out of such experience of liminality as the first followers of Jesus strived to follow his radically transformative good news and actions. They grew from a first-century Jewish renewal movement, during a period of liminality and upheaval for all Jewish people at that time, into a movement that traversed boundaries in every sense of the word; they took that good news from one city to another, from culture to culture, from ethnic group to ethnic group, welcoming all regardless of status, class, gender, ethnicity. Much of the story of the earliest Christians concerns how they faced crisis after crisis. And yet they endured, came through, and helped that good news transform the lives of countless other souls. As the story of the Church unfolded from century to century and from first to second and toward the third millennium, crisis would return to the life of the Church and of Christians on a periodic basis.

What was, in many ways, distinctive about February 2013 was that when, without public warning, although many had expected that one day this would happen, Pope Benedict XVI announced his resignation, the Church was placed in a position where it would not be sufficient simply to fall back upon ancient and quasiancient protocols, rituals, and realpolitik to determine its future. Nor would the Church, by necessity, be preoccupied with a period of mourning and the need to attend to appropriate memorials, protocols, and an eventual funeral for a deceased pontiff.

It was rather that the Church was offered the opportunity, however briefly, to channelize its energies elsewhere instead. It was given the chance to take stock, to look around, and try to determine where the real priorities for the Church lay. Many individuals and groups throughout the global Church began to voice their perspectives on what the Church for today and for the future most needed. Gradually some bishops and significant number of the cardinals preparing to gather in conclave, took soundings from the wider Church.

Many Catholics (and a majority of Vaticanologists and Church historians affirmed them in such a view) did not expect anything especially radical for the Church to emerge on the balcony of St Peter's Basilica whenever the cardinals had finally reached the required degree of agreement upon which of them would be the new universal shepherd to guide the Catholic Church into the twenty-first century proper. They observed, quite rightly, how the cardinal-electors had all been appointed by the two previous popes—48 by John Paul II and 67 in the much shorter pontificate of Benedict XVI.

The Roman Catholic Church has been through a period that can only be described as a "dark night" in recent decades. The turmoil and divisions were manifested in a variety of ways: from what some have called the "culture wars" to the battle for the soul and legacy of Vatican II, to the very different ways in which Catholics in different cultures, countries, and continents refract the faith and its mission; from the struggles between professional theologians and ecclesial offices and leaders, to divisions among the theological community itself; from conflict between religious orders, Rome, and episcopal conferences, to oppression and marginalization within the Church, as well as exclusion and exclusivity from and in the Church; from the clerical abuse crisis to financial scandals; from the growing and glaring social challenges of this planet that cry out for ecclesial action to ongoing wars and conflicts; and from the imperative of dialogue with other faiths, churches, and people of no faith that has sadly stalled the progress in far too many places to even the liturgy, the celebration of communion, of unity itself, which has also become a battleground. Battles over these and many other issues have made it a very draining and often exhausting period of the Church's history in which to be a Catholic.

So, when, in the Italian evening of 13 March, Cardinal Jean-Louis Tauran emerged to tell the waiting crowds and watching world the joyful news that "Habemus Papam," there was both anticipation and anxiousness around the Catholic world. In the media scrum, it was not immediately obvious to everyone who the cardinal who had actually been elected was, but when Tauran announced his chosen name, there was a gasp in so many places around the globe: the choice made by the new pope carried with it a very significant message, and so, for him and the Church in general, a very challenging set of responsibilities: the Church would now be shepherded forward into the future by *Papa Franciscus*.

No previous pope had ever dared try and live up to the responsibility of taking the name of Saint Francis of Assisi, the man who had been called by God to rebuild the Church and who had sought to bring the Church back to its radically transformative roots—above all, to be a Church of and for the poor, to embrace peace, service, dialogue, to care for nature and all creation, to follow the gospel rather than human ambition. And yet, Jorge Bergoglio, the Cardinal Archbishop of Buenos Aries, from Argentina, from "the ends of the earth" as he joked himself, had not shirked the demanding challenge. He came out onto the balcony and began his papacy as it has largely, thus far, continued: with humility, with an engaging style, and with dedication to the vision of Francis and to being open to dialogue with the world. Asking first for the blessing of the waiting people before he would take on the papal stole, he spoke of himself only as the Bishop of Rome, a deliberate statement with immense collegial and ecumenical significance. More was to follow. He renounced the right to live in the palatial papal apartment, choosing instead to live in simple rooms in the Casa Santa Marta, a guest house beside St Peter's Basilica. Latin America had its first pope, after all, and the Church had its first Pope Francis.

In the following months, his energy and vision have ushered in a period of tremendous excitement, hope, and now renewed anticipation. His key appointments, his daily homilies, his initial statements and teachings have all strived to live up to that vision of Saint Francis. He has made justice for the poor and wider questions of social justice, both his own and the Church's key priority. He has intervened to help promote peace and to denounce war and conflict, most significantly in holding a day for peace in Syria as the belligerents were pressing for an apocalyptic attack of devastation and destruction. He has given astoundingly frank, open, and revealing interviews. He has made it clear that the priority for the Church is to look forward not backward, that doctrinal minutiae and disputes are not more important than living the faith and putting it into practice itself. So far, it appears he has banished the neoexclusivism that characterized too much of the Church under his immediate predecessors. He has sought to follow Pope John XXIII's example in many respects. He wants a Church open to and engaged with the wider world. Like John XXIII before him, he, too, accentuates what people share in common rather than what divides them. And, again like John, he preaches mercy, compassion, and forgiveness rather than stern admonishments and banishment. Mercy, not moralizing, lies at the heart of the gospel—he cites Aquinas in seeing mercy as the greatest virtue of all.

He has, overnight, given renewed energy to ecumenical and interfaith ventures in dialogue. For the first time in many decades, Catholics and noncatholics alike, in tentatively yet increasingly positive, constructive, and hopeful terms, are speaking about the Church—likewise about his own office of the papacy. He has denounced ecclesial factionism and clerical ambition. His first major teaching document (following an encyclical, *Lumen Fidei* of 29 June which was in large part composed under his predecessor) was issued on 24 November 2013. Entitled *Evangelii Gaudium*, The Joy of the Gospel, it was a document that was soon being talked about around the world with its powerful messages about social and economic inequality, about the nature of the Church and its mission. Francis addresses multiple crises in this document. He speaks of the challenges "amid the crisis of communal commitments in the world."[1] He explores the financial crisis, of ideologies, cultural crises, crises of identity, of commitment and community. There is a realism to his outlook which is refreshing.

His gestures and his openness have themselves echoed his words, such as his washing the feet of young offenders at a correctional institution (including those of a young Muslim

---

[1]*Evangelii Gaudium*, Chapter II.

woman), his frequent embracing of the sick, and sharing his birthday breakfast with the homeless. His first visit abroad was to his home continent and World Youth Day in Brasil.

He has made curial reform and indeed reform of the Vatican's overall organizational practices and priorities another top priority. He instructed the nuncios and episcopal conferences of the world to elicit responses about questions concerning, divorce, remarriage, and family life ahead of the forthcoming Synod of Bishops, thereby at once helping at least to try and make the process more truly synodal than has been the case hitherto.

The Church was weary prior to the election of Francis. Catholics were weary. It is not that all of its problems, divisions, and challenges have disappeared overnight, and there are question marks over ambiguous or mixed messages on several issues that are coming out of Rome. But there is a sense of hope, of positive energy radiating throughout the Church for the first time in many, many years. Great obstacles lie ahead, but there is a vitality to the Church's life once more—something that has been absent in all too many areas of ecclesial life in recent decades.

All of the foregoing is a very roundabout way of saying that the book you now hold in your hands is as timely as it is possible to be. Just as the Church entire, including its leadership, is seeking to discern missional priorities, Raymond Helmick, a brother Jesuit of the pope, who has worked in overcoming conflict and division in war-torn regions and in interfaith and interchurch contexts around the globe for many decades, has produced this most pertinent of studies.

In many ways, this book could have been entitled "*Beyond* the Crisis in the Catholic Church," because Ray Helmick seeks it to serve a very positive and constructive end. This echoes *Evangelii Gaudium* where Pope Francis assures us that "Challenges exist to be overcome!" and therefore encourages the Church by asking for realism fired with enthusiasm for a better tomorrow: "Let us be realists, but without losing our joy, our boldness and our hope-filled commitment. Let us not allow ourselves to be robbed of missionary vigour!"[2]

This book addresses many of the most challenging questions facing Roman Catholicism today and yet does so in an engaging and

---

[2]Ibid., §109.

constructive fashion throughout. Helmick brings to his own Church the application of wisdom of decades spent working in situations of extreme conflict and violence in places such as the Middle East and Northern Ireland. He also brings his deep experiences in helping to promote ecumenical and interreligious dialogue to bear upon the situation in the Catholic Church. He equally applies the insights of his Jesuit background in seeking to discern how the Catholic Church might openly confront its most serious problems in order that its future will be a much brighter one. The book, in many ways, builds upon and takes to another level the incisive analysis put forward in his earlier work, *Living Catholic Faith in a Contentious Age*.[3]

The volume opens with an assessment of where the Church is at. Helmick pulls no punches in laying bare the crisis that the Catholic Church has found itself in in recent decades. He particularly lays emphasis upon the rapidly diminishing confidence in the Church of recent times—a loss of confidence in its clergy, religious, leaders, and institutions alike. Many Catholics have voted with their feet. Here, as throughout the volume, Helmick draws upon social scientific evidence, far-reaching statistics as well as serious theological and ethical scholarship. Refreshingly, although from the United States, he explores the Church in its truly global context rather than focusing primarily on the Church internal to the borders of the United States.

All in all, for Helmick, the present crisis comes down to questions of power, authority, and the malaise of the culture of clericalism that has overtaken too much of ecclesial life. Thus far, judging by statements emerging from Pope Francis, he and Fr Helmick are very much on the same page. Helmick draws his opening chapter and identification of the crisis to a close with a series of questions for his reader:

Does this analysis of the crisis of confidence in the Church ring true? If it does, we will not get out of it and be in a position to restore confidence until we recognize and admit it. Can we indeed have Church without this aura of clericalism and authoritarianism? There are many in the Church who doubt that. Their conviction that it is only by the exercise of their authority that the Church

---

[3]New York and London, Continuum, 2010.

is saved stands at the root of the most fundamental troubles of
the Church, now or at any time in its history. Is that the Church's
essential nature, or are there ways to address these glaring sources
of alienation? We should hope so. The Gospel affirms it to the
point of redundancy, and it will be the basic thesis of this book.
We need to understand how much the thirst for power is the
curse of the Church we have learned to love.[4]

Helmick then goes on to explore past crises in the Church and
looks at how the Church overcame such crises (or when it failed
miserably in either not trying to confront such crises or in going
about doing so in ways doomed to failure). He especially focuses
upon the modern period, so replete with one crisis after another
that it was. These chapters take the reader on a journey through
much of the Church's long story, all with the focus on how periods
of crisis can be overcome.

In particular, the book devotes especial attention to the Second
Vatican Council (1962–65) because Helmick particularly seeks to
add further insights to the voices of those who continue to call for
the full implementation of the Second Vatican Council as a means
for helping the Church to overcome its present crisis. Helmick
offers an extended commentary on the significance of the council in
a separate chapter in which he tries to explain for a new generation
why this event, which began over 50 years ago, was and remains so
vitally important.

In his previous work, Helmick believed that only a new council
would suffice. Now he raises a different, if provisional possibility,
in the light of the election of Pope Francis and the development of
his pontificate thus far. Helmick opines if the Church can first see
whether due attention to truly implementing the reforms intended
by the previous council might not take the Church a long way
to overcoming its present situation. One suspects that Helmick
knows the answer himself, which is, in some ways, yes and in other
ways no. Too many vital aspects of the council's documents were
effectively neutered in many ways by the factionism that came to
the fore at crucial junctures of the conciliar sessions (as well as
by subsequent maneuverings within Rome and beyond). And the

---

[4]Page 13.

world is very different now to what it was then, just as the Church is. The greatest and most transformative legacies of Vatican II can and must, therefore be fully embraced anew for today's world. Accentuating dialogue and an openness to, and engagement with, the wider world is, of course, key to much of this, and Pope Francis has made such an encouraging start on those matters. And the legacy of Vatican II can be built upon by new theological, social, and ethical explorations to take the Church and its mission long into the future. Perhaps a new council will, after all, prove to be the swiftest and most practical ways of bringing this about.

And Fr Helmick's book will stir much debate and even provoke disagreement. Indeed, it has to be said that, on occasion, some readers (including this one!) may find that the thoroughgoing constructive tone of the text gives certain ecclesial developments and Church leaders too generous a benefit of the doubt. For example, Pius XII's *Humani Generis* is looked at in a positive light for at least encouraging greater scientific research, while nonetheless noting its hardline clampdown on certain theological researches. Aspects of the more hagiographical and often questionable conclusions drawn in the biography of John Paul II by George Weigel can be, and have been, frequently challenged and so demand balance with alternative perspectives.

Benedict XVI's interpretation of Vatican II is generously taken at face value in some respects, yet the rhetoric of the ecclesial and theological agenda that often lay behind the Pope Emeritus' writings and speeches, especially when it came to the topic of the council, are areas that have caused much debate, with Ratzinger's antipathy toward *Gaudium et Spes* being especially well documented.

Indeed, the interpretation of Joseph Ratzinger, as theologian, as prefect of the CDF and as pope would be less generous and more probing elsewhere. Not a few commentators lay much of the responsibility for the nature and extent of the crisis facing the Church in recent times at his door and those of like ecclesial perspective. Many can testify that the inquisitorial nature of the Church did very much continue under Pope Benedict XVI as it has under Prefect Ratzinger. The methods sometimes became a touch more subtle, and much of the heavy lifting in relation to admonishments and punishments meted out to those deemed to have fallen doctrinally foul of the CDF was outsourced to more local ecclesiastical bodies: but the investigations picked up and continued nonetheless, and the pain and anguish suffered by the victims of such treatment remained very real and, in some cases, was accentuated.

Here, one only has to mention the examples of a number of brother Jesuits of both Pope Francis and Helmick. Many investigations of the works of such servants of the church have been found to be unnecessary, flawed, and inaccurate. Indeed, the overall treatment of these Jesuit theologians under Pope Benedict has been judged harsh and unfair by many neutral observers. They took a very great toll upon the health and well-being of those subject to such treatment.

A number of readers will also speak of the equal need for the treatment of still further aspects of the crisis in the Church in recent times, such as the clashes between Rome and women religious, or for a deeper exploration of the conflicts over theological ethics on multiple issues and the pastoral consequences of such (particularly with regard to social issues, sexual ethics, and human relationships). Of course, no one volume can treat every topic.

All of that having been said, although the overall intention of this volume remains constructive, by and large, Helmick does not pull his punches and so, all in all, the study constitutes an essay in which all concerned with a more positive future for the Church will find much food for thought.

Helmick explores the divisions in the Church of recent times from a practical starting point because he is truly concerned that the Church finds ways to deal with the multiple crises of authority, clerical abuse, authority, division, and decline of recent times. He explores the origins and deepening of the recent crisis at length across several chapters; from the clashes over contraception and *Humanae Vitae*, through the ups and downs of John Paul II's pontificate, and through to the clerical abuse crisis which Helmick approaches first and foremost in relation to the avalanche of cases that finally became public at the beginning of the century in his now home archdiocese of Boston, MA.

Throughout this work, Helmick interlaces the scholarly narrative with illuminating anecdotes from his own rich ministry and pastoral experiences. This is a volume that should appeal as much to a wider and more general audience as it will to scholars and students. And this is a book that wants to encourage *hope*. Indeed, with change and reform and positive engagement back on the agenda with the election of Pope Francis, Church pastors and leaders alike would find much food for thought in these pages.

For these and many other reasons, we were delighted that Fr Helmick offered this book for publication in the *Ecclesiological Investigations* Series, not least of all in that it seeks to promote dialogue within and across churches and that it concerns contemporary ecclesiological issues yet also explores historical periods and global contexts for the Church in the service of the present. It is a book about bridge-building, and the Ecclesiological Investigations Network was established and exists primarily in order to help build bridges.

It is not just Fr Helmick nor even simply Roman Catholics around the world who are hoping that the crisis of confidence in the Catholic Church can be overcome and, indeed, is already beginning to be overcome in significant ways. So many people of other Christian churches, of other faiths, and people of goodwill who claim no particular faith are equally hoping and, in their own diverse ways, praying, that the Church can rediscover its own faithfulness to its own core mission, values, and virtues once again in order that it will serve the global human family all the better with its rich treasure house of resources from across the centuries of traditions, interpreted and appropriated in the best possible fashion for the world today and all its needs.

As the book was being written, the famous interview—effectively a last will and testament—from Milan's Cardinal Martini appeared. Ray Helmick took great inspiration from those words of the dying Cardinal—yet another brother Jesuit. Above all else, Martini said the Church was some 200 years behind the times and urged Catholics to break free of the fear that had been paralyzing the Church for far too long. Let us hope, with the contributions of scholars such as Ray Helmick and the tentative signs of a more open, inclusive, and collaborative vision we see unfolding from the heart of Rome right now, that such fear may swiftly become a thing of the past and that confidence both *in* the Church and *throughout* the Church may return.

Gerard Mannion
Georgetown University, Washington, DC
Ecclesiological Investigations International
Research Network (www.ei-research.net)
Feast of St Colman of Lismore

PREFACE

Raymond G. Helmick, S.J.

On the evening of 8 February 2013, I thought I had finished the last chapter of this book. The chapter dealt with the reign of Pope Benedict XVI, which had left the crisis of confidence described here untouched, and speculated on what might lie ahead in another pontificate. Pope Benedict proved me wrong on Monday morning, 11 September, when he announced his resignation. My reading of the state of the Church had been rather glum. As a result of the events that followed that announcement, and the advent of Pope Francis, this has become a much happier book.

People have tended to trace the crisis of confidence to the sex abuse scandal, a situation that had been ongoing long before it suddenly became a paramount issue in 2002. It should be evident enough, though, that the falling away from Catholic practice, the loss of priests, and the scarcity of new priestly vocations had been underway long before.

I've chosen to trace the problems of the Catholic Church much farther back in its history. The concentration of Church leadership on control of the Christian population, their requiring of obedience to their rulings rather than on the Gospel values of Jesus, the defensiveness and self-righteousness in the face of any criticism, traceable to the time of Constantine, had served the Church ill in major times of crisis; notably, the eleventh-century period of divisive conflict between East and West and the Reformation crisis of the sixteenth century had served the Church ill, and it was consistent behavior through many centuries. Some heroes of the Church's history have won praise for their hardness in such circumstances.

After a long period of power, the Church had met open hostility from its own society in the French Revolution. Its frightened leadership had become disastrously out of step with the world it lived in through most of the nineteenth and early twentieth centuries, vehemently opposed to the very things—growth of knowledge, technology, and civil freedom—we most value in those periods. The Church allied itself with the most regressive forces of those times, losing its contact with the abused industrial proletariat and having to rely on the patience and devotion of the rural peasantry. The reign of Pope Leo XIII and his initiation of a new social doctrine of the Church had seen a break in this blindness to the times, but the quest for control remained the characteristic of Church governance.

The special character of Pope John XXIII, his extraordinary experience of having to live Christian love under harrowing circumstances at many stages of his life, his understanding of Christian responsibility for the centuries-long terrorizing of Jews, prepared him to bring the Church to a time of remarkable insight into the Second Vatican Council which he initiated. John saw a Church in need of reform, and had learned from such theologians as Yves Congar how such a reform had to be conducted; *in* the Church rather than to it, governed by love of the Church as a communion in the love of God. Finding himself raised unexpectedly to the office of Pope, he called the Council almost at once. His prescription for it was expressed in his opening address. The Council should not be an occasion for condemnation but should bring the Church actively into the life of the world—*aggiornamento*; and not by departing from its ancient principles but by deep penetration into its original and essential sources—*ressourcement*. John's way of doing this was to *consult* the Church, not as a driver but as an enabler, allowing the assembled bishops the freedom to examine its conduct, its liturgy, its responsiveness to the Scriptural resources which were the channel of its tradition, its respect for the person in every way, its self-understanding. By that very fact he had put the bishops into full contact with the aspirations of their people and made possible, thus, a consultation of the entire Church.

The great pioneering Pope was dead after a first year of the Council, but he had accustomed his bishops to this freedom of examination. The sense of direction they gave to the Church addressed long-established and even ancient ways in which it had failed to be faithful to the teachings of Christ. The Church found ways for its active role in the world to spread out, in freedom and fidelity, from the activity of the center to comprehend the entire membership.

I have given the Council centrality in this study, the middle four of its dozen chapters, as it brought the Church to an awareness of its potentiality for an active life of faith by its total membership. The present crisis of confidence arose subsequent to the Council. Those who distrust the Council and its teaching agree on its centrality to the present state of the Church and believe that it ruined everything in what had been a calm and ordered Church. Others of us see rather that a refusal of the central leadership to accept the basic prescriptions of the Council has left our people appalled. They had seen the promise of a restored Church and then found that it never happened, that instead the Church was led into a condition of more centralization and control than it had ever experienced before.

Many great decisions of the Council did take root and made great differences in its conduct. The injustices to Jews have been largely reversed. An ecumenical outlook toward other Christians has had its ups and downs but is regarded as the proper direction for the Church, and respect for those of different faiths has grown. Religious liberty and freedom of conscience, things that were effectively rejected by the preconciliar Church, have won recognition as of the essence of Christian life. Yet, we have seen the most essential findings of the Council, its endorsement of the role of all the bishops in collegial governance of the Church and its recognition that the Church, of its nature, is all its people, the People of God, basically negated, frustrated by a new rigid centralization, the college of bishops reduced, by careful steps, to the status of franchises, kept under tight control. Our people have disappeared from the Church out of disillusion. Christianity, instead of being the life of the people, has become something done by somebody else, and not very well.

The sex abuse scandal, coming on top of all that disappointment, proved explosive and gave an already estranged people the cynical feeling that the Church was some sort of fraud.

How will the Church revive? In its earliest days, the Church grew and attracted new members because, in the cold and often ruthless bureaucracy of the Roman Empire, it was a community of real loving care and fellowship for its members and of concern for the poor and suffering that its people encountered. These were the very things that Jesus had preached and practiced. On those grounds, Christians multiplied to the point that the Empire could no longer defeat or do without them. This picture was never perfect, of course. They were a community of sinners, and knew they were, but this was the spirit. Conversions to Christianity came by personal choice to join in this attractive way of life.

At a later stage, as the Germanic tribes of Northern Europe were converted, the objective was to convert the kings, who would then command the baptism of all their people. This top-down way of spreading the influence of Christianity meant that its characteristic must become control. That has been much of the subsequent history of the Church, a distinct weakening of its essential Christian character, long tolerated by people, some of whom were devout believers in Christian faith, other simply conforming to the expectations of their society. Now that the people have gotten a whiff of what they see as hypocrisy, conformity can have no further place.

A new growth of Christianity can come now only by a return to the love and care of its original premises, to the things that are redolent of the life of Jesus. This will not be accomplished by control. When we speak nowadays of a "new evangelization," compulsion or scolding will have no effect. It can only be done by living a Christian life, giving an example. It is for this reason that we find such a burst of new energy and hope in our badly battered Church as the new Pope Francis appears to be so intent on restoring those essential aspects of Christian life, in his own person and in the model he gives in the spirit of St Francis.

This book had a bleaker look before the election of Pope Francis. During the conclave period, wise heads told us not to expect that any single man could bring about real restoration by himself, but a Pope is important. Pope John XXIII, by his own example of faith, brought about a true earthquake of conversion to Christian conviction in the Church. It may seem strange to speak of a need for conversion to Christianity in the Church, but that is the case.

Seeing the spread of disillusion and disappointment in the Church of recent years, I began arguing, in the atmosphere of the sex abuse scandal, that we would need another Council to meet our needs. It may well be that we can achieve them simply by implementing the decisions that were so central to the Council but have been so deliberately stifled: collegiality and the understanding of the Church as People of God.

1

The nature of the crisis

People generally agree that the Catholic Church is suffering a crisis. We see diminished numbers of Catholics in the pews. The supply of new priests from our own communities has practically dried up. A great proportion of our religious women are at, or close to, retirement age, with few new recruits expected. And the Catholic community divides sharply between those who want to see a restoration of a vanished past and those who look for a new configuration of Catholic life.

The Archdiocese of Boston launched, in 2011, a program called "Catholics Come Home." Admirable in its generous welcome to Catholics who have not been attending church, it seemed rather odd to have it proclaimed in sermons to the people who were actually there at Sunday Masses when it was directed to those who were not. We heard of a campaign that would be run with media ads, for which we sought people's support, and, of course, the Mass-goers who were present were asked to extend the invitation in person in their families and among friends.

Yet, an element was missing. We had here an appeal built on the supposition that something must be wrong with people who were not there in the pews listening to us. We were not questioning what we may have done wrong in our presentation of Catholic faith that we should have lost so many people. The statistics are such as should surely catch our attention. Of those we regard as Catholic, or who so regard themselves, we see only about 17 percent of a Sunday now, the numbers still diminishing, down from very high percentages in earlier years.

In this basically Protestant country, blossoming now into surprising religious diversity, Catholics are still the largest single Christian denomination. Yet, ex-Catholics, who have wandered into other churches or who have left out of church practice altogether, come second.[1] Still, we seem extraordinarily reluctant to ask the question: what is this all about? If we raise this question, we are at a risk of being taken as saying the wrong thing, a kind of disloyalty. What we don't quite admit is that the crisis is one of confidence. It does not much help to assume that those whose confidence is shaken are at fault.

All of us are aware of the sexual abuse crisis, which went on for an indiscernible length of time in the past, but which only became a matter of general focus with the *Boston Globe* articles beginning on Epiphany, 6 January 2002. Catholics have reacted with anger, disillusionment, and disappointment. The response from authority sources in the Church has been seen as defensive, often evasive, sometimes simply self-deceiving, as when high authority figures have claimed that the whole scandal is merely an attack on the Church by its enemies. This element is true, of course, since the scandal was ready-made for anyone who was looking for a cudgel with which to beat the holy Church, but the real problem lies in the dismay of those who love the Church and yearn within it for the confidence of faith. The people seated there in the pews are as badly hurt as anyone.

The crisis, in fact, goes back much further. We can see it in a long, steady decline both in Church attendance and in vocations to priesthood and religious life, which goes back as far as the first great hemorrhage of priests in the late 1960s. An element of simple secularization has to be admitted, as the Church, religion, and faith tend to occupy less space on the horizon of the contemporary world, but that doesn't adequately account for the decline among people who truly love the Church and the faith and who wish it were not such a disappointment. They retell, in their sorrow, the same sad

---

[1] The Pew Forum on Religion and Public Life constantly analyzes these statistics and bases forecasts on them. The Glenmary Research Center for Religious Congregations has kept updated figures since 1970. Divergent estimates between them, the Official Catholic Directory for 2010 and the 2010 General Social Survey of the National Opinion Research Center are discussed in a column of *America Magazine*, 28 May 2012, "U.S. Catholic Population at 59 Million."

stories as they hear from those who greet the decline of the Church with glee.

Some blame the Second Vatican Council for breaking the atmosphere of unchanging certainty about all things that prevailed in the Church before that time. Mark Massa's admirable book, *The American Catholic Revolution*,[2] identifies that characteristic of the otherwise turbulent 1960s with the simple realization that, in the Catholic Church, change happens—as in all things.

At the time, the world received the Council with great enthusiasm and joy. The "opening of the windows" proclaimed by Pope John XXIII gave breath to a Church that had become formalized into a kind of total institutionalization. Why did he do it? In part, he saw the practice of Church behavior as routinized, becoming its own end. People went to Mass, confessed their sins, abstained from meat on Fridays, and catechized their children as a matter of habit, one which would likely not sustain them in the rapidly changing world that had emerged after the two world wars. Faith makes radically challenging demands, but well-oiled Catholic practice seemed to conceal the challenge. Christian and Catholic life was, in fact, rather self-satisfied at the time.

Still, a canker ate at the Catholic Church and, indeed, at all of Europe's Christian churches. None of them had done very well during World War II. Despite occasional acts of courage, they had all run for cover during the decades of Fascism, too often preferring their institutional safety over moral concerns. Opposition—the Resistance movement—during the time of the Nazi conquests had come from mavericks, people whom their own church institutions regarded as trouble, and who had to fear that if their church authorities knew of their activities they would turn them in. They had to discover whom they could trust. It turned out that some of these were Catholic, some Protestant, some Socialists or Communists, some atheists or agnostics; regardless, it was to them that the resistors had to turn.

Ecumenical interest and activity had been about among Protestants since early in the century, as manifested in the Edinburgh mission

---

[2]Mark Massa, S.J., *The American Catholic Revolution: How the '60s Changed the Church Forever* (New York: Oxford University Press, 2010), V, Chapter 8, "Things Change," 147ff.

conference of 1910 and in the network of Councils of Churches that had sprung up as a result, which would culminate in the World Council of Churches in 1948. The Catholic Church had stood aloof and disapproving for most of that time, and was in any case hardly welcome to the Protestant participants: for too many centuries, Catholics and Protestants had inveighed against each other and denied each other's true Christianity. Yet, Catholic resistance to ecumenism was self-exclusion as well. Now, the mavericks of the Resistance gained in honor, as the persons whose integrity any of the churches had to recognize, and ecumenism became increasingly attractive to Catholics.

Americans had not shared that Continental experience of the Resistance; what's more, European ecumenical ideas had to cross the ocean in books, a process that took some 15 years. (Ireland, where ecumenism would meet unfriendly soil, had the exceptional experience that the war had deepened mutual suspicions between Protestants and Catholics.) An important straw in the wind occurred when Jesuit Father Leonard Feeney of Boston drove his inveterate religious exclusivism and anti-Semitism to the point of denying the possibility of salvation to anyone other than Catholics. This egregious case brought a necessary condemnation of so extreme a position from Rome, where Pope Pius XII himself had an immediate hand in writing the decision.[3] Still, during all this time, Catholic theologians in Europe and America had begun, often to the grave disquiet of church authorities, to explore these new territories. In France, center for some of the most important fresh thinking, the very perceptive Papal Nuncio, Archbishop Angelo Giuseppe Roncalli, the future Pope John XXIII, studied closely the work of Dominican Father Yves Congar on *True and False Reform of the Church*, which authorities had not managed entirely to suppress,

---

[3]This episode, one of the things that opened the way to the Second Vatican Council, is not adequately chronicled. Theologian and future Cardinal Avery Dulles published a touching recollection of Feeney after his death, "Leonard Feeney: In Memoriam," *America Magazine*, 25 February 1978. Father Richard Schmarek, who was close to the whole episode and helped with the lifting of Feeney's excommunication year later, has a yet unpublished book manuscript about it. Too seldom commented upon, the text of the condemnation can be found in the traditional collection: Denzinger-Schönmetz, *Enchiridion Symbolorum, Definitionumet Declarationum de rebus fidei et morum* (Herder edition of 1963) Ep. S. Officii ad archiep. Bostoniensem, 8 August 1949, ##3866–73, pp. 770ff.

taking copious notes in the book and wondering whether genuine Church reform would be possible.[4]

Roncalli had direct experience of the Holocaust (Shoah) crimes against the Jews, had worked strenuously for their rescue and had understood well the roots of virulent anti-Semitism in age-old Christian prejudice and persecution. He was convinced, by the time he convened the Council, that this situation required radical rethinking on the part of the Church.[5]

Some commentators see tension between the two major engines of the Council, aggiornamento, good Italian for the updating of our understanding of the faith, and ressourcement, this time French for the return to sources. Yet, for most of us, there was no contradiction here. The original sources of revelation and tradition were the very meat of the aggiornamento, gave it life. We were paying attention to Gospel sources in a way that had not been done earlier when they and their spirit had been constantly subordinated to the doctrinal pronouncements of institutional authority. The understanding that the Church was "people of God" gave us a stake in the living of faith that was not merely conformity to someone else's authoritative perception.

From the start, there was alarm over this development, especially among those who still held power in the establishment. They were a minority voice at the Council, vastly outnumbered in the voting, but heavily represented in the Roman Curia. They had the advantage of holding the ring of power and, to a great extent, choosing their

---

[4]This important theologian, whose work was paralleled by that of Marie-Dominique Chenu, Henri de Lubac and several others, published in 1950 Vraie et fausse reform dans l'Eglise. The Holy Office at once prohibited its reprinting or translation into other languages, and Congar himself was sent into exile. But the future Pope read it, and his opening address to the Council powerfully evoked Congar's vision of authentic reform. Congar himself was one of the first theologians he appointed to the Council's preparatory commission and had great influence through the course of the Council. The Liturgical Press, recognizing the resemblance of the present crisis to that of the earlier time, reissued the book, translated by Paul Philibert, as True and False Reform in the Church, in 2011. This history is mentioned in the Translator's Preface, pp. xi–xii.

[5]Pope John XXIII's special interest in this theme of the Council, his employment of Cardinal Augustin Bea to promote it, his revision of the Good Friday liturgy, and his early contacts with Jewish scholar Jules Isaac (1877–1963), are narrated in John W. O'Malley, What Happened at Vatican II (Cambridge, MA: Belknap Press of Harvard University Press, 2008, 2010), pp. 218–20.

own successors. The new Pope, Paul VI (r. 21 June 1963–6 August 1978), who took over the Council from its second session, seemed often to regard the bishops of the Church, assembled in Council, as a runaway body. He took several key questions out of their hands to be resolved only by himself and his counselors, notably matters of contraception, ordination of married men or ordination of women. Often he seemed to do end runs around the Council, as when he made his visit to the Holy Land just as the Council was contemplating the *Nostra Aetate* decree about the relation of Catholics to Jews and other religions, subsequently drawing the Council back from phrasings that we still strain to reach today, or when his visit to Patriarch Athenagoras (r. 1948–72) in Istanbul undercut the ecumenical outreach of the Council.

A number of the newly "liberated" Catholics began to do quite bizarre things. Liturgy, opened now to change, was subjected to a lot of self-indulgent and self-promoting experiment. Where before it had been obscure and distant ritual in a language most people did not understand, it now often became performance, with super-star performers. The grounding of children in faith was often subjected to simplistic reductionism. Strange, arbitrary teachings surfaced in ways that were terribly off-putting to traditionalists, indeed to the advocates of the *ressourcement* itself. We might say that these things were hardly surprising given the rigid culture they displaced.

An atmosphere of resistance and retraction could be felt even during the concluding years of the Council, but the acid test came with the issuance of the birth-control Encyclical, *Humanae Vitae: On the Regulation of Birth*, on 25 July 1968. Reserving this question to himself, to the exclusion of the Council, Pope Paul expanded the commission created by John XXIII to study the question deeply, in the light of the population explosion that had the world's attention at the time; yet then Paul VI declined to accept the recommendation of the majority, which he himself had crafted, and twice over. The Church had come away from the view of sexuality as "necessary evil" and had begun to acknowledge that it had a purpose, co-equal to that of procreation, in fostering/ expressing the love of married partners. Paul's commission recommended overwhelmingly an opening to what was called "responsible parenthood," but the Pope, on the advice of a small fraction of the advisers, chose instead to issue an absolute prohibition of artificial contraception.[6]

One can reconstruct by now the insights that gave reason to his choice. The sexual revolution of the 1960s was already producing the kind of anarchy and selfishness we have seen since. What seemed then a threatening cloud of the exhaustion of the world's resources has since been counterpoised by the dangers of an aging population that has to be supported by too small a base of active working young adults. Still, the Pope's solitary decision on the matter marked a major watershed, since in the eyes of many, even of its own members, the Church *magisterium* had lost its qualification to speak on matters of sexuality. Many walked with us no more, and a great part of the Church was thereafter left not trusting magisterial decisions and without any authoritative bearings in these matters. It is an ancient teaching of the Church that magisterial teaching must win reception, and this did not. Yet the highest authority levels of the Church kept insisting on it as a matter of first importance.

We became a very divided Catholic community. Increasingly, from this time, judgments became common, from right and left alike, that those of different outlooks did not truly qualify as Catholic, as genuine members of the Catholic communion. The remaining years of the pontificate of Paul VI were characterized by anxiety on his part. Newspapers all over the world had preset headlines that began "Pope warns . . ." and they accurately forecast whatever new worries he conceived.[7]

What was going on here? The ferment in the Church took place against the background of new philosophical understandings which we can characterize as postmodernism. Distrust of religious institutions had an earlier origin in the period of religious wars, to which we shall turn in Chapter 3 (p. 1.). Here, we should note that postmodernity's emphasis on the primacy of individual experience inclined members of advanced Western societies to think in terms of

---

[6]The Encyclical and its consequences will be the topic of a chapter later in this book.

[7]A good account of the papacy of Paul VI can be found in Peter Hebblethwaite, *Paul VI: The First Modern Pope* (NY/Mahwah, NJ: Paulist Press, 1993). A moving, thinly fictionalized reflection upon his reign may be found in the late Edward Sheehan, *Cardinal Galsworthy* (New York: Viking, 1997).

narrative, of particular experience. We take this habit as a virtue of our time. The meta-narratives which gave substance to overarching institutions have yielded to the uniqueness of individual experience, leading to a skeptical, critical mindset.

The concept of a universal Church has to embrace a great deal of individual difference, a relatively novel phenomenon, and one which a very centralized structure finds difficult to deal with. Nonetheless, church scholarship had already moved beyond the comfortable old cultural assumptions, and this was particularly pronounced in biblical studies. For we had received our license from Pope Pius XII, in his 1943 Encyclical *Divino Afflante Spiritu*, to read our Scripture critically, and that had led to a far more nuanced understanding of its historical, cultural, and linguistic roots. Doctrinal tradition and developing ethical discussion proved more difficult, as the masters of institution felt more challenged when these matters were discussed. Seeing things in terms of individual narrative, we suppose that many of the things our traditions insist on are individually or socially constructed, and thus they can be de-constructed or re-constructed. Levels of creativity are now arising from this intellectual freedom, levels of creativity that were not available to us before.

What's more, we become conscious, in this postmodern narrative thought, that sin can be structural and institutional, not merely individual. This goes some way to accounting for the damage done when church bodies played such a "safe" game during World War II's time of deep crisis. Abuses of power, exclusivity, structures which oppress can all be sin in which we, as members of the Church, take part. Thus in today's philosophical milieu, when we question the structures of the Church, we are asking moral questions as well as social ones.

Our Church authorities become very worried when they discern what they call "situational ethics," a term often of rather indefinite ambience and extension. Doubtless there are expressions of relativism (a favorite term of Pope Benedict's) with regard to Catholic faith or behavior that would damage the Church in its obedience to the Spirit. With all due allowance made for that risk, it must be said that for us not to understand or to reject on principle these phenomena of the postmodern age does grave harm to the Church.

The new Pope, after the very brief interlude of John Paul I, "the smiling Pope" (reigned only 33 days, 26 August 1978 to

28 September 1978), was the magnetic Polish personality, Karol Wojtyla, Pope John Paul II, whose term would last from 16 October 1978 to 2 April 2005, the second longest papacy in history. He was himself the superstar, traveling the world in a way no Pope had ever done, generating enormous enthusiasm with his World Youth Day meetings, brimming with confidence.[8] He was essential to the bringing down of the Communist empire, stunning in his ecumenical outreach to other churches and his openness to interreligious comity, an opener of new vistas for Catholicism like his predecessor John XXIII, beloved even by those who took his teaching least seriously. At the same time, though, he was a man of *integrationist* authority, clawing back power to the central offices of the Vatican, but doing so for an ever-decreasing, church-going public, despite the remarkable personal acclaim he achieved. Features of his reign were the appointment of bishops who became practically franchises of the central firm and the recruitment of young men into the priesthood, "the John Paul priests," who would be unblushing advocates of this centralization and increasingly alienated from those they hoped to lead. *The term "Restoration" became talisman to a new era.* Authority tended to marginalize from the official structures those who would not go along with the wide-ranging Restoration.

Adherence to the Church became continuously less as this reign went on, despite the popularity of the Pontiff. Church attendance dropped off drastically. Numbers of priests fell precipitously, while recruitment to women's religious life all but disappeared. A particularly alarming phenomenon was the number of women who departed from Catholic life and practice. In critical times in the past, the participation of men in the Church's life had often shrunken, but it was the women who remained and brought up their children to the faith. This trend was now threatened as never before.

For many women, particularly the "feminist theologians" who have become such a terror to authorities, a "hermeneutic of suspicion" affected their approach to Scripture. They had to suspect that the writers, translators, transcribers, and those who chose the

---

[8]George Weigel, *Witness to Hope: The Biography of Pope John Paul II* (New York: Harper Perennial, 1999, 2001, rev. edn, 2005), gives us an encyclopedic account of John Paul's reign up to that date. Analytic assessment can be found in Gerard Mannion, ed., *The Vision of John Paul II: Assessing His Thought and Influence* (Collegeville, MN: Liturgical Press, 2008; paperback 2009).

canon of scripture were steeped in an androcentric society and worldview from which they could not easily be freed. This bias is reflected in all aspects of their traditional work; moreover, it taints our view to the point that we must seek to root it out and find new ways to make the Gospel message valid for women (and men!) today, even while acknowledging that we, too, live in a male-dominated society and must contend with similar biases in our own minds.

A reaction set in against clerical authoritarianism, and reciprocally, a counter-reaction, a clerical insistence on deference and even submission. In parts of the world where secular society had oppressed Catholics, as in Ireland, Communist Poland or an earlier United States, clergy had been the only educated class of Catholics who could raise voices against the oppression and protect their fellows. That had given them tremendous internal power within their own communities. None but Catholic clerics, with the active encouragement of Pope John Paul II, could have enabled the rise of the Solidarity movement in Poland, leading to the overthrow of Communist domination, but once Polish society had accomplished that, it turned to resisting domination by Church authorities themselves. Clerical influence had dominated Ireland's Catholic community through the centuries of British Protestant supremacy. As a bitter by-product thereof, its dominance, seen as the incapacity of Catholic Ireland to act independently of clerics, underlay Protestant fears that Catholics were unfit for a democratic life.[9] In the United States, the automatic deference to clergy was melting as educational levels rose among lay Catholics. Clericalism had always been the greatest danger to the Church, but now, after the high hopes of the Council years, the appearance of arrogance became more damaging than ever. That had been a perception of the Catholic clergy from well before the time of the sex crisis, and submissiveness of the laity was always admixed with a measure of anticlericalism.

The conscious difference between clergy and laity, product of many centuries' development, the sense of the clergy's worthiness and entitlement to deference and obedience, from Pope and bishops down to the lower ranks of priests and religious, was wrapped up in one psychological perception almost universal among the Catholic public and the clergy themselves: that these were celibates,

---

[9]This writer published an analysis of this phenomenon in *The Month*, August 1977, "Church Structure and Violence in Northern Ireland."

and therefore better than other people. Women could be left out of the power structure. Clergy were seen as asexual and therefore superior. We can compare this to the erstwhile difference between colonial masters and their subjects, upon whom they could look down *de haut en bas*. For that reason, when the abuse crisis showed the sexual behavior of clergy as full of shocking hypocrisy and betrayal, the repercussions were explosive.

The crisis of confidence which we note, then, preceded by far the sexual-abuse crisis that broke upon us in 2002, but that event exacerbated it enormously. It all links up with that sense of clerical arrogance. Clericalism turned out to be the Achilles' heel of the Church as a power structure, a lurking bomb once the perception of hypocrisy ignited it.

Let this not be a complaint about celibacy. It is not, let us observe, the first time that clerical sexuality has shown itself a problem. Celibacy, in this writer's perception, is of great value in the Church. Of its nature, it is a gift of exclusive service to others: the man, or woman, for others on the model of Christ himself. It is a covenanted status in our human faith community, just as much a covenant as is marriage. Simple bachelorhood is not such.

I would question the rule of mandatory celibacy for all the clergy—not a universal value, and never imposed by the other churches or by Eastern Catholics. It may well be that it should be expected only, or mainly, from those in religious life. As covenant, it should be freely and fully adopted and known as such. That said, I do not believe that the celibacy rule is the reason so few young men enter the priesthood in Western cultures today. We should not put this down to a lack of generosity in the young, but to a perception that there is something false behind much of the Church they see. It doesn't smell right.

It may well be that we are losing the valuable service of married men who would be ideal priests and pastors. It may well be also that we have many priests who have accepted the rule of celibacy only because it is a required condition for ordination.[10] There are other reasons besides service to others for men to enter the clergy.

---

[10]This is not the place to go into this complex history. A good introduction to it can be found in Stefan Heid, *Celibacy in the Early Church: The Beginnings of a Discipline of Obligatory Continence for Clerics in East and West*, trans. Michael J. Miller (San Francisco: Ignatius Press, 2000).

They may see it as a life of security, a legitimate opportunity for career advancement and power, or simply as a way to serve one's fellow men and women with dignity and simplicity. Those who enter it for those reasons and accept the celibacy rule just because it is the only way in are not really entering into a covenant, and for them the celibacy may well be a burden entered into reluctantly for other reasons.

Such thinking conditioned the general Protestant abandonment of clerical celibacy at the time of the Reformation. The Reformers and their public had seen too many cases of coerced or merely pretended celibacy to think of it as covenant. Yet, then again, they lost something of great value when they made this choice, as some Protestants begin to recognize in our own time.

Once we could make a distinction between the life of the religious vows of poverty, chastity, and obedience and the quite different life of "secular" diocesan clergy. Parish clergy, in fact, live generally on small salaries. All of us religious priests have heard them jibe that we take the vow of poverty but they live it. And they, without a vow of obedience, are obliged to promise obedience to their bishops, an obedience likely to be very exacting. Consequently, since the time of the universal requirement of celibacy, introduced after a complicated history, little difference will be seen in these ways of life. Even those in religious orders, with vows, have joined in the hemorrhage of clergy over the period we are looking at, as if there were no difference in the character of their obligations.

Still, the problem is not with celibacy as such. It is with the status of entitlement and assumed superiority, which has become so much associated with celibacy that the clergy have got into trouble. With this, its value as the expression of a life of faith has been critically compromised. For a person to whom an expectation of deference is the value of celibacy, the appearance of celibacy will be more important than the reality.

Power—the lust for power—is the heart of the matter. We should always remember that rape, the rape of altar boys, the rape of women, is primarily an imposition of power more than a matter of sexuality. A culture built on power and authoritarianism will generate it. Sexual abuse, whether of women or of children, occurs far more widely in many other parts of society, including families, than it does in clergy, but that assertion of power is regularly its context.

Does this analysis of the crisis of confidence in the Church ring true? If it does, we will not get out of it and be in a position to restore confidence until we recognize and admit it. *Can we indeed have Church without this aura of clericalism and authoritarianism?* There are many in the Church who doubt that. Their conviction that it is only by the exercise of their authority that the Church is saved stands at the root of the most fundamental troubles of the Church, now or at any time in its history. Is that the Church's essential nature, or are there ways to address these glaring sources of alienation? We should hope so. The Gospel affirms it to the point of redundancy, and it will be the basic thesis of this book. We need to understand how much the thirst for power is the curse of the Church we have learned to love.

2

How the Church has handled grave crises in the past

Often since the clamor over the Church's sex-abuse scandal broke over the world with *The Boston Globe*'s articles on 6 January 2002, I have said and written that it is a Reformation-size crisis, to which we should make a response commensurate with its size, and that a merely defensive stance would not measure up to our needs. This chapter should not become a history lesson, but in teaching this topic as a course, I have emphasized two previous crises, to both of which the Church did give basically defensive responses. The result was that both provoked lasting division among Christians. These are the Reformation itself and the great East-West divide in the Church in the eleventh century.

On occasion, I see references to other great times of crisis, such as the French Revolution, and one might add the Constantinian period, which made such substantive changes in the character of the Church, the Investiture Crisis, which led to the much-admired Gregorian Reform, or the Conciliar period of failed reform efforts in the fourteenth to fifteenth centuries. In too many of these situations, the response of Church leadership had elements of the defensive posture—we are always right, and that means our opponents are always wrong—that I will criticize in this chapter. But those two periods of major division among Christians are the most comparable to the present. If we respond as poorly in our own time as Church leaders did in those, we may expect not to find that people break away into rival churches but this time rather that people simply walk away.

ᴊ-tell, let me recount a recent conversation
ᴊg seminarian which, I found, illustrates the
ᴊon he receives for dealing with other religions.
ᴊn to a meeting of Christians and Muslims. The
ᴊted both the regional Massachusetts Council of
ᴊ Boston Archdiocese. The Muslims belonged to a
ᴊgland group. The topic was forgiveness. The young
man ᴊᴊ   ᴊ, during the meeting, the question of the sin against
the Holy Spᴊ.ᴊt, the sin that cannot be forgiven (Mk. 3:29; Mt. 12:32;
Lk. 12:10), and identified it, in his understanding, as apostasy. He
wanted to know if Muslims regarded any sin as unforgivable, and
that led to a discussion of apostasy in Islam. Was it possible for a
Muslim to convert to Christianity without sin?

That conversation was kept quite civil but, conspicuously, two
of the Muslim participants in the meeting were converts from
Christianity, one of them from Catholicism. Our conversation
continued in the car on the way home, and ran to discussion of
objective and subjective sin. Inasmuch as sin is the act of a person, not
an object in itself, the subjective element would seem the important
one, and we spoke of the primacy of conscience, a central Catholic
theme, often not a comfortable one for our authorities, which had
surfaced in ways it had not before at the Second Vatican Council.
Eventually, the discussion led to a question about Islamic faith itself:
could the young man see God active in the faith of Muslims, or did
he believe it was all deception? Not having been asked so stark a
question before, he floundered a bit, and then came down firmly
with the judgment that it was deception and that his Christian
responsibility was to convert Muslims from their faith to ours.

All that leads to a question of how well this generous young man
is being prepared, in his seminary, for a life dealing, as Catholic
pastor, with people of other faiths. Has he been taught to reflect on
the insights of *Nostra Aetate*, the Second Vatican Council's decree
on the Church's relation to Jews, to Muslims, to those of other
faiths, or the discussion that has gone on in the Church over the
many decades since? How will he deal with those—the second-
largest religious category of Americans after Catholics themselves—
who have left the Catholic Church and gone over to other Christian
denominations, to other faiths, or to none? What are his thoughts,
or on what is he prepared to base a relation, with regard to those
who have left the Catholic Church because they have found it, its

leadership, its community insupportable—in its record on sex abuse, perhaps to themselves, in its habits of domination, in its intolerance or unforgiving habits, or in other ways? Can he see them even as having offered something of value to the Church by their expression of dissent or dismay? Is any such conversation carried on in the teaching of his seminary?

Assuming that this is the condition in which we, as the Catholic Church, live today, we need to see how this compares with the other great periods of crisis the Church has experienced, notably the two cited: the time of the eleventh-century schism and that of the sixteenth-century Reformation. What lived values did the response of Church leadership to those crises show?

1054: The East-West division

Christians of Orthodox and Catholic tradition generally think of themselves as separate churches. We date the separation to the event of 16 July 1054, on which a papal Legate, Cardinal Humbert, head of a delegation of eleven from Rome, entered the church of Hagia Sophia and laid upon the altar a Bull of excommunication against the Patriarch of Constantinople, Michael Cerularius, Leo of Achrida (an Albanian Metropolitan who had co-signed, with Caerularius, a document condemning the Western use of unleavened bread in the Eucharist) and their associates. An anomaly in the proceeding was that Pope Leo IX, who had commissioned Humbert to deal with Constantinople, had already died in April. The Patriarch reciprocated in kind, excommunicating Humbert and his fellow legates.[1]

We often hear of this as the mutual excommunication between the two churches, but, in fact, only those individuals, none of whom recognized the validity of the action, were excommunicated. And the relation between Eastern and Western churches did not, in fact, cease. Friendly exchanges continued between them often through the eleventh and twelfth centuries, despite recurrent friction and even a massacre of the Latin Catholics in their city by the Orthodox citizens

---

[1] A basic narrative can be found in the article "Great Schism," *Oxford Dictionary of the Christian Church* (New York: Oxford University Press, 2005).

of Constantinople in 1182.[2] It took the invasion and destruction of Constantinople by Crusaders in 1204, with the imposition of a Latin patriarch of the city, to break the link. After that, relations hardened.

Two efforts were made to reunite these churches, once at the Second Council of Lyons in 1274,[3] again at the Council of Florence in 1439.[4] Neither was accepted by the Orthodox patriarchs or their people, who believed a Council required a ratification by their own churches which was never given. A great part of the motivation for the Greeks was the expectation that the Western countries would come to their defense against the Turks, help that never arrived. In 1484 a Synod of Constantinople, a city now under Ottoman Turkish rule, definitively repudiated the Florence union.[5]

We need to know what the quarrel was about and why it has continued so long. Lurking in the background is the controversy over the term *filioque* in the creed, a divergence in Trinitarian doctrine, with the Holy Spirit proceeding from the Father alone or from the Father and the Son. The term was devised in fourth-century Spain by Christians who used it to oppose the Arian denial of the full divinity of the Son and his equality with the Father. Greek theologians preferred to emphasize the Father's role of primacy as source of deity.[6] The argument has produced vehement denunciations over the centuries, but the churches lived with this difference long before the schism.

The real quarrel is that *filioque* was not in the original creed of the Council of Nicaea (325),[7] as amended by the First Council of Constantinople (381)[8] with a few additions on the Holy Spirit, a

---

[2]Timothy Gregory, *A History of Byzantium* (Hoboken, NJ: Wiley-Blackwell, 2010), 309.
[3]The full Acta in Norman Tanner, S.J., *Decrees of the Ecumenical Council* (Two volumes, Sheed and Ward and Georgetown University Press, 1990), I, 303–31.
[4]Acta regarding the Orthodox, Tanner, I, 506–59, including texts of all the agreements. Of particular interest is the decree *Laetenter* with the agreement of the Greeks, 523–8.
[5]This merited the attention of Edward Gibbon, *The Decline and Fall of the Roman Empire, Vol. 7* (UK: Wildside Press edition, 2004), 142–3, note 7. A better account in Steven Runciman, *The Great Church in captivity* (Cambridge: Cambridge University Press, 1985), 193–4.
[6]*The HarperCollins Encyclopedia of Catholicism* by Richard McBrien, Harold Attridge, pp. 529–30 gives an overview.
[7]Text, Tanner, I, 5.
[8]Ibid., 24.

formula approved by all the churches, but was added by unilateral decision in the West, without the approval of the East. The Emperor Charlemagne, especially, who regarded it as a sign of his full succession to the ancient Empire even while a Byzantine emperor still reigned in the East, had insisted on it.[9] It was not approved for general liturgical use in the West until 1014[10] but had been a battle cry in East-West conflicts before that. In the time of ninth-century Patriarch Photius, a saint in the Orthodox Church, this and other contentions had led to depositions of patriarchs and nullification of councils.[11] Yet though the quarrel persists to this day the unity of the Church had survived. We can conclude that this issue did not break the unity of the Church.

Other issues of practice were also disputed between the churches, from the date of Easter to the use of leavened or unleavened bread for the Eucharist. Eastern patriarchs objected to the Latin celebration of Masses on the weekdays of Lent, omission of the Alleluia during Lent, the depiction of Christ as a lamb. The strongest dispute was over the celibacy of priests and deacons, with the East defending their right to marry. The disputed Council of Trullo held in Constantinople in 692 prescribed excommunication for anyone who attempted to separate a priest from his wife or any priest who abandoned a wife.[12] Pope Sergius I refused to sign the canons of this council, despite the fact that the Emperor Justinian sent a military force to Rome to compel him, but the mainly Italian imperial army at Ravenna came to his rescue.[13] An 8th Council of Toledo in Visigothic Spain did ratify it, but later had to retract it.[14]

---

[9]The 1911 edition of the *Catholic Encyclopedia*, in its article "Filioque," details this argument.

[10]Gregory Dix, *The Shape of the Liturgy* (London: Continuum, 2005), 487.

[11]Adrian Fortescue, *The Orthodox Eastern Church* (Piscataway, NJ: Gorgias Press LLC, 2001), 147-f.; Andrew Louth, *Greek East and Latin West: The Church, AD 681-1071* (St. Vladimir Seminary Press, 2007), 171; Shawn Tougher, *The Reign of Leo VI (886–912): Politics and People* (Leiden, The Netherlands: Brill, 1997), 69.

[12]George Ostrogorsky, *History of the Byzantine state*, trans. Joan Hussey (New Brunswick, NJ: Rutgers University Press, 1957), 122f.

[13]Andrew J. Ekonomou, *Byzantine Rome and the Greek Popes: Eastern influences on Rome and the papacy from Gregory the Great to Zacharias, A.D. 590–752* (New York: Lexington Books, 2007), 223.

[14]Roger Collins, *The Arab Conquest of Spain, 710–97* (Oxford: Blackwell Publishing, 1989), 19.

None of these was the cause of the schism. Instead it was a matter of jurisdiction. Originally Christians had recognized four patriarchal sees as founded by Apostles: Jerusalem, Antioch, Alexandria, and Rome. Rome had precedence as the See of two Apostles, Peter and Paul, the See of Peter as chief of the Apostles and heart of Empire.[15] When Constantinople became principal capitol city of Empire it too acquired a patriarch, its apostolic character explained in terms of a visit by St Andrew, brother of Peter, to Byzantium.[16] The Second Ecumenical Council (381), First Council of Constantinople, declared in its Canon 3: "The Bishop of Constantinople, however, shall have the prerogative of honor after the Bishop of Rome; because Constantinople is New Rome."[17]

Jurisdiction in the Church was thus vested in a Pentarchy,[18] the five patriarchates, in order, of Rome, Constantinople, Alexandria, Antioch, and Jerusalem, as confirmed at the Fourth Ecumenical Council, that of Chalcedon in 451. These jurisdictional claims were the central issue that built up the estrangement as East and West drifted apart within the Empire.

Languages had become separate, as the number of people who spoke both Latin and Greek gradually shrank. Imperial control in the West fell apart increasingly after the city of Rome was sacked by the Goths in 410. Relations between the churches became remote as the West was overrun by Germanic tribes. In Greek view, the popes became an appendage of the Frankish kings from 752 to 844, reducing themselves to military leaders and "shedding the blood of Christians and pagans alike."[19]

The Greeks claim that Canon 28 of Chalcedon grants equal privileges to Constantinople and Rome, making the Pope "first among equals." They do not recognize a primacy of one over the

---

[15]Bernhard Schimmelpfennig, *The Papacy* (New York: Columbia University Press, 1992), 27.
[16]Article "Ecumenical Patriarchate of Constantinople," *Encyclopædia Britannica*, 2005.
[17]Tanner, I, 32.
[18]Article "Pentarchy," *Encyclopedia Britannica*, 2005. Never accepted as a formula by the Latin Church, the term Pentarchy was especially formulated by the Emperor Justinian: Cf. Milton V. Anastos, *Aspects of the Mind of Byzantium (Political Theory, Theology, and Ecclesiastical Relations with the See of Rome)* (Ashgate Publications, Variorum Collected Studies Series, 2001).
[19]Such is the opinion of John Romanides, *Franks, Romans, Feudalism and Doctrine*, part 1, p. 8.

other. The Romans counter that the papal legates were not present for the vote on this canon and protested it afterwards, and further that it was not ratified by Pope Leo the Great in Rome.[20]

Patriarch Michael Cerularius circulated, in 1054, to the bishops of the West, a letter condemning such Western practices as the use of unleavened bread as "Judaistic." Cardinal Humbert translated the letter into Latin for Pope Leo IX, who ordered him to draw up a refutation of every charge, with a defense of papal supremacy. Leo's letter based the supremacy argument on the forgery known as *The Donation of Constantine*, which he believed to be genuine.[21] The Patriarch rejected the argument with such hostility that Humbert and his legates stormed out of the palace, further angering the Patriarch. The laying of the excommunication on the altar of the Hagia Sophia during the celebration of the liturgy followed.

The Bull of excommunication listed 11 complaints against Michael and "the backers of his foolishness." Top of the list was promoting men who had been castrated to episcopacy. It went on through rebaptism, and finished with the refusal of communion or baptism to women who were menstruating and refusal to be in communion with those who tonsured their heads or shaved their beards. The doctrinal issue of rejecting the procession of the Holy Spirit from the Son figured in the list, but merited only seventh place.[22]

What are we to make of this tragic development that has kept the Christian churches divided and abrasive to each other for so many centuries? The issues—claims to jurisdiction, assertions of

---

[20]Tanner, I, 99f. But the text as given in Tanner reflects the way the Canon was recorded in Rome. Referring to the First Council of Constantinople, of 381, which gave first place to Rome, Canon 28 of Chalcedon thus reads: ". . . we issue the same decree and resolution concerning the prerogatives of the most holy church of the same Constantinople, new Rome. The fathers rightly accorded prerogatives to the see of older Rome, since that is the imperial city; and moved by the same purpose the 150 most devout bishops apportioned equal prerogatives to the most holy see of new Rome, reasonably judging that the city which is honoured by the imperial power and senate and enjoying privileges equaling older imperial Rome, should also be elevate to her level in ecclesiastical affairs *and take second place after her*." (Emphasis added).

[21]The exchange can be found in Migne's *Patrologia Latina*, Vol. 143 (cxliii), Col. 744–69. Also Mansi, *Sacrorum Conciliorum Nova Amplissima Collectio*, Vol. 19 (xix), Col. 635–56.

[22]A text is available at http://www.acad.carleton.edu/curricular/MARS/Schism.pdf. Consulted 31 May 2012.

power—can only strike us as petty, basically the *amour propre* of ambitious men. They have had other long-term consequences than the division itself, namely a priority given to power and control as ultimate concerns of leadership in the Church. When it came to the contention with Holy Roman Emperors over the appointment of bishops in the West these values would subsequently hold sway in the Gregorian Reform.

Our tradition has generally acclaimed the courage and commitment of Pope Gregory, who determined to preserve the Church from domination by the political powers. We admire his great success in this, but ought to acknowledge that it committed the Church to a pursuit of power and made it vulnerable to the connivances of power-hungry men within its own system.

Assertion of an unchallenged autonomy in the Pope, who need consult no one in the governance of the Church, obtained as benchmark claim for the centuries to come. Such structures, and the accoutrements of power that go with them, accord ill with the Gospel injunctions to humility, forgiveness, and service, or the injunction that those leading in the name of Christ must never make their power felt or dominate others as the rulers of the Gentiles do.[23] These habits appear to have been common well before the great break came, but we could have so much different a Church, united and known by its love, if this crisis with the Orthodox of the eleventh century had been dealt with otherwise.

Efforts to mend relations with the Orthodox churches have come in more recent years. Pope Paul VI and Patriarch Athanagoros solemnly lifted the eleventh-century excommunications during the Second Vatican Council and publicly embraced in the Hagia Sophia.[24] In the offices of the Pontifical Council for Promoting Christian Unity in Rome hangs a painting, gift of Athanagoros to the

---

[23]Mt. 20:25 f.; Mk 10:42 f.; Lk. 22:25 f.: "And He said to them, 'The kings of the Gentiles lord it over them; and those who have authority over them are called "Benefactors." But it is not this way with you, but the one who is the greatest among you must become like the youngest, and the leader like the servant.'"
[24]*JOINT CATHOLIC-ORTHODOX DECLARATION OF HIS HOLINESS POPE PAUL VI AND THE ECUMENICAL PATRIARCH ATHENAGORAS I,* 7 December 1965, from the Vatican website, http://www.vatican.va/holy_father/paul_vi/speeches/1965/documents/hf_p-vi_spe_19651207_common-declaration_en.html. Consulted 22 June 2012.

Pope, of the Apostles Peter and Andrew embracing.[25] Customarily each year Pope and Patriarch send representatives to take part in the major feasts of one another's churches, an orthodox representative at St Peter's on the feast of Saints Peter and Paul, a papal one in Istanbul on the feast of St Andrew. But these gestures come late, and cannot yet overcome the inherited atmosphere of suspicion and resentment.

Our more immediate concern is how far the attitudes of the power-holders in the Church now duplicate those of the eleventh-century imbroglio. The Church undergoing the crisis of our time is as much tested in the integrity of its Christian faith and practice as that of the earlier period, in which we can only judge that Church leadership was critically lacking in Christian character. To their shame, power-holders in the Church of the eleventh century had shown themselves to be more interested in the maintenance of their leadership position than in the interests of their community and its faith.

The Reformation

The ills of the Church during the intervening time between the eleventh-century divide and the Reformation arise clearly from these same characteristics in the exercise of Christian leadership. The preoccupation with relations of Church and State had grown constantly since Constantine first conferred large civil responsibilities on the Church.[26] Until then, it had been an outsider group, barely if at all tolerated by the Roman imperial State, alien to its culture and marginalized. Now imperial government saw in its structure new possibilities for the control of the empire.

In the West, where bishops of Rome found themselves increasingly the sole source of order as barbarian invaders ravaged the empire,[27] they allied themselves with the Frankish kings, gave the title of

[25]Observed by this writer on a visit in 1994.

[26]John Howard Yoder, *The Priestly Kingdom*, 2nd edn (Notre Dame: University of Notre Dame Press, 2001), ch. 7, "The Constantinian Sources of Western Social Ethics," 135–47.

[27]Thomas F. X. Noble, *The Republic of St. Peter: The Birth of the Papal State, 680–825* (Philadelphia: University of Pennsylvania Press, 1984), 22–53.

Holy Roman Emperor to their protector Charlemagne, and entered a long struggle for control with this new empire for centuries to come.[28]

Bishops and abbots, through the wealth gratefully given them for their restoration of order, had gained such power that the Ottonian emperors claimed a right to choose them within their realm. Their legitimacy was understood as stemming from their coronation by popes, and that placed them and their Salian successors in the position of needing to contest control of the papacy itself.[29] The system bred violence, corruption, and rival efforts at reform by religious and imperial forces until, at last, the able churchman Hildebrand, as Pope Gregory VII, brought the Emperor Henry IV to heel, deposing him from his office pending his submission, symbolized by his humiliation at Canossa.[30] The empire disintegrated. Gregory and succeeding popes, through to the end of the thirteenth century, could claim supreme power, civil as well as religious, and the title of reformer. But insistence on the power prerogatives, which became a principal concern of churchmen and popes, produced its own forms of corruption.

By the opening of the fourteenth century a French king, Philippe le Bel, successfully trumped the power claims of Pope Boniface VIII[31] and the papacy found itself reduced, for the 70 years described as the "Babylonian captivity of the Popes," to practical vassalage under the kings of France, their interests concentrated ever more heavily on revenue.[32] When in 1377 Pope Gregory IX reluctantly returned to Rome, just the year before his death, his French cardinals revolted against his successor, Urban VI, fled back to France, and for the

---

[28]James Bryce, 1st Viscount Bryce, *The Holy Roman Empire*, 1864, pp. 62–4.

[29]Uta-Renate Blumenthal, *The Investiture Controversy: Church and Monarchy from the Ninth to the Twelfth Century* (Philadelphia: University of Pennsylvania Press, 1988), 34–6.

[30]Herald Zimmermann, *Der Canossagang von 1077. Wirkungen und Wirklichkeit* (Mainz: Akademie der Wissenschaften und der Literatur; Wiesbaden: In Kommissionbei F. Steiner, 1975), esp. ch. 5.

[31]E. R. Chamberlain, "The Lord of Europe," Chapter III in *The Bad Popes* (New York: Barnes and Noble, 1998), 102–20.

[32]*The Avignon Papacy*, P. N. R. Zutshi, *The New Cambridge Medieval History: c. 1300–c. 1415*, Vol. VI, ed. Michael Jones (New York: Cambridge University Press, 2000), 653ff. See also Adrian Hastings, Alistair Mason and Hugh S. Pyper, *The Oxford Companion to Christian Thought* (Oxford: Oxford University Press, 2000), 227.

next 40 years, those of the "Great Western Schism," papal office was claimed by rival popes in Rome and Avignon.[33]

Church governance had become a sorry spectacle. Demands for reform "in head and members" dominated Christian life. Councils, sometimes summoned by popes, sometimes by episcopal initiative,[34] once by the Emperor Sigismund, claimed power in the Church equal or superior to that of a pope. Conciliar decision to depose both rival popes led, for a time, to three popes asserting simultaneous claims while the civil powers reached for military solutions to the problem they presented.[35] The Roman winners of the fight for papal office firmly suppressed, often with violence, all resistance to their supremacy prerogatives, among which was political control over a great part of Italy. This gave rise to the widespread impression that the papacy was the enemy of all reform.

All this constituted the context of the Reformation, which began with Martin Luther's protest against the sale of indulgences. This attracted the support of princes who saw an opportunity to break the papal thrall, and provided an arena for all the grievances that had accumulated over the centuries. An *ecclesia semper reformanda* had found its voice.

We should ask what was truly at stake here. The contest, the steady refusal of a series of popes to brook the claims of councils, clearly involved a question of jurisdiction, basically the same question that had occupied center stage in the battles with the Eastern patriarchates and with the civil authority of emperors and kings. Can we construe it as actually a question of doctrinal truth?

---

[33]Among the many studies of this period, one of the better is Johan Huizinga, *The Waning of the Middle Ages* (1924, reissued by Courier Dover Publications, 1999).

[34]Successive Councils of Vienne (1311–12), Constance (1414–17) and the migrating Council of Basel (1431), Ferrara (1438), Florence (1439), and Rome (1443–45), of which the most important is Constance, the one convened by the Emperor Sigimund in despair at the rival claims of popes, are all recorded in full in Tanner, I, 333–592.

[35]The Council of Pisa, 1409 but not included in the recognized list, deposed both papal claimants, Gregory XII (the one considered legitimate since by the Catholic Church) in Rome and Benedict XIII in Avignon, electing in their place Alexander V. But neither of the others accepted his deposition and the Church was left with three popes. After joining with Sigismund in convening the Council of Constance, Alexander was seized by his advisor, Cardinal Cossa of Bologna, died quickly and was succeeded by Cardinal Pedro di Luna, regarded as an antipope, who took the name Benedict XIII.

Many subsequent determinations have cast papal supremacy as strictly a doctrinal matter, an essential content of Christian faith.[36] It is contested still by Orthodox and Protestant churches, many of whom recognize the role of the successor of Peter as a cement of unity among Christians and as *primus inter pares*.

The primacy definition of the First Vatican Council,[37] a separate matter from the infallibility definition, affirmed submission to the papal primacy of jurisdiction involving government and discipline of the Church as necessary to Catholic faith and salvation. The Second Vatican Council[38] reaffirmed this teaching, but added new emphasis on the role of bishops. Bishops, it says, are not "vicars of the Roman Pontiff." Rather, in governing their local churches they are "vicars and legates of Christ." Together, they form a body, a "college," whose head is the pope. The entire episcopal college is responsible for the well-being of the Universal Church.

The centrality of the papal office is affirmed again in the declaration of the Congregation for the Doctrine of the Faith, *Dominus Jesus*, signed by its then Prefect, Cardinal Joseph Ratzinger, now Pope Benedict XVI, and by its then Secretary, Archbishop Tarcisio Bertone, now Cardinal Secretary of State. It was approved by Pope John Paul II and published on 6 August 2000.[39]

This document denies the title "church" to those "ecclesial communities," the Reformation bodies, "which have not preserved the valid Episcopate and the genuine and integral substance of the Eucharistic mystery." It recognizes that those who are baptized in these communities are, by Baptism, incorporated in Christ and thus are in a certain communion, albeit imperfect, with the Church. Those bodies, though, the Orthodox churches, which "while not existing in perfect communion with the Catholic Church, remain united to her by means of the closest bonds, that is, by apostolic succession

---

[36] Walter Kasper, *The Petrine ministry: Catholics and Orthodox in Dialogue: Academic Symposium held at the Pontifical Council for Promoting Christian Unity* (Matwah, NJ: Paulist Press, 2006), 188.

[37] Dogmatic Constitution of the Church of Christ, *Pastor Aeternus*.

[38] Dogmatic Constitution on the Church, *Lumen Gentium*, 22.

[39] CONGREGATION FOR THE DOCTRINE OF THE FAITH, DECLARATION *"DOMINUS IESUS"* ON THE UNICITY AND SALVIFIC UNIVERSALITY OF JESUS CHRIST AND THE CHURCH, from the Vatican website, http://www.vatican.va/roman_curia/congregations/cfaith/documents/rc_con_cfaith_doc_20000806_dominus-iesus_en.html. Consulted 22 June 2012.

and a valid Eucharist, are true particular Churches. Therefore, the Church of Christ is present and operative also in these Churches, even though they lack full communion with the Catholic Church, since they do not accept the Catholic doctrine of the Primacy, which, according to the will of God, the Bishop of Rome objectively has and exercises over the entire Church."[40]

But in his encyclical letter on ecumenism of 1995, *Ut Unum Sint*, preparing for the coming millenial celebration, Pope John Paul had written: "Whatever relates to the unity of all Christian communities clearly forms part of the concerns of the primacy. As Bishop of Rome I am fully aware, as I have reaffirmed in the present Encyclical Letter, that Christ ardently desires the full and visible communion of all those Communities in which, by virtue of God's faithfulness, his Spirit dwells. I am convinced that I have a particular responsibility in this regard, above all in acknowledging the ecumenical aspirations of the majority of the Christian Communities and in heeding the request made of me to find a way of exercising the primacy which, while in no way renouncing what is essential to its mission, is nonetheless open to a new situation."[41]

The question, then, whether or how recognition of the juridical primacy of the Bishop of Rome is the essential lynchpin of Christian faith, still bothers the Catholic Church, which in our own time has committed itself to the ecumenical quest for the unity of Christians, and knows well that this unity must find its expression in diversity.[42] Given the crisis of confidence which now troubles the Church, we must hope that this carefully nuanced commitment to the unity of Christians will shape our present response. We have to recognize

---

[40]*Dominus Jesus*, 17.

[41]Ioannis Paulus PP II, *Ut Unum Sint*, from the Vatican website, http://www.vatican.va/holy_father/john_paul_ii/encyclicals/documents/hf_jp-ii_enc_25051995_ut-unum-sint_en.html. Consulted 22 June 2012, #95.

[42]Most interesting, among the small number of responses to the Pope John Paul's plea for help in exercising the papal primacy, has been the contribution of John R. Quinn, the now retired Archbishop of San Francisco and past President of the National Conference of Catholic Bishops in the United States. He addressed the question first in a lecture he gave, on 29 June 1996, on the occasion of the centennial of Campion Hall, Oxford, "The Claims of the Primacy and the Costly Call to Unity" (www.ewtn.com/library/**BISHOPS**/OXFORD.HTM. Consulted 6 June 2012), then in a book, *The Reform of the papacy: The Costly Call to Christian Unity*, published in 1999 by The Crossroad Publishing Company.

that the response of Church leadership to the two previous major crises, in the eleventh and sixteenth centuries, to which we have compared it, had given such priority to the maintenance of juridical power that their commitment to unity stands in question, and that the crisis response of our own time wavers in this matter.

The unity we seek as constitutive of the Church is one of faith: faith in God in Christ through the working of the Holy Spirit. That is the basis of the *communio*, our association together as one body in Christ.

Any association of persons has its defining purpose and its interests, whether it be a local stamp club or the Church. There is no true association if it has no structure, as much or as little structure as it needs for its purpose. The small Pauline house churches had minimal structure by our standards for the universal communion in Christ. But the existence of a structure already implies that the association has some form of leadership.

We always hope that the leadership will have purposes and interests identical with those of the association itself. But inevitably, in any association, leadership has some interest in continuing to be the leadership. This may or may not well serve the interests of the association, but we learn to live with some degree of divergence. If that divergence increases, the association is in great trouble, and at the point when the protection of its power becomes the priority interest of leadership things may have gotten beyond repair. Dislodging corrupt and entrenched leaders may have become difficult or even impossible.

Thinking such thoughts puts us in the situation of a Martin Luther, whose initial complain, about the sale of indulgences, was hardly unorthodox and very low-key. Archbishop Albrecht of Mainz and Magdeburg, to whom it was first addressed, saw it at once as challenge to his authority, and doubtless his income.[43] He delated it to the Medici Pope Leo X in Rome, who treated Luther as an upstart to be marginalized, but Luther had hit a chord that found popular resonance. Over a next 3 years of escalating mutual insults, attempts to define Luther as heretic and the dispatch of a Cardinal Legate, Cajetan, who found himself unable to arrest Luther or force him to

---

[43]Hillerbrand, Hans J., article "Martin Luther: Indulgences and salvation," *Encyclopædia Britannica*, 2007.

recant, the quarrel became entrenched.[44] Political leaders rallied to his cause. By now, in his responses to Cajetan, Luther had denied the biblical basis of papal authority.[45] Leo X excommunicated him early in 1521 leaving the punishment, as was customary, to the "secular arm."[46] The Bull *Exsurge Domine*, had demanded that Luther recant 41 theses, including his 95-thesis document as a whole, but Luther had publicly set fire to the bull and decretals at Wittenberg on 10 December 1520. That brought Luther to judgment at the Diet of Worms, the general assembly of the estates of the Holy Roman Empire,[47] but the Elector Frederick III of Saxony took him under his protection, sequestering him in the Castle of Wartburg,[48] where he did his translation of the New Testament from Greek into German and authored many polemical writings.[49]

Election in January 1522 of a new Pope, the reform-minded Dutchman Adrian VI, who had been the childhood tutor to the Emperor Charles V, brought a changed situation. The instructions the Pope gave to his agent, Francesco Chiericati, contained a frank admission that the disorder of the Church was perhaps the fault of the Roman Curia itself, and that it should be reformed.[50] This represented a chance, despite the reluctance of the emissary, that the response to Luther might be other than merely defensive, but the Pope died in September 1523 before he could do more and things went back to full adversarial mode.

---

[44]Michael A. Mullett, *Martin Luther* (London: Routledge, 2004), 83. On his financial troubles, Mullett, 42, also Heiko Oberman, *Luther: Man Between God and the Devil* (New Haven: Yale University Press, 2006), 189.

[45]Mullett, 82.

[46]Martin Brecht (trans. Wolfgang Katenz), "Luther, Martin," in Hans J. Hillerbrand (ed.), *Oxford Encyclopedia of the Reformation* (New York: Oxford University Press, 1996), 2:463.

[47]Richard Marius, *Luther* (London: Quartet, 1975), 155.

[48]Diarmaid MacCulloch, *Reformation: Europe's House Divided, 1490–1700* (London: Allen Lane, 2003), 132.

[49]*Luther's Works*. Jaroslav Jan Pelikan, Hilton C. Oswald and Helmut T. Lehmann (eds), Vol. 48: Letters I, Philadelphia: Fortress Press, 1999, c.1963, 48:246; Mullett, 133.

[50]Hans Joachim Hillerbrand, *The division of Christendom: Christianity in the sixteenth century* (Westminster: John Knox Press, 2007), 141. See further Ludwig von Pastor, *The History of the Popes, from the Close of the Middle Ages*, Ralph Francis Kerr, ed., 1908, B. Herder, St. Louis, Vol. 7, pp. 348–9.

The adversarial character of Church response, with the growing acerbity of the challenge and the many other reformers who flocked to the cause of rebellion, led to wars, denunciations, and the identification of the sides with the political quarrels of the time. By the time of the Council of Trent, often interrupted by warfare and running from 1545 to 1563, both sides were intent on condemnation. Catholic and Protestant alike understood everything decided at the Council as a way to reject and dismiss the other. This included even such things as the Decree on Justification,[51] which, in the twentieth century, would be discovered by such Protestants as Karl Barth as expressing common faith.[52] The Protestant confessions, of Augsburg[53] or Westminster,[54] were understood the same way. Theological discussion ran in unrelated channels. The Reformers, denying any superior doctrinal authority of the Pope, based their perceptions purely on Scripture, to which they gave diverse but always literalist interpretations, while for the Catholics the defense of a history of doctrinal and jurisdictional tradition had priority. Both sides doubted the genuine Christianity of the other and we all spent the next four centuries screaming at each other.

Will we do otherwise now, as confidence in the sagacity and in the honesty of the traditional leadership, what we call the *Magisterium*, is at so low an ebb in a large part of the Catholic community and in the educated public at large? Another faction in the Church

---

[51]For full text, Tanner II, 671–83.

[52]Karl Barth, *Church Dogmatics*, Volume IV, Part 1: *The Doctrine of Reconciliation*; Part 2: *Doctrine of Reconciliation: Jesus Christ the Servant As Lord*; Part 3, 1st half: *Doctrine of Reconciliation: Jesus Christ the True Witness*; Part 3, 2nd half: *Doctrine of Reconciliation: Jesus Christ the True Witness*; Part 4 (unfinished): *Doctrine of Reconciliation: The Foundation of the Christian Life (Baptism)*. Catholic theologian Hans Küng's doctoral thesis, *Justification. La doctrine de Karl Barth et une réflexion catholique*, was finally published in English in 1964. It located a number of areas of agreement between Barthian and Catholic theologies of justification, concluding that the differences were not fundamental and did not warrant a division in the Church. (The book included a letter from Karl Barth, attesting that he agreed with Küng's representation of his theology.)

[53]The Augsburg Confession (1530) in Latin with a parallel English translation and with notes on the differences in the 1540 edition (Articles I–VII); from Philip Schaff's *Creeds of the Evangelical Protestant Churches* at the Christian Classics Ethereal Library.

[54]*Westminster Confession of Faith*, http://www.reformed.org/documents/wcf_with_proofs/. Consulted 22 June 2012.

concludes that any doubt of either that sagacity or the honesty of the official leadership is a plain disloyalty to the Catholic faith itself. Our faith, though, is not properly invested in the institution as such but in God, who made us and loves us, in Christ his Son who saved us, and in the Holy Spirit who guides us to all truth.

The one side believes that the Holy Spirit lives only in the Vatican and, to a much lesser degree, in the episcopal residences. Do their inhabitants believe that of themselves? The others are likely to lay claim to a presence of the Holy Spirit somewhere that simply suits their predilections. The promise of his permanent presence and protection stands as very definite in the teaching of Jesus himself, so we shouldn't really worry that the Church will fail. Yet the promise would seem to be that the Spirit informs the Church as a whole, speaking so very quietly that we have to listen to one another with great care.

3

The Monolith Church as it emerged from the French Revolution

Care for one another and a quest for reconciliation did not characterize the way Christians, Protestant or Catholic, engaged one another after the Reformation breach. Instead, the aftermath of the religious quarrels saw more than a century of savage warfare, hardly the vision of the Carpenter of Nazareth. Brutality and intolerance engulfed Europe's people as the opposing sides strove to destroy one another or force the other to conformity. Strong convictions about doctrine and authority yielded nothing to any urgings of mercy or forgiveness. As a result, by the time of the Peace of Westphalia in 1648, Europeans came away from the experience with a profound skepticism about all their religious institutions. Most people were still ready enough to submit, though more from fear of a frequently threatened divine retribution or the certainty of state persecution than from affection. They vested their belief in an angry God. But churches, all of them, were suspect, and for the first time in Europe it became socially respectable to announce oneself as atheist or agnostic and break relations with the Church.

This development coincided, to the great disadvantage of the Christian churches, with another, which we can call the emergence of the Modern World.

Understanding of the world had already changed from the time of Copernicus and his heliocentric model of the universe.[1] That Church authority should have seen this as contrary to a doctrine of faith was the Church's misfortune. Galileo Galilei, in fact, was a better theologian than those who judged and condemned him, as he saw that the Scriptures taught about the relation of God to humanity and were not the place to seek knowledge of astronomy.[2] But the persecution he suffered set up a long-term perception that Christian faith was at odds with the newly proclaimed scientific method, which constituted the first building block of the Modern World. The repercussions of that method, giving birth to modern technology, affected every aspect of life so much that belief in a conflict between religion and science could not but work out to the discrediting of faith.

A second major element of the Modern outlook, the glorification of reason, from the beginnings of the Enlightenment in the late seventeenth century,[3] came also to be seen as making faith superfluous. The Catholic Church, particularly, seemed to its leaders such a burden on intellectual growth that the deist Voltaire could make its defeat a program: *écrasez l'infâme*. A third element, political liberalism,[4] which proceeded from the age of enlightened despots through demands for the accountability of governments to a growing insistence on representative forms, gave shape to a Modern outlook that would dominate as the intellectual mainstream of European and American culture for the next two centuries.

In the Modern Era, these Three Holy Things, science, enlightenment, and liberalism, came to be venerated as the answer to all the questions of life and history. Religious people, excluded from that mainstream, took to what twentieth-century Latin Americans would call "European theology," theologies that spanned the whole spectrum of Catholic and Protestant, right and left, but had as their common denominator a

---

[1] Nicolaus Copernicus Gesamtausgabe: *Urkunden, Akten und Nachrichten: Texte und Übersetzungen,* 23ff.

[2] Annibale Fantoli, "The Disputed Injunction and its Role in Galileo's Trial," 139, in Ernan McMullin (ed.), *The Church and Galileo* (Notre Dame, IN: University of Notre Dame Press, 2005), 117–49.

[3] Too large a subject to annotate. A good general source is Ellen Wilson and Peter Reill, *Encyclopedia of the Enlightenment* (2004).

[4] This liberalism was not the economic free-market concept but rather the expectation of accountability in government.

response to the question: "Why should anyone believe these things in the Modern World?" Apologetics took over professional theology in the face of the prevailing skeptical mindset. It was not until the awful experiences of the twentieth-century wars brought about a realization that the Three Holy Things had failed to answer all the questions that the intellectual mainstream once again become interested in all the wisdom sources, including the religions, while still retaining as much as ever its suspicion of the religious institutions. Liberation theologians[5] in Latin America then began seeing the apologetic European theologies as essentially adolescent. Either you believed the Gospel revelations or you didn't, but the test, the "Questioner," was how you responded to them, how central to your faith was care, even "preferential option" for the poor.[6] The Gospel has more to say as well: forgiveness and reconciliation, things that constituted a more important measure of a life of faith than simple doctrinal submission.

The churches, then, finding themselves increasingly marginalized in a Europe that blamed them for the paroxysm of violence it had experienced in the religious wars, a charge they could hardly evade, lost ground throughout the succeeding centuries. Interests of dynasties took precedence over those of churches, and kings, in Portugal, in Spain, in France, could bend the Church to their wills. A typical episode was the expulsion of the Jesuits, known for their defense of the popes, from each of those kingdoms in turn, until in 1773 Pope Clement XIV was browbeaten into suppressing the order altogether.[7] Rivalry for power had characterized church/state relations throughout the Middle Ages, but now the Westphalian system, defined in terms of nation states, gave kings and rulers supremacy over all the churches through its principle "*cujus regio ejus religio*."[8] Territorialism had been redefined, with every king entitled to determine what religious denomination all his subjects must belong to—or be punished.

---

[5]The paradigmatic book is Gustavo Gutiérrez, *A Theology of Liberation: History, Politics and Salvation* (Maryknoll, NY: Orbis Books, 1988).

[6]James B. Nickoloff, ed., *Gustavo Gutierrez: Essential Writings* (Maryknoll, NY: Orbis, 1996), 145.

[7]Bertrand M. Roehner, "Jesuits and the State: A Comparative Study of their Expulsions (1590–1990)," *Religion* 27(2) (April 1997): 165–82.

[8]The concept had reigned since the 1555 Peace of Augsburg, but the actual phrase was first coined in 1582 by the legist Joachim Stephani (1544–1623) of the University of Greifswald. Cf. Steven Ozment, *The Age of Reform 1250–1550* (New Haven: Yale University Press, 1986), 259, n. 13.

But the experience of massive rejection by the forces of the French Revolution still came as a shock to Catholic authorities. People associated them with the oppressive secular regimes that had mastered them even while trivializing them. Bishops were banished, priests went to the guillotine, churches and cathedrals were desecrated and rededicated to a goddess-like Reason. Napoleon could confiscate church property and estates at will and did so right across his conquests. As signal of his power he insisted on crowning himself rather than receive the crown from the hands of the Pope Pius VII, whom he had summoned to Paris to crown him. He would permit no sign of submission to a Pope.

A nineteenth-century Church responded by battening down the hatches. Pope Pius VI, first papal victim of the revolution, died a prisoner in France in August 1799. He had made his close relative, Barnaba Niccolò Maria Luigi Chiaramonti, who had taken the name Dom Gregory as a Benedictine monk, a Cardinal. When the armies of the Revolution invaded Italy in 1797 Cardinal Chiaramonti advocated patience and submission to the Cisalpine Republic they established. In his Christmas homily he argued that there was no opposition between a democratic form of government and being a good Catholic: "Christian virtue makes men good democrats. . . . Equality is not an idea of philosophers but of Christ . . . and do not believe that the Catholic religion is against democracy."[9]

Chiaramonti's election to the papacy as Pius VII in 1800, after a 3-month stalemate, resulted from the inability of the Habsburg emperor to impose any of his three candidates, any one of whom would have been implacably opposed to France. His willingness to cooperate with the Revolution did not save him from the humiliation of Napoleon's coronation, to which he consented as the price of regaining control of some territories of the Papal States, but when Napoleon invaded and confiscated the Papal States in 1809 he arrested and imprisoned the Pope. At the fall of Napoleon and his exile to Elba in 1813 the Pope was released and reinstated in his states, by terms of the Concordat of Fontainbleau,[10] his unhappy reign ending in 1823, but not before he had condemned for heresy, in 1814, Melkite bishop, Germanos Adam, who had shown

---

[9]Thomas Bokenkotter, *Church and Revolution: Catholics in the Struggle for Democracy and Social Justice* (New York: Doubleday, 1998), 32.
[10]Frank McLynn, *Napoleon* (London: Pimlico, 1998), 593–4.

conciliarist tendencies in wanting a Council called to restore the fortunes of the Church.[11]

On the death of Pius VII, the forces of reaction took full control. Cardinals known as the *zelanti* elected, over the opposition of France, Cardinal Annibale Francesco Clemente Melchiore Girolamo Nicola Sermattei della Genga, who reigned as Pope Leo XII from 1823 to 1829. Della Genga had been a secretary to the aristocratic Pope Pius VI, outraged at his imprisonment. He had served as papal diplomat in several of the courts and countries invaded by Napoleon. When Napoleon abolished the Estates of the Church in 1798 he was exiled as a state prisoner to the Abbey of Monticelli. On release in 1814 he carried the congratulations of Pius VII to the restored King Louis XVIII. He was later promoted to Cardinal and from 1820 made Vicar-General of His Holiness for the Diocese of Rome.

Upon his election, Leo embarked on a course of deep conservatism. "He was determined to change the condition of society, bringing it back to the utmost of his power to the old usages and ordinances, which he deemed to be admirable; and he pursued that object with never flagging zeal."[12] Condemning Bible societies and putting all education in the Papal States strictly under priestly control, all secondary education, as well as the proceedings of all courts, to be carried out in Latin. All charitable institutions came under his own direct supervision. "The results of his method of governing his states soon showed themselves in insurrections, conspiracies, assassinations and rebellion, especially in Umbria, the Marches and Romagna; the violent repression of which, by a system of espionage, secret denunciation, and wholesale application of the gibbet and the galleys, left behind it to those who were to come afterwards a very terrible, rankling and long-enduring debt of party hatreds, of political and social demoralization, and—worst of all—a contempt for and enmity to the law, as such."[13]

He prohibited Jews from owning property, leaving them only the briefest time to sell what they had. He required all Roman

---

[11]Adrian Fortescue and George D. Smith, *The Uniate Eastern Churches* (Piscataway, NJ: First Gorgias Press, 2001), 210.
[12]Luigi Carlo Farini, *Lo stato Romano, dell'anno 1815 a 1850* (Turin, 1850), vol. I, p. 17, quoted by Thomas Adolphus Trollope, *The Story of the Life of Pius the Ninth*, vol. I (Richard Bentley and Son, 1877), 39f.
[13]Trollope, p. 41.

residents to listen to Catholic catechetical teaching, driving most Roman Jews to emigrate, to Trieste, Lombardy, and Tuscany.[14] He imposed rigorous dress codes for all citizens, particularly for women, excommunicating any seamstress who made gowns deemed too revealing. His obscurantism and a superstitious character of his piety made him a mockery to the more liberal opinion of his time.

Leo was succeeded briefly by Pope Pius VIII, elected in March 1829 and dying early in December 1830. His one Encyclical, *Traditi Humiliati*,[15] warned against the danger of vernacular translations of the Bible "with new interpretations contrary to the Church's laws. They skillfully distort the meaning by their own interpretation. They print the Bibles in the vernacular and, absorbing an incredible expense, offer them free even to the uneducated. Furthermore, the Bibles are rarely without perverse little inserts to ensure that the reader imbibes their lethal poison instead of the saving water of salvation." In a further Brief, *Litteris Altero*,[16] he condemned the Masons as secret societies and had more to say against Bible translations. During his brief pontificate, Catholic Emancipation occurred in the United Kingdom, and the July Revolution (1830) in France—after which he recognized Louis Philippe (1830–48), who had toppled Charles X, as the *de facto* king of France.

After that brief reign, Bartolomeo Alberto Cappellari, known as Father Mauro in the Camaldolese order, became Pope as Gregory XVI. His reign, from 1831 to 1846, recapitulated that of Leo XII. Not yet a bishop though a Cardinal, he had to be consecrated quickly by his rival for the election, Cardinal Bartolomeo Pacca. Coming to the throne in the midst of political upheaval and the seizure of nearby Ancona by the new king of France, he repeatedly had to call upon Austrian troops to put down red-shirted republican guerrillas. He and his Secretary of State, Cardinal Luigi Lambruschini, dedicated themselves to opposing the arrival in Italy of gas lighting and railways, fearing they would promote commerce and increase the power of the bourgeoisie, leading to demands for liberal reforms which would undermine the monarchical power of the Pope over central Italy. He liked to call railroads "*chemin d'enfers*" (roads to Hell), playing on the French term *chemin de fer* ("iron roads"). To

---

[14]Farini, *loc. cit.*
[15]24 May 1829.
[16]25 May 1830.

his great credit, he issued an Encyclical, *In Supremo Apostolatus*, in 1839 condemning the Atlantic slave trade.[17] He also condemned the French priest Hugues Felicité Robert de Lammenais[18] for his liberalism and what he regarded as religious indifferentism.[19]

The quarrel with Lammenais epitomized a major preoccupation of all these popes with the defense of Ultramontanism, a cultivation of the centralization of Church authority in Rome and the Pope, contrasted in the nineteenth century with Gallicanism, the control or at least influence of the state. Lammenais, prominent as a preacher and writer, polemicist against the state's indifference to the Church's religious freedom claims, accounted himself thoroughly ultramontanist. He had defended the Church against interference by Napoleon and greeted the Bourbon restoration of Louis XVIII in 1815 with great enthusiasm, as portending a regeneration of the Catholic Church. His earlier works had the approval of Pope Leo XII, who invited him to Rome and offered him an influential position.

He gave no approval, though, to monarchist absolutism. His ultramontanism led him to call for general freedom of religion and thoroughgoing democratization, and that made him suspect to Pope Gregory XVI, who wanted no part of either. With his colleagues Montalembert and Lacordaire he set off for Rome in 1831 looking in vain for the new Pope's approval but his principles led him to a full breach with the Church.

We must make an assessment here. Church leadership had met, throughout the century, with insult and attack. Church influence was in full decline. The response was essentially to insist on prerogative, draw the defense perimeter, and require uttermost deference from the remaining adherents. The Church had effectively lost the proletariat. It tried in every way to frustrate the aspirations of bourgeoisie for

---

[17]Website *Papal Encyclicals Online*, http://www.papalencyclicals.net/Greg16/g16sup.htm, *In Supremo Apostolatus*, Apostolic Letter condemning the slave trade, written by Pope Gregory XVI and read during the 4th Provincial Council of Baltimore, 3 December 1839. Consulted 13 July 2012. At a time when American Catholics generally had no objections to the institution of slavery, the Pope reviewed the history of Christian and New Testament positions on slavery, recommended the full liberation of slaves and condemned in severe terms the slave trade and the reduction to slavery of "negroes, Indians and other wretched peoples" as "a shame to the Christian name."

[18]*Singulari Nos*, 25 June 1834.

[19]*Mirari Vos*, 15 August 1832.

fear that they might trample on those precious prerogatives. Popes and the Church as they shaped it thus put themselves out of range for any true engagement with the world of their time. Nothing but domination would do.

The pursuit of those vanishing prerogatives of power had to do fundamentally with political privilege, little to do with the Gospel, with love of God or man, with reconciliation or the service of the needy other. This was hardly new, or an aberration, as the contesting of power with the state had been a theme of Christian history ever since the Constantinian settlement. Gospel could surface, as with Gregory XII's brave condemnation of slavery, but in general it was not a primary interest of the leadership.

It seemed all this might change with the election, in June of 1846, of Giovanni Maria Mastai-Ferretti as Pope Pius IX. His nineteenth-century predecessor Pius VII had held the record for the longest pontificate in history, other than possibly for Peter, but Pius IX would exceed him, remaining in office for 32 years until 1878. He began his pontificate with the reputation of a liberal.

Pope Pius VII had personally supported his study for the priesthood when it seemed he was disqualified because of epilepsy, and it was in gratitude to that Pope that Mastai-Ferretti took the name Pius. As Archbishop of Spoleto, he had generously obtained pardon for the participants in an abortive insurrection during the general upheaval of 1831.[20] He organized relief with great efficiency after an earthquake and had a reputation for generosity to the poor. Moved to Imola and made a cardinal, he dedicated himself to the better education of his priests and to charity, regularly visiting prisoners in the jail and organizing programs for street children. An Italian patriot, known to be a supporter of administrative changes in the Papal States and a critic of Pope Gregory XVI, he sympathized with the nationalist movement in Italy and was even rumored to have joined the Freemasons.[21]

His election, after a deadlock in the conclave between conservative candidates, was greeted with joy by the Romans. Prince Metternich of the conservative Austrian Empire had sent a Cardinal, Archbishop Carlo Gaisrick of Milan, to veto Mastai-Ferretti's election, but he

---

[20]Josef Schmidlin, *Papstgeschichte*, vol. IV (Köstel-Pusztet München, 1939), 8–10.
[21]Dudley Wright, *Roman Catholicism and Freemasonry* (London: William Rider & Son, Limited, 1922), 172–5.

arrived too late. Elsewhere in Europe his election was received with enthusiasm.[22] Even English Protestants saw him as an enlightened man who would bring freedom and progress to Europe.[23] He began his reign with a general amnesty of all political prisoners in the Papal States.[24]

Then the bottom fell out. Disparate revolutionary movements convulsed every part of Europe in 1848.[25] The Pope, sovereign ruler of the Papal States as well as head of the Catholic Church, regarded himself as above the conflict and refused to declare war on Austria. In a calculated move in November, assassins claimed his Minister of Justice, Pellegrino Rossi. They disarmed the Swiss Guards and made the Pope a prisoner in his palace. The Pope, in disguise, fled to Gaeta, a fortress belonging to the Kingdom of the Two Sicilies.[26] He was briefly guest on board the USS Constitution, "Old Ironsides," then on Mediterranean station, along with King Ferdinand II, the first time any pope had been on the equivalent of US territory.[27]

Revolution and Roman Republic quickly failed, but this traumatic experience put an end to the Pope's liberalism. Returned to Rome in 1850, his main concerns for the rest of his long pontificate were the assertion of his authority and his prerogatives as head of the Papal States.

Doctrinal authority was an issue from the start. In 1854 he solemnly defined as doctrine the Immaculate Conception of the Virgin Mary, meeting all the requirements that would later be invoked for the definition of papal infallibility. He produced a record number of encyclicals, 38 in all, using them not so much for teaching as for condemnation of errors or offenses. Of these the most memorable is

---

[22]Seppelt-Löffle, *Papstgeschichte* (München, 1933), 408, where he adds: "For the next twenty months, Pius IX was the most popular man on the peninsula; cries of 'Long Live the Pope' were unending." (My translation).

[23]Pougeois, *Histoire de Pie IX, son pontificatet son siècle* (Paris: J. Pougeois, 1877), I, 215. Schmidlin, IV, 23.

[24]Eamon Duffy, *Saints and Sinners, a History of the Popes* (New Haven: Yale University Press, 1997), 223.

[25]Michael Rapport, *1848: Year of Revolutions* (New York: Basic Books, 2010).

[26]Schmidlin, 35. The palace was the Quirinale. Only after his return to Rome in 1850 did the Pope take up residence in the Vatican, where his successors have lived ever since.

[27]Tyrone G. Martin, *A Most Fortunate Ship: A Narrative History of "Old Ironsides"* (Annapolis, MD: Naval Institute Press, 1997), 291–9.

the 1864 *Quanta Cura*, which contained the Syllabus of Errors, seen ever since as an index of how reactionary the nineteenth-century Church had become. It condemned a list of fully 80 propositions, many of them political or social, as heresy. Any encroachment of the state on prerogatives of the Church found its way onto this list. It attacked many forms of secularism, rationalism, or modernism. In its own day, the list proved controversial. Influence of the Church had declined steadily over the century and this convinced people that its author was an enemy of progress.[28] Catholics were at the same time generally glad to see it defending the liberty of the Church, and in this period not offended by the way it claimed exclusive privilege for its expression of truth over any other confessional stand. American Catholics saw the Pope's view of the relation of Church and state consonant with those of their founding fathers, especially regarding the temporal rights of the Church in areas of education, marriage, and family.[29]

The weightiest action of the pontificate was the First Vatican Council, convened by the Pope in 1869 just as his secular sovereignty over the territory of the Papal States came most under threat. Since his return to Rome in 1852 from his exile in Gaeta, these had come under the shelter of the French Second Empire and Napoleon III, who protected them from domination by Austria. The French had not been able to prevent the seizure of all the papal provinces except Latium, the area just around Rome itself, in September 1860 by *risorgimento* King Victor Emmanuel II of Italy. Now France itself came under threat from Prussia, and without French protection the last remnants of the Pope's civil power would stand at risk. The Pope saw the assertion of his doctrinal power as the best antidote to the temporal loss.[30]

In defining the Immaculate Conception as doctrine, the Pope had decided with the Franciscans over the Dominicans in a centuries-old controversy.[31] But it opened the question whether the Pope had the power to define something as infallible doctrine without the bishops. Pius IX wanted to see a further definition of the infallible

---

[28]John Gilmary Shea, *The Life of Pope Pius IX* (New York: T. Kelly, 1877), 279.
[29]Gilmary, 282.
[30]Raffaele De Cesare, *The Last Days of Papal Rome* (London: Archibald Constable & Co., 1909), 422f.
[31]August Franzen, *Papstgeschichte* (Freiburg: Herder, 1988), 340.

teaching of the Pope, by himself, and have it confirmed by the bishops in Council.

The subject of papal infallibility had come up before, as extensively studied by Brian Tierney.[32] The *Dictatus Papae*, attributed to Pope Gregory VII (1073–85) but apparently originating in 1090, had asserted that no one can judge the pope (Proposition 19) and that "the Roman church has never erred; nor will it err to all eternity, the Scripture bearing witness" (Proposition 22).[33] In the fourteenth century, the Franciscan Spirituals, a faction influenced by Joachim di Fiore and the Joachimist Peter Olivi, argued the obligation of Christians who wished to live lives of perfection to the maintenance of apostolic poverty, on the model of Christ and his apostles who had possessed absolutely nothing, separately or jointly.[34] Pope Nicholas III, they claimed, had defined this irrevocably in his Bull *Exiit qui seminat* of 1279, and it stood therefore as infallible doctrine. Avignon Pope John XXII, seeing that this would make it impossible for the Church to have any possessions, condemned this view by his Bull *Cum inter nonnullos* in 1323, as "erroneous and heretical."[35] He returned to the topic in 1324 in the Bull *Quia Quorendam*, denying as "coming from the Father of lies," the premise of his enemies, which said: "What the Roman pontiffs have once defined in faith and morals with the key of knowledge stands so immutably that it is not permitted to a successor to revoke it."[36] For the next couple of centuries, until this argument died down, his successors were insistently opposed to any definition of infallibility.

In more recent times, Popes since Pius IX have seen infallibility as granting increased power to the Holy See and diminishing that of bishops. Those popes of the earlier period regarded it as a limitation on their freedom and their power if they were bound by the pronouncements of their predecessors. Pius IX, though, insisted

---

[32]Brian Tierney, *Origins of Papal Infallibility, 1150-1350: A Study on the Concepts of Infallibility, Sovereignty and Tradition in the Middle Ages* (Leiden: Brill Archive, 1972), esp. 179–81.

[33]M. C. Miller, "Power and the Holy in the Age of the Investiture Conflict: A Brief History with Documents." (New York: Bedford Series in History & Culture, 2005), 81–3.

[34]Christopher Kleinhenz, *Medieval Italy: An Encyclopedia* (New York: Routledge, 2003), I, 373.

[35]Klaus Schatz, *Papal Primacy* (Collegeville, MN: Liturgical Press, 1996), 117f.

[36]Tierney, 186.

so vehemently on a doctrine of his personal infallibility "in matters of faith and morals" that expressing opposition was regarded as disloyal, even if the objectors were bishops.

Definition of infallibility by the First Vatican Council has had profound psychological influence on the subsequent understanding of the Church, whether by Catholics or by non-Catholics. Folk-theology often took it as meaning that Councils of the Church would never again be needed, as the Pope could do all the teaching on his own. More sophisticated thought has considered that infallibility a commonplace mark of serious teaching in the Church, expecting that the Church's doctrinal life would commonly bear its mark. People have tended to read the frequent encyclical letters of popes as at least touched by infallibility.

James Gibbons, subsequently made a Cardinal as Archbishop of Baltimore, attended the Council as an auxiliary bishop and voted for the infallibility definition. Asked later in life the extent of papal infallibility, he responded "that during the last interview I had with His Holiness he addressed me constantly as Cardinal *Jibbons*."[37] Pope Benedict XVI, speaking impromptu to priests in 2005, remarked: "The Pope is not an oracle; he is infallible in very rare situations, as we know."[38] Pope John XXIII said once: "I am only infallible if I speak infallibly but I shall never do that, so I am not infallible."[39]

To define the infallibility doctrine, the First Vatican Council had to establish first a doctrine of papal primacy. Long acknowledged, in much lesser form, by the Orthodox and many other churches, the Petrine primacy received this definition in the words of the Dogmatic Constitution *Pastor Aeternus* (18 July 1870), Chapter III: "... we teach and declare that, by divine ordinance, the Roman Church possesses a pre-eminence of ordinary power over every other church, and that this jurisdictional power of the Roman pontiff is both episcopal and immediate. Both clergy and faithful, of

---

[37]William V. Shannon, *The American Irish* (Amherst: University of Massachusetts Press, 1989), 120. Ashley Horace Thorndike, *Modern Eloquence* (New York: Modern Eloquence Corporation, 1928), 2.

[38]"Pope Has No Easy 'Recipe' for Church Crisis," *Zenit*, 29 July 2005, retrieved 8 July 2009, zenit.org.

[39]Quoted from Hans Küng, after his audience with Pope Benedict XVI, by John Wilkins, "The 'straight arrow' theologian and the Pope," *National Catholic Reporter*, 12 November 2010.

whatever rite and dignity, both singly and collectively, are bound to submit to this power by the duty of hierarchical subordination and true obedience, and this not only in matters of faith and morals, but in those which regard the discipline and government of the church throughout the world. . . . This is the teaching of the catholic truth, and no one can depart from it without endangering his faith and salvation."[40] The Constitution goes on to say (in Chapter IV):

> Therefore, faithfully adhering to the tradition received from the beginning of the Christian faith, to the glory of God our saviour, for the exaltation of the catholic religion and for the salvation of the Christian people, with the approval of the sacred council, we teach and define as a divinely revealed dogma that when the Roman pontiff speaks *ex cathedra*, that is, when, in the exercise of his office as shepherd and teacher of all Christians, in virtue of this supreme apostolic authority, he defines a doctrine concerning faith or morals to be held by the whole church, he possesses, by the divine assistance promised to him in blessed Peter, that infallibility which the divine Redeemer willed his church to enjoy in defining doctrine concerning faith or morals. Therefore, such definitions of the Roman pontiff are of themselves, and not by the consent of the church, irreformable.
>
> So then, should anyone, which God forbid, have the temerity to reject this definition of ours: let him be anathema.[41]

Strong words, but they contain within themselves powerful conditioning limits on the reach of the doctrine. Most centrally, the infallibility of the Pope is defined in terms of an undefinable: "that infallibility which the divine Redeemer willed his church to enjoy in defining doctrine concerning faith or morals."

How are we to envision that? We have the promise of John 16:13: "But when He, the Spirit of truth, comes, He will guide you into all the truth; for He will not speak on His own initiative, but whatever He hears, He will speak; and He will disclose to you what is to come." It is buttressed by Isaiah 11:2: "The Spirit of the LORD will rest on him–the Spirit of wisdom and of understanding, the Spirit of

---

[40]Tanner, II, 813f.
[41]Ibid., 816.

counsel and of power, the Spirit of knowledge and of the fear of the LORD." John 14:17 describes him as "the Spirit of truth. The world cannot accept him, because it neither sees him nor knows him. But you know him, for he lives with you and will be in you." And at John 14:26 we have: "But the Counselor, the Holy Spirit, whom the Father will send in my name, will teach you all things and will remind you of everything I have said to you."

But the Spirit's guidance cannot be confined to hierarchical pronouncements. Yves Congar is a good guide in this matter. The whole membership of the Mystical Body of Christ, is the Church, and within it each individual member is a gift of the Spirit to the Church as a whole. The Spirit uses the "graced initiatives" of many individuals to build up a community made up by the brotherly contributions of all its members.[42]

The particular work of the Spirit, though, is to unify these diverse individuals and gifts into an ecclesial unity as he did at Pentecost. In fact, Congar would argue, only in its unity does the Church have access to the fullness of the Spirit's gifts.[43] This unity could only be achieved by God himself, honoring and never violating the very diversity and individuality he has created.[44]

Such an understanding of Spirit-led unity must be both sociological and ecumenical, the oneness of the Church not only an institutional ideal but an experienced personal reality, a relationship of different ethnic groups and commitment to ecumenical dialogue among the representative of diverse faith traditions.[45]

We have to see the promise of indefectibility of the Church, too, in terms of the agonizing question put by Jesus when, in describing the judge's reluctant conceding of justice to a poor widow, not because he is just but only because she persists in her demands and he fears she will wear him out, the Lord says (Lk. 18:6–8): "Hear what the unrighteous judge says. And will not God vindicate his elect, who

---

[42]Yves Congar, *I Believe in the Holy Spirit*, trans. David Smith, 3 volumes (New York: Crossroads Publishing, 2006), General Introduction, I, vii–x. This entire study by Yves Congar cast great light on the entire long history of the understanding of this leading by the Holy Spirit, especially rich in the Orthodox tradition. Cf. Elizabeth Theresa Groppe, "The Contribution of Yves Congar's Theology of the Holy Spirit," *Theological Studies* 62 (2001), 452–7, and Groppe's *Yves Congar's Theology of the Holy Spirit* (New York: Oxford University Press, 2004), 4–8, 100f.
[43]Congar, 2, 206.
[44]Ibid., 17.
[45]Ibid., 21.

cry out to him day and night? Will he delay over them? I tell you, he will bring about justice for them quickly. However, when the Son of Man comes, will he find faith on earth?" This cannot be a merely rhetorical question.

The conditions under which the popes may exercise their infallibility also deserve our attention. He must be speaking *ex cathedra*, that is, invoking supreme apostolic authority in his office of shepherd and teacher of all Christians. He must be defining a doctrine concerning faith or morals as necessarily to be believed by the whole Church. The number of times all those conditions have been fulfilled is very few, far fewer than the teachings of Ecumenical Councils.

Some would count only the two explicit dogmatic definitions of Marian doctrine by Pius IX in his 1854 Encyclical, *Ineffabilis Deus*, by which he defined the Immaculate Conception, and Pius XII in the 1950 Apostolic Constitution, *Munificentissimus Deus*, by which he defined the Bodily Assumption of Mary into Heaven. In both those instances all the criteria were invoked.[46]

Historian Klaus Schatz considered including as a claim to infallibility the *Tomus Leonis ad Flavianum*, Pope Leo the Great's

---

[46]*Ineffabilis Deus*, ". . . by the inspiration of the Holy Spirit, for the honor of the Holy and undivided Trinity, for the glory and adornment of the Virgin Mother of God, for the exaltation of the Catholic Faith, and for the furtherance of the Catholic religion, by the authority of Jesus Christ our Lord, of the Blessed Apostles Peter and Paul, and by our own: "We declare, pronounce, and define that the doctrine which holds that the most Blessed Virgin Mary, in the first instance of her conception, by a singular grace and privilege granted by Almighty God, in view of the merits of Jesus Christ, the Savior of the human race, was preserved free from all stain of original sin, is a doctrine revealed by God and therefore to be believed firmly and constantly by all the faithful."

"Hence, if anyone shall dare – which God forbid! – to think otherwise than as has been defined by us, let him know and understand that he is condemned by his own judgment; that he has suffered shipwreck in the faith; that he has separated from the unity of the Church; and that, furthermore, by his own action he incurs the penalties established by law if he should are to express in words or writing or by any other outward means the errors he think in his heart."

Munificentissimus Deus, 44f. ". . . by the authority of our Lord Jesus Christ, of the Blessed Apostles Peter and Paul, and by our own authority, we pronounce, declare, and define it to be a divinely revealed dogma: that the Immaculate Mother of God, the ever Virgin Mary, having completed the course of her earthly life, was assumed body and soul into heavenly glory.

"Hence if anyone, which God forbid, should dare willfully to deny or to call into doubt that which we have defined, let him know that he has fallen away completely from the divine and Catholic Faith."

letter received in 449 by the Council of Chalcedon, which was a deciding element in the Council's teaching on the two natures of Christ precisely because it had come from the Pope.[47] But the letter makes no claim to personal infallibility but rather commends the teaching of Leo to the consideration of the Council, which itself is to decide the matter. It contains no threatening language of anathemas, though those were common in Conciliar statements of the period. The same applies to the letter of Pope Agatho on the two wills of Christ, received by the Third Council of Constantinople in 680.[48] The reception of both these papal letters evidenced and helped to build up the respect in which teaching of the bishops of Rome was held throughout the Church, but there was no appeal to infallibility.

The Monothelite dispute, though, raises the question of papal infallibility more directly with the endorsement given the doctrine by Pope Honorius in 635. The quarrel had arisen when the Emperor Heraclius sought to unify his realm by offering a middle ground between the two-nature teaching of Chalcedon and the many Non-Chalcedonians of Syria, Mesopotamia, and Egypt, Monophysites who insisted that Christ had only one nature. The Emperor proposed what seemed to him a convenient compromise, saying that Christ had two natures, as asserted at Chalcedon, but only one will. His Patriarch of Constantinople, Sergius, advocating the position, wrote to Pope Honorius, and in return received the reply that the Pope agreed and that there should be no more discussion of the matter. The doctrine generated far more heat, including an incident in which Pope Martin I, for refusing to endorse the Emperor's opinion and entering once more into the prohibited discussion of it, was kidnapped from Rome, imprisoned in Constantinople, and so severely tortured that he died of his sufferings. But Honorius was condemned and anathematized in the letter of Agatho and by the Third Council of Constantinople. Whether because of the formulas used by Honorius in favor of Monothelitism or simply because he was so condemned as heretic in his very office as Pope, the episode

---

[47]Klaus Schatz, S.J., *Papal Primacy: From Its Origins to the Present* (English translation, Liturgical Press, 1996), 42–6. Cf. also Francis A. Sullivan, S.J., *Creative Fidelity: Weighing and Interpreting Documents of the Magisterium* (Wipf & Stock Publishers, 1996), ch. 6.
[48]Joseph Brusher, S.J., *Popes Through the Ages* (New York: D. Van Nostrand & Company, 1959).

raises question about papal infallibility, and defenders of the 1870 infallibility definition have had to address it.[49]

Harder to deal with as instances of papal statements that did make the invocations of full Petrine authority in favor of positions that Catholic teaching would not now embrace, are the actions of two medieval Popes.

Boniface VIII reigned as Pope at the beginning of the fourteenth century, after a period in which popes had broken the authority of emperors in Germany and heard the kings of England acknowledge that they held their power only as vassal of the Pope. He was about to see his own power shattered by a king of France who would reduce the papacy to dependency for a great deal of time to come, challenged eventually by its conciliarist bishops and thrown on the defensive. He chose that moment to issue, in 1302, his Bull *Unam Sanctam*, claiming supreme authority of the popes in both Church and State. During this Avignon century, popes would reject use of the term "infallibility," but the language of *Unam Sanctam* unmistakably meets the requirements of the 1870 infallibility decree:

> Urged by faith, we are obliged to believe and to hold that there is One Holy Catholic and truly Apostolic Church. And this we firmly believe and simply confess: outside of Her, there is neither salvation, nor the remission of sins, just as the Bridegroom in the Canticles proclaims: 'One is my dove, my perfect one. One is her mother; elect is she who bore her.' (Canticles 6:8. . . . And so, the one and only Church is one body, one head, (not two heads like a monster), Christ certainly, and the vicar of Christ, [who is] Peter and the successor of Peter. For the Lord said to Peter himself, 'Feed my sheep.' (Jn 21:17) . . .
>
> Of this one and only Church there is one body and one head – not two heads, like a monster – namely Christ, and Christ's vicar is Peter, and Peter's successor, for the Lord said to Peter himself, 'Feed My sheep.' He said 'my' generally, not solely of these or of those. By this, it is understood that all (*universas*) were committed to him. Therefore, if either the Greeks or others declare themselves not to be committed to Peter and his successors, they necessarily

---

[49]Cf. J. Chapman's 1910 article "Pope Honorius," in the 1911 edition of *The Catholic Encyclopedia*. Steven O'Reilly, article "Guilty Only of Failure to Teach" in *This Rock* (San Diego, CA: Catholic Answers, Inc., 2000), 28–31.

admit themselves not to be among the sheep of Christ, just as the Lord says in John, 'there is one sheepfold, and only one shepherd.' (John 10:16) We are instructed in the Gospel sayings that in Her and within Her power, there are two swords, specifically, the spiritual and the temporal. For the Apostles say, 'Behold, there are two swords here,' that is, in the Church. But when the Apostles were speaking, the Lord did not respond, 'it is too much,' but 'it is sufficient.' (Luke 22:38) Certainly, whoever denies that the temporal sword is in the power of Peter, misunderstands the word of the Lord, saying: 'Put your sword into its sheath.' (Matthew 26:52) Therefore, both are in the power of the Church, namely, the spiritual sword and the material. But indeed, the latter is to be exercised on behalf of the Church; and truly, the former is to be exercised by the Church. The former is of the priest; the latter is by the hand of kings and soldiers, but at the will and sufferance of the priest . . .

But this authority, even though it may be given to a man, and may be exercised by a man, is not human, but rather divine [power], having been given by the divine mouth [of Christ] to Peter, and to him as well as to his successors, by [Christ] Himself, [that is, to him] whom He had disclosed to be the firm rock, just as the Lord said to Peter himself: 'Whatever you shall bind,' (Matthew 16:19) etc. Therefore, whoever resists this authority, such as it has been ordained by God, resists the ordination of God. (Romans 13:2) Otherwise, he would be proposing two principles to exist, as did Manichaeus, and this we judge to be false and heretical. For Moses testified that God created heaven and earth, not in the beginnings, but "in the beginning." (Gen. 1:1) Moreover, that every human creature is to be subject to the Roman pontiff, we declare, we state, we define, and we pronounce to be entirely from the necessity of salvation.[50]

It would be hard to find in the Church of our own time anyone who believed what Boniface here so solemnly asserted. Another embarrassment for those who defend papal infallibility comes from Pope Eugenius IV, who issued his Bull *Cantate Domino*, issued in 1442 in the context of the Council of Florence, as representatives

---

[50] I use here the translation of Ronald L. Conte, Jr., in Dr Johann Karl Ludwig Gieseler, *A Text-book of Church History* (New York: Harper Brothers, 1857), 351.

of the various oriental churches were making their submission to the Roman Church, submissions that would all be repudiated by their churches when these representatives returned home. Defining the faith of the Church, the Pope writes:

It firmly believes, professes, and proclaims that those not living within the Catholic Church, not only pagans, but also Jews and heretics and schismatics cannot become participants in eternal life, but will depart 'into everlasting fire which was prepared for the devil and his angels' (Matt. 25:41), unless before the end of life the same have been added to the flock; and that the unity of the ecclesiastical body is so strong that only to those remaining in it are the sacraments of the Church of benefit for salvation, and do fastings, almsgiving, and other functions of piety and exercises of Christian service produce eternal reward, and that no one, whatever almsgiving he has practiced, even if he has shed blood for the name of Christ, can be saved, unless he has remained in the bosom and unity of the Catholic Church.[51]

What conclusion can we draw? The history of solemn papal definitions contains a number of such proclamations, uttered with all the threatening assertions of the forfeit of eternal salvation for dissenters that popes and the Catholic faithful would firmly repudiate if asserted in our time. We might limit the infallibility claim to statements made since the solemn definition of 1879, but then we have only the one instance to show, the Assumption definition of 1950, though it is clear the Pius IX meant to make the claim in 1853. Of the two Marian doctrines one must say that they stand less at the center of Catholic faith than the Creed or the Christological statements of the earlier councils. One accepts them on the basis of the *decet*, "it is fitting," without explicit Scriptural basis. To some extent, Pope Pius IX's action in defining the Immaculate Conception in 1853 was a way of saying: "I can do it, and by myself." Pope Pius XII, in 1950, echoes this in saying: "I can too."

We must see paradox, then, in the atmosphere regnant in the Church that we are a Church of infallible statements. An aura of infallibility is given to statements that carefully do not claim it, such

---

[51]*Documents of the Christian Church*, ed. Henry Bettenson, 2nd edn (Oxford: Oxford University Press, 1963), 159–61.

as the Apostolic Letter Pope John Paul II issued in 1994, *Ordinatio Sacerdotalis*, reserving priestly ordination to men only. The great hue and cry raised by the American bishops in 2012 over religious liberty, in response to the mandate in the health-care law to provide contraceptive services in Catholic institutions that were not churches evokes that feeling of infallible certainty for the 1968 birth-control Encyclical *Humanae Vitae*. But this is not, in fact, the way the Catholic faithful live. They are attentive to their leaders though often bewildered by their vehemence, disillusioned by their conduct and dubious about their absolutism; finding their careful way through the dilemmas of life in accordance with their understanding of the Gospel, insofar as it has been made real to them in their Church.

The Council had to disperse abruptly when the Italian troops arrived and seized the city of Rome, putting an end to the long history of the Papal States. We hear often that it was left incomplete, having dealt with papal primacy and infallibility and not gotten on to its remaining task of defining the office of episcopacy. Its energy, however, had really been thoroughly expended in the infallibility definition. That was its purpose, and it made a fitting climax to the nineteenth-century papacy's fear of everything in its world as enemy, its certainty that it alone was right and the only resource for mankind. Engagement with the real developments in its world was beyond its reach.

Pius IX lived as "the prisoner of the Vatican," ever indignant and pitied by the Catholic world, another 8 years, dying of a heart attack and the epilepsy that had plagued him all his life in 1878, a month after his old adversary King Victor Emmanuel II.[52] When he heard that the king was close to death, Pius IX lifted all the excommunications he had imposed on him.

---

[52]J. N. D. Kelly, *The Oxford Dictionary of Popes* (Oxford: Oxford University Press, 1987), 310.

4

Between the two Vatican Councils: The Church striving to find itself

A dispirited and at the same time super-authoritarian Catholic Church came out of the experience of the First Vatican Council, seen with renewed suspicion by the already hostile Protestant world of the English-speaking countries. Most Catholics in the United States had only recently come as impoverished refugees from Europe, some because of the famine in Ireland, some because of the failed revolutions of 1848. They hardly commanded respect from the hardy Americans proud in their independence. A curious contention broke out in England, when Prime Minister William Ewart Gladstone concluded that Catholics had "forfeited their moral and mental freedom" in submitting to the Council's infallibility decree. The Catholic Church, he wrote had become "an Asian monarchy: Nothing but one giddy height of despotism, and one dead level of subservience." The Pope, he believed, would conceal his "crimes against liberty beneath a suffocating cloud of incense."[1] John Henry Newman, leaping to the defense, showed some hesitancy about the infallibility ruling himself, as he argued the supremacy of conscience, with which papal infallibility could not be in conflict. Responding to Gladstone in a published Letter to the Duke of Norfolk he offers

---

[1]From a pamphlet published by Gladstone in 1874, *The Vatican Decrees in their Bearing on Civil Allegiance*, cited by Philip Magnus, *Gladstone: A Biography* (London: John Murray, 1963), 235–6.

a toast: "I shall drink to the Pope if you please; still, to conscience and to the Pope afterwards."[2] The Council, he argued, "left the Pope just as it found him," which hints at an assessment similar to that of our last chapter. The definition, Newman, believed, was very moderate and specific with regard to what specifically could be declared infallible.[3]

The time between the two Vatican Councils, close to a century, would define the Church as it would come under the responsibility of Pope John XIII in 1959, when he determined that it had need of an Ecumenical Council to restore its life. Over the interval between these two Councils the Church would have striven, off-again on-again, with some reversions, to break out of the institutional solipsism in which it had wrapped itself since the French Revolution, even as it coped with a world unhinged, careening from catastrophe to catastrophe. By the end of the period, the Church would have regained some of its relevance to the world it lived in by engaging some of the real problems of its time. It would deal with people who defined their world in fundamentally secular terms, in which motives of faith or discipleship had no part. But it would still understand itself mainly in terms of institutional structure rather than a living communion in the faith.

The papacy of Leo XIII came as a breath of fresh air into this atmosphere. Vincenzo Gioacchino Raffaele Luigi Pecci was 68 years old when he became Pope in 1878, first Pope born in the nineteenth century, and would have a long pontificate, longer than any other than his immediate predecessor Pius IX,[4] dying at the age of 93 in 1903.

We remember him most for his attention to the rights of working people, a signal witness of Christian love in the papal chair. His concern for the poor showed early in his career when, as administrator of Papal States provinces, first of Benevento and then of the more important Spoleto, he discovered that bakers did not always provide the full pound weight for a loaf of bread. He had all the bread weighed, confiscated any that was below the prescribed weight and

---

[2]Letter to the Duke of Norfolk in *The Genius of John Henry Newman: Selections from His Writings*, ed. I. Ker (Oxford: Oxford University Press, 1990).

[3]This exchange is discussed by Stanley L. Jaki, O.S.B., in *Newman's Challenge* (Grand Rapids, MI: William B. Eerdmans, 2000), 170.

[4]Pope John Paul II in the twentieth century would rule longer than either of them.

distributed it free to the poor.[5] As Archbishop of Perugia from 1846 to 1877, he would found homes for homeless children and the elderly, as well as soup-kitchens, open bank branches that focused on low-income people and offer low-interest loans.[6] Appointed Camerlengo in 1877, the Cardinal responsible for arranging papal elections, he was then obliged to reside in Rome.

As Pope, he issued the landmark Encyclical *Rerum Novarum* in 1891, the charter document of Catholic social doctrine, the first time papal teaching had authoritatively addressed social inequality and issues of social justice.[7] It defended the rights of labor to unionize and laid down the duties of capital, introducing the concept of subsidiarity, the principle that political and social decisions should be taken at a local level, if possible, rather than by a central authority, into Catholic thought. The Encyclical's title, "Of New Things," shows the Pope's consciousness that he was embarking into new theological territory. He had sided with the German bishop Wilhelm Emmanuel von Ketteler, whose classic 1864 book, *Die Arbeiterfrage und das Chistentum*, had called upon the Church to side with the suffering working classes.

Papal teachings since Leo's time have expanded on these themes, the rights and obligations of workers and the limitations of private property. Leo XIII had called both communism and capitalism flawed systems. As the emphasis continued, Pope Pius XI would issue his Encyclical *Quadragesimo Anno*, on the *Reconstruction of the Social Order*, to expand on Leo's teaching on its fortieth anniversary in 1931.[8] Pope Pius XII wrote constantly on a great variety of social issues throughout his reign (1939–1958). Pope John XXIII authored his *Mater et Magistra*, on *Christianity and Social Progress*, in 1961,[9] Pope Paul VI his *Populorum Progressio*, on world development issues, in 1967, and Pope John Paul II his *Centesimus Annus* on

---

[5]Benno Kühne, *Papst Leo XIII* (New York and St. Louis: C&N Benzinger, Einsideln, 1880), 37.

[6]Kühne, 78.

[7]Papal Encyclicals Online, http://www.papalencyclicals.net/Leo13/l13rerum.htm. Consulted 27 June 2012.

[8]On the website of the Holy See, http://www.vatican.va/holy_father/pius_xi/encyclicals/documents/hf_p-xi_enc_19310515_quadragesimo-anno_en.html. Consulted 27 June 2012.

[9]Website of the Holy See, http://www.vatican.va/holy_father/john_xxiii/encyclicals/documents/hf_j-xxiii_enc_15051961_mater_en.html. Consulted 27 June 2012.

the hundredth anniversary, 1991. The labor legislation of the United States, owing much to the influence of Monsignor John Augustine Ryan (1869–1945) in the time of the Roosevelt New Deal, is an important part of this heritage.[10] Given this honorable and deeply ingrained tradition, we may find it shaming today to see how little attention the attrition and near destruction of unions and labor influence in the United States of our own time receives from our Catholic bishops.

Child of the ancient Italian nobility, like most of the popes over many centuries, Leo XIII was wary of any ideas of democracy and free thought, in particular the separation of Church and State. Yet in a breakthrough from the antipathy of previous nineteenth-century popes, Leo had urged on French Catholics loyally to accept the Third Republic. He was disturbed to see the declining influence of French Catholicism in a state that sought constantly to limit the power of the Church under the banner of *laicité*.[11]

In 1891, an American Paulist author, Walter Elliott, had written a biography of the Paulist founder, Isaac Hecker, which described Hecker's efforts to reach out to American Protestants by pointing out the compatibility of Catholic principles, such as individual freedom, community, service, and authority, with American values. Leo XIII's problem was not actually with America but with the French. When Elliott's book was translated into French 6 years later with a laudatory introduction by Abbé Felix Klein, it won great popularity with progressive French priests who wanted to engage with the new French society and took Hecker as a kind of patron saint of modernity for his devotion to liberal Catholicism.[12]

This struck Leo as a watering down of Church authority. In 1895, in an Encyclical *Longinqua Oceani* ("Wide Expanse of Ocean"), the Pope had taken a positive view of the success of Catholicism in the

---

[10]Cf. Patrick W. Gearty, *The Economic Thought of Monsignor John A. Ryan* (Washington, DC: The Catholic University of America Press, 1953).

[11]*Religion and Society in Modern Europe*, by René Rémond (Author), Antonia Nevill (Translator) (Malden, MA: Blackwell Publishers, 1999). Evelyn M. Acomb, *The French Laic Laws, 1879-1889: The First Anti-Clerical Campaign of the Third French Republic* (New York: Columbia University Press, 1941).

[12]Cf. Frank K. Flinn and J. Gordon Melton, *Encyclopedia of Catholicism* (New York: Facts on File, 2007), 19. David J. O'Brien, *Isaac Hecker: An American Catholic* (Mahwah, NJ: Paulist Press, 1992), 384. Thomas E. Woods, *The church confronts modernity* (Woods, New York: Columbia University Press, 2004), 179.

United States, noting, however, that she "would bring forth more abundant fruits if, in addition to liberty, she enjoyed the favor of the laws and the patronage of the public authority,"[13] and warning the American hierarchy not to export their separation of Church and State to other countries. In 1898, he expressed his disquiet that Church and State in America were "dissevered and divorced," and wrote that there should be a closer relationship between the Catholic Church and the State, along European lines. Finally, in 1899, he sent an Encyclical letter, *Testem Benevolentiae* ("Witness to Our Benevolence"), addressed to Cardinal James Gibbons, Archbishop of Baltimore, in which he condemned "Americanism" by name. While Catholicism had long allowed nations to tolerate other religions, he wrote, the Church believed that the Catholic Faith must be favored, to the exclusion of other religions, whenever possible.[14]

Cardinal Gibbons and many other American bishops replied to Rome, defending Hecker from any of the named "heresies," such as undue insistence on interior initiative in the spiritual life, which would lead to disobedience, attacks on religious vows, and disparagement of the value of religious orders in the modern world (his Paulists did not take religious vows, only promises), minimizing Catholic doctrine, or minimizing the importance of spiritual direction. The Pope had not actually said that Hecker was guilty of any of these offenses, but had asserted that, if such opinions did exist, the hierarchy were to eradicate them. The effect was to curtail the activity of progressive Catholics and strengthen the most conservative tendencies in France.[15]

Pope Leo also advocated a strong revival of Thomistic theology. Not much the theologian himself, one of the first acts of his papacy had been to elevate his Jesuit elder brother Giuseppe Pecci, a prominent Thomist theologian, to the cardinalate.[16] The Pope's fostering of Thomism constituted a great intellectual gift to the Church. By his Encyclical *Aeterni Patris* of 1879, he made it normative not only in the training of priests in seminaries but also in the education of the

---

[13]Woods, 179.
[14]To be found on the website of EWTN, http://www.ewtn.com/library/PAPALDOC/ L13TESTE.HTM. Consulted 27 June 2012.
[15]Cf. John Tracy Ellis, *The life of James Cardinal Gibbons* (Milwaukee: Bruce Publishing Company, 1963), 147–8.
[16]Kühne, 247.

laity at universities.[17] For the advancement of scholarship he also opened the hitherto secret Vatican archives and personally fostered the work of Ludwig von Pastor and his 20-volume scientific study of the papacy.[18]

The papacy of Leo XIII had re-enlivened the Catholic Church. The authoritarian streak that had characterized the nineteenth century did not die with him. He maintained the "prisoner of the Vatican" hostility of Pius IX toward the Italian kingdom even as he exhorted the French to accede to the Republic. But his activism had served the worthiest of causes and the Church came out of his reign with a respect that it had not enjoyed for a long time. He had promoted a synthesis between Catholic teaching and secular culture, between faith and science, divine revelation and reason.

His successor, Pope Pius X, Giuseppe Melchiorre Sarto, not the customary man of noble family but the son of an impoverished village postman, had risen to be Cardinal Patriarch of Venice. For the duration of his papacy, 1903 to the fateful August of 1914, he faced a Europe in the throes of tensions that would lead, with the assassination of an Austrian Archduke at Sarajevo, to the catastrophe of World War I. His piety so impressed his age that he became the first Pope to be canonized a Saint since Pius V in the sixteenth century.

The election of Cardinal Sarto to the papacy came only after a Polish Cardinal laid down a veto from the Austrian Emperor Franz Joseph against Leo XIII's Secretary of State, Cardinal Mariano Rampolla, the last time the secular power had interfered so directly in a papal election. Because of those circumstances Cardinal Sarto at first refused the office, accepting it only after the pleas of many cardinals and a period of prayer in the Pauline Chapel.

As Pope, he combined a strong sense of compassion and practice of personal poverty with, his contemporaries tell us, a certain rigidity and stubbornness in his opinions. With the habits of a pastor, he took up the practice of preaching every Sunday, which no other Pope of the twentieth century has done. When earthquake shook Messina in 1908 he filled the papal palace with refugees long before

---

[17]On the website of the Holy See, http://www.vatican.va/holy_father/leo_xiii/encyclicals/documents/hf_l-xiii_enc_04081879_aeterni-patris_en.html. Consulted 27 June 2012.
[18]Ludwig von Pastor, *Errinnerungen* (Kerle, 1950).

the Italian government began to act.[19] He had imbibed the deep defensiveness of Pius IX, in whose honor he took the name Pius for himself, and tended to see all the world outside of the Church itself in terms of hostility.[20] Insistent on authority, he took as his motto *Instaurare Omnia in Christo*, "to restore all things in Christ." His first Encyclical, *E Supremi Apostulatus*, would proclaim "We champion the authority of God. His authority and Commandments should be recognized, deferred to, and respected."[21]

His first interests were in the liturgical life of the Church. Within 3 months of his coronation he had issued a *motu proprio* titled *Tra le Sollecitudine*, in which he ordered replacement of the Classical and Baroque music commonly heard in churches by Gregorian chant, declaring that "[t]he primary and indispensable source of the true Christian spirit is participation in the most holy mysteries and in the public, official prayer of the church."[22] For this purpose, he commissioned the monks of the Solemnes Abbey in France to study the sources for traditional chant and present it in a normative form.[23] The hesitancy of Catholics to receive Holy Communion for fear of a guilty reception, a heritage of a guilt culture in the Middle Ages, disturbed the Pope and he was determined to bring about a restoration, first emphasizing the frequent reception of the Sacrament of Penance so that Communion could be received worthily, and then, by his Decree *Quam singulari* of 1910, advancing the age of First Communion, "Age of Reason," from 12 to 7 years old. Once he gave communion to a 4-year-old child who, when asked by the Pope whom he would receive in Communion, answered "Jesus."[24]

---

[19]Hans Kühner, *Lexikon der Päpste* (Fischer: Frankfurt, 1960), 183.

[20]Joseph Lortz, *Geschichte der Kirche* (Münster: Aschendorff, 1934), 113.

[21]Vatican website, http://www.vatican.va/holy_father/pius_x/encyclicals/documents/hf_p-x_enc_04101903_e-supremi_en.html, Encyclical of Pope Pius X, *E Supremi*, On the Restoration of All Things in Christ, #4. Consulted 2 July 2012.

[22]Vatican website, http://www.adoremus.org/MotuProprio.html, II. Consulted 2 July 2012.

[23]Steven M. Avella and Jeffrey Zalar, "Sanctity in the Era of Catholic Action: The Case of St. Pius X," *U.S. Catholic Historian* 15, no. 4, Spirituality and Devotionalism (Fall 1997), 57–80.

[24]Vatican website, http://www.papalencyclicals.net/Pius10/p10quam.htm, *Quam singulari*, Decree of the Sacred Congregation of the Discipline of the Sacraments on First Communion, 8 August 1910. Consulted 2 July 2012.

Nothing characterized the reign of Pius X more than his campaign against "Modernism."

Defining the term, in the sense which the Pope so severely condemned, has its difficulties. Pius certainly shared the antipathy of nineteenth-century popes like Leo XII, Gregory XVI, and Pius IX toward anything that smelled of democracy or the weakening of monarchical autocracy. Thinkers as far back as John Locke and Emmanuel Kant, or the atheistic philosophy of Jean-Jacques Rousseau seem to have figured in the Pope's concept of the "modern," as well as any hint that there had been development of doctrine within the Church. Lamennais' adversary Charles Périn defined Modernism in 1881 as, in its more extreme form, "the ambition to eliminate God from all social life," which he goes on to associate with "liberalism of every degree and shade."[25] The Pope saw Modernism especially in the work of the French priest-scholar Louis Marie Olivier Duchesne, who had influenced the efforts of Alfred Firmin Loisy to bring Catholicism into sympathy with science, especially the social sciences, and who invented the term "Catholic Modernism." A professor at the *Institut Catholique* in Paris, Loisy had questioned the sole authorship of the five books of Torah by Moses or that the early chapters of Genesis were literal history. He had thus seen development of doctrine even within the Scripture and in other ways broke with scriptural literalism.

Scripture lay truly at the heart of Pius X's condemnation of Modernism. He associated it with a number of more liberal Protestant Scripture scholars of the nineteenth century, such as Adolf von Harnack, and actually embraced a literalism as stringent as any professed in the Protestant Fundamentalism of the American Bible Belt.

Leo XIII had taken pains to put the teachings of Thomas Aquinas at the center of Catholic seminary studies. Under Pius X, a very absolutist Neo-Thomism would become doctrinally mandatory in seminaries, remaining so well into the mid-twentieth century.[26] He gave strong encouragement to a group called *Sodalitium Pianum*, or League of Pius V, who functioned as a network of informants to smell out Modernist thinkers, accusing many persons of heresy,

---

[25]Charles Périn, *Le Modernisme dans l'Église d'après les lettres inéditesde Lamennais* (Paris/Lyons: Librairie Victor Lecoffre, 1881).
[26]Gerard Noel, *Pius XII: The Hound of Hitler* (UK: Bloomsbury 2009), 8.

often on such flimsy grounds that they acquired the nickname, of a "Clerical Smersh."[27] Umberto Benigni, who would later become the special ally to Fascism within the Roman Curia, received the special task, as head of the Department of Extraordinary Affairs within the Secretariat of State, to distribute anti-Modernist propaganda and gather information on culprits. Pius X himself, when asked whether he had compassion for his Modernist foes, would respond: "They want them to be treated with oil, soap and caresses. But they should be beaten with fists. In a duel, you don't count or measure the blows, you strike as you can."[28]

In July of 1907, the Holy Office, as the doctrinal Congregation within the Curia was then called, issued a decree, *Lamentabili Sane Exitu*,[29] "A Lamentable Departure Indeed," condemning 65 propositions as modernist or relativist. They concerned the nature of the Church, revelation, Scriptural exegesis or the divinity of Christ. An Encyclical, *Pascendi Domenici Gregis*, "The office divinely committed to Us of feeding the Lord's flock," followed in September,[30] characterizing Modernism as the "synthesis of all heresies (#42)" and condemning, in the most vehement language, all its forms.

By a further personal decree, a *motu proprio* of 1 September 1019, *Sacrorum Antistitum*,[31] the Pope prescribed an *Oath Against Modernism*, "to be sworn by all clergy, pastors, confessors, preachers, religious superiors, and professors in philosophical-theological seminaries." A requirement of all candidates for priestly or Episcopal ordination or for any teaching post that they take this oath would remain in place until July 1967, when the Congregation for the Doctrine of the Faith would finally rescind it. By that time many holes had been driven through it. Cardinal Newman had taught the development of doctrine well before the oath. The 1943 Encyclical

---

[27] Avella and Zalar, 57–80.

[28] John Cornwell, *Hitler's Pope* (Waltham, MA: Penguin Books, 2000), 37.

[29] Denzinger-Schönmetzer, *Enchiridion Symbolorum Definitionum et Declarationum de rebus fidei et moribus* (Freiburg im Breisgau: Herder, 1963), ##3401–66.

[30] Pascendi Dominici Gregis, Encyclical of Pope Pius X on the Doctrine of the Modernists, Vatican website, http://www.vatican.va/holy_father/pius_x/encyclicals/documents/hf_p-x_enc_19070908_pascendi-dominici-gregis_en.html. Consulted 7 July 2012.

[31] On the Vatican website, http://www.papalencyclicals.net/Pius10/p10moath.htm. Consulted 6 July 2012.

of Pope Pius XII, *Divino Afflante Spirito*, had invited historical and other critical reading of the Scripture by Catholic scholars. Successive popes had praised democracy, and Catholic social teaching had been developing ever since Leo XIII. The Second Vatican Council, further, had by then affirmed freedom of religion and the priority of conscience among many decisions contrary to the strictures of *Lamentabili* and *Pascendi Domenici Gregis*. It was time for the oath to go. Even today it is still taken voluntarily before priestly ordination by such groups as the Priestly Fraternity of St Peter.[32] And the schismatic Traditionalist movement of Archbishop Marcel Lefebvre, which still refuses, despite vigorous invitations to reconciliation by the present Pope Benedict XVI, to accept the Second Vatican Council, maintains its title, Society of Saint Pius X.

The Pope had been able to distance himself from the anguishes of his time, absorbed in internal institutional affairs as he pursued those theologians he regarded as danger to the Church. Much of the Catholic public stood staunchly with him, concerned with the status of the papacy and glad of his manifest piety. Yet, as he lay dying in early August of 1914, the entire world of European civilization entered the agony of World War I in a way his successor could not ignore.

On his election to the papacy, Giacomo Paolo Giovanni Battista della Chiesa took the name Benedict XV.[33] The conclave that chose him, deeply divided over both the issue of Modernism and the war alliances, settled on the obscure Archbishop of Bologna, only 4 months a cardinal and so little known that Cardinal Gibbons

---

[32]Founded in Switzerland in 1988, with the approval of Pope John Paul II. Their website, http://www.fssp.org/en/index.htm (consulted 6 July 2012) documents *motu proprio*s of both John Paul II and Benedict XVI and celebratory homilies by Cardinal Joseph Ratzinger (1990) and Cardinal Dario Castrillon Hoyos (2003 and 2008).

[33]The election of Benedict X in 1058, with the aid of a political faction, was opposed by Hildebrand, the future Gregory VII, with the support of other powerful forces. Cardinals who had been against Benedict's election promptly elected, in 1059, Hildebrand's candidate, Nicholas II, who deposed and excommunicated Benedict. After a year of warfare he renounced the papacy and was imprisoned, dying in captivity in 1073. However, when the next Pope to choose the name Benedict was elected in 1303, the Catholic Church had not definitively judged Benedict X an Antipope. The numbering of Popes Benedict remains therefore an anomaly, those officially numbered Benedict XI on through the present Pope Benedict XVI regarded by the Church as the 10th through 15th validly elected popes of that name.

of Baltimore, arriving at the conclave, like Cardinal O'Connell of Boston, too late to vote, asked of Cardinal Della Chiesa, "Who's he?"[34] The crusading anti-Modernist curial cardinals, led by Secretary of State Cardinal Merry del Val, mounted a challenge to the election, demanding a recount of the vote to ascertain that Della Chiesa had not voted for himself.[35] Pius X had taken care at the beginning of his pontificate, to exclude Leo XIII's Secretary of State, Cardinal Mariano Rampolla, Della Chiesa's mentor,[36] who had been Leo's agent in urging French Catholics to accept the democratic republic and work to render it hospitable to the Church.[37] Della Chiesa, from having been Sostituto, the officer in the Secretariate of State responsible for diplomatic contact with nations, was consequently demoted for his association with Rampolla, and moved from one minor diplomatic post to another until, in 1907, he became Archbishop of Bologna.

The new Pope's concern turned necessarily to the making of peace. But the long isolation of a Church preoccupied, other than during the interval of Leo XIII, with itself, had left papacy and Church with little influence in the councils of Europe. Benedict's peace efforts would do much to restore the dignity of the Holy See and set the parameters within which later popes of the twentieth century would become spokesmen for peace. But he was stymied throughout his short reign, his neutrality questioned, especially after Italy itself entered the war on the Allied side in 1915. An initial statement, which he issued 8 September 1914, only 5 days after his election, had called the powers to peace, but this was still in the days when the feeling in the Vatican was that the war would be over by Christmas.[38] The battles of the Marne and Ypres in that September settled the Western Front into long-term trench warfare, ending any such hope. The adhesion of Turkey to the Austro-Hungarians and the Germans stopped the expected Russian steam-roller and rendered the Eastern Front just as static. Hence, when Benedict issued his first Encyclical, *Ad Beatissimi*, on 1 November, All Saints

---

[34]John F. Pollard, *The Unknown Pope, Benedict XV (1914-1922) and the Pursuit of Peace* (London: Geoffrey Chapman, a Continuum imprint, 1999), xiii.
[35]Pollard, 62f.
[36]Ibid., 19.
[37]Ibid., 11.
[38]Ibid., 85.

Day of 1914, he made a massive effort to define the causes of the war which he called "the suicide of civilized Europe."[39]

> But it is not the present sanguinary strife alone that distresses the nations and fills Us with anxiety and care. There is another evil raging in the very inmost heart of human society, a source of dread to all who really think, inasmuch as it has already brought, and will bring, many misfortunes upon nations, and may rightly be considered to be the root cause of the present awful war. For ever since the precepts and practices of Christian wisdom ceased to be observed in the ruling of states, it followed that, as they contained the peace and stability of institutions, the very foundations of states necessarily began to be shaken. Such, moreover, has been the change in the ideas and the morals of men, that unless God comes soon to our help, the end of civilization would seem to be at hand.[40]

In the same Encyclical, he sought to tame the frenzy of the anti-Modernist campaign. Even while nominally endorsing Pius X's actions, he added:

> The success of every society of men, for whatever purpose it is formed, is bound up with the harmony of the members in the interests of the common cause. Hence We must devote Our earnest endeavors to appease dissension and strife, of whatever character, amongst Catholics, and to prevent new dissensions arising, so that there may be unity of ideas and of action amongst all.[41]
>
> As regards matters in which without harm to faith or discipline – in the absence of any authoritative intervention of the Apostolic See – there is room for divergent opinions, it is clearly the right of everyone to express and defend his own opinion . . . but let it be done with due moderation, so that no one should consider himself entitled to affix on those who merely do not agree with his ideas the stigma of disloyalty to faith or to discipline.[42]

---

[39]Vatican website, http://www.vatican.va/holy_father/benedict_xv/encyclicals/documents/hf_ben-xv_enc_01111914_ad-beatissimi-apostolorum_en.html. Consulted 9 July 2012.
[40]*Ad Beatissimi*, #5.
[41]Ibid., #22.
[42]Ibid., #23.

It is, moreover, Our will that Catholics should abstain from certain appellations which have recently been brought into use to distinguish one group of Catholics from another. They are to be avoided not only as "profane novelties of words," out of harmony with both truth and justice, but also because they give rise to great trouble and confusion among Catholics.[43]

We might well wish that such wholesome admonitions as these were heard in our own time.

For Christmas, 1914, the Pope made his first direct intervention in the war, appealing for a 24-hour cease-fire. British, German, and Austrian governments responded positively, the French and the Russians did not.[44] After many other exhortations to peace and establishing organizations for the welfare of prisoners, location of missing persons and appeals for the repatriation of sick POWs,[45] Benedict issued his "Peace Note" in August 1917.[46] His plan contained seven points: (1) that "the moral force of right . . . be substituted for the material force of arms," (2) "simultaneous and reciprocal diminution of armaments," (3) a mechanism for "international arbitration," (4) "true liberty and common rights over the sea," (5) a "renunciation of war indemnities," (6) occupied territories should be evacuated, and (7) "an examination . . . of rival claims."[47] Benedict also called for outlawing conscription,[48] a call he repeated in 1921.[49]

---

[43]Ibid., #24.

[44]Pollard, 112f. It is noteworthy that such a cease-fire actually did take place that first Christmas of the war, initiated by the front-line troops themselves, who first broke into familiar carols, then emerged from their trenches to exchange small gifts, and finally initiated a football match in the No-Man's-Land. Malcolm Brown and Shirley Seaton, *Christmas Truce: The Western Front, December 1914* (London: Trans-Atlantic Publications, 1984). I have personally met a man who, after hearing reference to this event in a parish sermon in Boston, told me his grandfather had scored the winning goal.

[45]Pollard, 113.

[46]Cf. Italo Garzia, *La Questione Romana durante la I guerra mondiale* (Naples, 1981), 111.

[47]John R. Smestad Jr., "Europe 1914–1945: Attempts at Peace," Loyola University, New Orleans, *The Student Historical Journal 1994–1995*, XXVI.

[48]"Pope in New Note to Ban Conscription," *The New York Times*, 23 September 1917.

[49]"Pope would clinch peace. Urges abolition of conscription as way to disarmament," *The New York Times*, 16 November 1921, from *Associated Press* report.

It is not hard to see the consonance of this plan with many of Woodrow Wilson's *14 Points*, issued later that same year, particularly with Wilson's League of Nations proposal. But Wilson himself, stolid Presbyterian that he was, rejected the Pope's plan out of hand. The British were interested but the Germans ambivalent. Coming from a Catholic Church which, for most of the century, had seemed an irrelevance, the Pope's appeals for peace were seen essentially as unwelcome interference by both sides. In Europe, each side saw him as biased in favor of the other and was unwilling to accept the terms he proposed. Still, although unsuccessful, his diplomatic efforts during the war did contribute to an increase of papal prestige and served as a model in the twentieth century: to the peace efforts of Pius XII before and during World War II, the policies of Paul VI during the Vietnam War and the position of John Paul II before and during the War in Iraq.[50]

We must, at this stage, ask a fairly stark question: how well had the central offices of the Catholic Church done, over a century's span, on actual Christianity? Holiness there certainly was in the Church throughout this time, but decisions and policies and major efforts of central authority that represent the priorities of Jesus, as we hear them in the Gospel, are another matter. The decision of Pope Gregory XVI in 1839 to condemn slavery and advocate the liberation of all slaves gave a sharp glimmer, in an age otherwise of near-total self-absorption, of Christian practice. Leo XIII's practical expression of commitment to the poor through his social policies, so important to his lengthy pontificate as they constitute its most lasting characteristic and so constant in the actions of Jesus, was a major breakthrough of genuine Christianity. And of course the dedication of his pontificate to peace by Benedict XV witnessed in a very concrete way to the compassionate love of Christ for all mankind. That such actions had become exceptional and even seen as breaches of what everyone understood as the papacy's commitment to the monarchist ways of a bygone world rendered Benedict's strenuous efforts practically ineffectual.

By the time his successor, Pope Pius XI, Ambrogio Damiano Achille Ratti, came to the throne, 11 February 1922, the twin powers of communism and fascism, toxic outcomes of the world conflict,

---

[50]Pollard, 136.

had already begun to hold the world in their grip. Barely older than Benedict and therefore of the same generation, the new Pope, long-time librarian of the Ambrosian Library in Milan and subsequently Prefect of the Vatican Library,[51] had brief diplomatic experience as nuncio to Poland, from which he was expelled but only after being the only foreign diplomat who refused to flee Warsaw when the Red Army approached it in August 1920.[52] He served very briefly as Archbishop of Milan before his election as Pope.[53]

As Pope he would be tempted to choose fascism over communism, and even to see it, in its conservatism, as a way to reestablish the influence of the Church. But Pius had strong elements of social conscience, which worked against those instincts. Even at the height of the quarrel with Republican Spain he broke with the nineteenth-century monarchism of the papacy to write that that the Church is not "bound to one form of government more than to another, provided the Divine rights of God and of Christian consciences are safe," and specifically referred to "various civil institutions, be they monarchic or republican, aristocratic or democratic."[54] In 1926, he would condemn the powerful monarchist Action Française movement, which had won the allegiance of much of the French clergy and hierarchy. The movement had defined Catholic interests in merely utilitarian and nationalistic terms, but seemed to its adherents to be the guarantee of stability and the greatness of France.[55]

Particularly threatened was the world Jewish community, long subjected to Catholic assumptions of its rejection by God and now already singled out as scapegoat for the tragedy of Europe. Mexico, Spain, and Russia had all taken to stifling Catholic practice and murdering Catholic clergy. The papacy still did not recognize the Italian kingdom, which had taken away its political independence,

---

[51]Lucio D'Orazi, *Il Coraggio Della Verita Vita do Pio XI* (Roma: Edizioni logos, 1989), 27.

[52]Mrg R. Fontenelle, *Seine Heiligkeit Pius XI* (France: Alsatia, 1939), 34–44.

[53]Fontenelle, 40.

[54]Encyclical *Dilectissima Nobis*, ENCYCLICAL OF POPE PIUS XI ON OPPRESSION OF THE CHURCH OF SPAIN, 3 June 1933, #3. From the Vatican website, http://www.vatican.va/holy_father/pius_xi/encyclicals/documents/hf_p-xi_enc_03061933_dilectissima-nobis_en.html. Consulted 16 July 2010.

[55]René Rémond, "Action française," in Lawrence D. Kritzman (ed.), *The Columbia History of Twentieth-Century French Thought* (New York: Columbia University Press, 2006), 8.

as legitimate, and had therefore no diplomatic relations with it. This became a more acute problem when Benito Mussolini made his march on Rome in October 1922 and established himself as Prime Minister, eventually assuming the title *Il Duce* by 1925.

Pius turned for help to the Jesuit historian, Fr Pietro Tacchi-Venturi, a man who held no official position in his order or in the Vatican, deeply conservative and instinctively anti-Semitic, but already an intimate of Mussolini, who became the "normal instrument for messages between the Pope and Mussolini,"[56] so much so that it becomes increasingly difficult for the Pope to extricate himself from his adviser's political preferences.

"The Roman Question" had dominated the lives of all the popes since the kingdom of Italy had stripped away the Papal States in 1870. Temporal sovereignty, much as it always involved the risk of embroiling the popes in merely mundane affairs, had become the accepted norm for many centuries. It came to be seen as the necessary guarantee of the Church's independence, free from the interference it had suffered from German emperors at the time of the investiture crisis, from French kings during the Avignon period, from all the contending polities that had tried to resolve, to their own advantage, the differences of contending popes during the schism period, from the revolutionary armies of France or the grip of Napoleon. Tacchi-Venturi's constant contact with Mussolini would lead, by 1929, to the Lateran Treaty,[57] by which the Pope regained his sovereignty as head of the Vatican City State, *Stato della Città del Vaticano*, an internationally recognized state although the smallest in the world, only the area of St Peter's Basilica and the papal palace, museum, and gardens. Besides the Treaty of Reconciliation, this would contain, as annex, a Financial Convention, which would make some compensation for the loss of the Papal States, and a Concordat, intended to guarantee the Church's freedoms in the Italian state.[58]

Concordats were a favorite instrument of Pius XI in his relation with states, considering them a protection of the Church's rights

---

[56]Owen Chadwick, *Britain and the Vatican During the Second World War* (Cambridge: Cambridge University Press, 1988), 62.

[57]Text, http://www.aloha.net/~mikesch/treaty.htm. Consulted 17 July 2012.

[58]Michael Riccards, *Vicars of Christ: Popes, Power, and Politics in the Modern World* (New York: Crossroad, 1998).

against governments inclined to interfere with them. He would sign them with 21 different countries during his reign.[59] When Hitler assumed power as Chancellor in Germany, 30 January 1933, he took the initiative himself of requesting a concordat. The papal Nuncio, Eugenio Pacelli, the future Pope Pius XII, promptly negotiated the *Reichskonkordat*, which was signed on 20 July 1933. Pius XI had then, for both Italy and Germany, benchmarks against which to complain when the terms were not fulfilled.[60] The Pope would issue an Encyclical in 1931, *Non Abbiamo Bisogno*,[61] in which he called the Italian dictator to book for violations of the Lateran Treaty. His relations with Mussolini deteriorated from that point on.

Despite heavy contrary influences, Pius would reject any racist anti-Semitism. On 14 March 1937, Passion Sunday, he published the German-language Encyclical *Mit Brennender Sorge*,[62] a scathing condemnation of Nazi totalitarianism and anti-Semitic racism. Printed copies had to be smuggled into the country to be read from the pulpit of every church,[63] to the outrage of Hitler, who tried to confiscate every copy and prohibit its further circulation. The writing had been done by Munich Cardinal Michael von Faulhaber and the Cardinal Eugenio Pacelli, who by then had become papal Secretary of State.[64] This was followed in April, 1938, by a *Syllabus Against Racism*, which was to be followed in all Catholic seminaries and universities.[65]

---

[59]Pinchas Lapide, *Three Popes and the Jews* (Portland, Oregon: Hawthorn Books, 1967), 91.

[60]Guenter Lewy, *The Catholic Church and Nazi Germany* (London: Weidenfield and Nicholson, 1964).

[61]Vatican website, http://www.vatican.va/holy_father/pius_xi/encyclicals/documents/hf_p-xi_enc_29061931_non-abbiamo-bisogno_en.html, *NON ABBIAMO BISOGNO*, ENCYCLICAL OF POPE PIUS XI ON CATHOLIC ACTION IN ITALY. Consulted 17 July 2012.

[62]Vatican website, http://www.vatican.va/holy_father/pius_xi/encyclicals/documents/hf_p-xi_enc_14031937_mit-brennender-sorge_en.html, *MIT BRENNENDER SORGE*, ENCYCLICAL OF POPE PIUS XION THE CHURCH AND THE GERMAN REICH. Consulted 16 July 2012.

[63]John Manners, *The Oxford History of Christianity* (Oxford: Oxford University Press, 2002), 374.

[64]August Franzen, *Remigius Bäumer Papstgeschichte* (Freiburg: Herder, 1988), 394.

[65]Konrad Repgen, "Judenpogrom, Rassenideologie und katholische Kirche, 1938," *Kirche und Gesellschaft*, No. 152/153, Koln, 1988, 28ff. Urging this was another socially concerned Jesuit, Fr Gustav Gundlach.

Pius would take it upon himself to expand on Leo XIII's enlightened social teaching, issuing his own Encyclical *Quadragesimo Anno*,[66] issued, as its title indicates, on the fortieth anniversary of *Rerum Novarum*, 15 May 1931. German Jesuit Fr Oswald von Nell-Breuning helped with the writing.[67]

But the Pope saw this new and serious social teaching of the Church radically opposed by the tenets of Marxism and the radical communism of the Soviet state. On the feast of St Joseph, workingman patron of the universal Church, 19 March 1937, only 5 days after *Mit Brennender Sorge*, he issued his Encyclical *Divini Redemptoris*[68] denouncing these teachings as "a barbarism worse than that which oppressed the greater part of the world at the coming of the Redeemer," which "exceeds in amplitude and violence anything yet experienced in the preceding persecutions launched against the Church"[69] Clearly, he took the communist threat more seriously even than that of fascism and Nazism.

Europe was already hurtling toward World War II when two heavy heart attacks, occurring with hours of each other on 25 November 1938, left the Pope crippled and helpless for his remaining few months, until a third attack felled him on 10 February 1939. His vigorous response to the many madnesses of his world had mattered little in the counsels of those who governed Europe's fate. The cardinals who assembled to choose a successor quickly settled on the most experienced diplomat among them, the Vatican Secretary of State, also the Camerlengo of the college, Eugenio Marìa Giuseppe Giovanni Pacelli, who would reign as Pope Pius XII from 2 March 1939, his 63rd birthday, to 9 October 1958.

This learned, aristocratic, and pious man would become the symbolic emblem of the papacy to friends and enemies for many years to come. Generations would argue over how he handled

---

[66]Vatican website, http://www.vatican.va/holy_father/pius_xi/encyclicals/documents/hf_p-xi_enc_19310515_quadragesimo-anno_en.html, *QUADRAGESIMO ANNO*, ENCYCLICAL OF POPE PIUS XION RECONSTRUCTION OF THE SOCIAL ORDER. Consulted 16 July 2012.

[67]Obituary, *The New York Times*, 23 August 1991, when Nell died at the age of 101.

[68]Vatican website, http://www.vatican.va/holy_father/pius_xi/encyclicals/documents/hf_p-xi_enc_19031937_divini-redemptoris_en.html, *DIVINI REDEMPTORIS*, ENCYCLICAL OF POPE PIUS XION ATHEISTIC COMMUNISM.

[69]*Divini Redemptoris*, #2.

himself and his responsibilities through the Second World War and the *Shoah*, the terrible Holocaust of the Jews.

How do we assess popes? The primacy and infallibility decisions of the First Vatican Council had brought about a kind of apotheosis of popes. "Cult of personality" would be a concept of the twentieth-century Soviet Union, certainly not the first time rulers had demanded that for themselves. But after Vatican I it seemed presumptuous, whether to Catholics or to most others, to speak of a pope, any pope, other than in flamboyant terms of adulation, seeing in him a kind of hypostasis of the Catholic Church itself. We can see that in the urge to canonize any pope of that period. One could easily create an index from the typical sermons heard in Catholic parishes: how often do you hear of Jesus Christ or his Gospel as compared to how often you hear of popes, a current pope, and citations of his teachings? This has perhaps tilted a little back toward Jesus Christ in the years since Vatican II, but not too far. Wisdom in his sayings, or fidelity to basic Gospel values can hardly be questioned, as he is the standard by which they are judged.

This study has been discussing popes by a different standard, seeing most of the popes of the nineteenth century as having done great damage to the Church, its faith, and the Gospel by their insularity. Pope Leo XIII stands out as a brilliant exception, especially for his realization that the Gospel summons us all to care for the poor, those treated unfairly, etc. Those had not been the principal thoughts of popes for some time. But even Leo was captive to much of the dismal legacy of that century. Pius X alone has received canonization as a saint among all the popes since the one sixteenth-century exception, Pius V, but in terms of his effect on the Church we have to account him a reversion. For Benedict XV, there was little choice but to dedicate his papacy to the pursuit of peace, but he had been left little moral capital in his office with which to work. So much of Pius XI's work meets our strong admiration, but he too was working with an office whose historic influence on anyone who was not habituated to the adulation had been fearfully squandered through its long isolation from the world. Truly there was little a pope could do.

Pius XII knew this.

Austere, remote, served his meals always in solitude with little human contact, a walking icon to Catholics, he received with a constant gracious kindness the worshipful throngs who came to see him, feeling privileged to receive from this hieratic figure his blessing on themselves, their rosaries, their medals and other holy objects.[70] He touched deftly those things, basically in the inner life of the Church, that came under his actual influence. Grandly intellectual, he would produce during his reign 41 encyclicals and nearly a thousand other messages and addresses, which would appear in the Vatican daily *Osservatore Romano*, touching on aspects of Catholic life and practice ranging from his great Encyclical on Scripture through education, especially the training of priests, medicine, the lives of saints, teaching on Mary as Mother of God and many other topics, eternal and contemporary.

Doctrinally he was always anxious to define the teaching authority of the Church's *magisterium* but in a difference from many of his predecessors, he was equally determined not to close doors to theological investigation.[71] In this way, he prepared the way for the openness of the Second Vatican Council. Teaching on politics, war, and peace came within his purview, but always with a realization that the world's leaders would listen only reluctantly and with prejudice.

The great benchmark of his teaching was the Encyclical *Divino Afflante Spirito*,[72] published in the midst of war, 30 September 1943, the feast of St Jerome, the ancient biblical scholar and author of the Latin translation of Scripture that we know as the Vulgate. Scripture was the hottest of hot potatoes in the teaching of the Church. Leo XIII, in the wake of the early critical studies by liberal Protestant scholars of the nineteenth century, had made an effort to unlock the gate to serious historical study, in his 1893 Encyclical *Providentissimus*

---

[70]These are the recollections I received throughout my years growing up in the atmosphere of his papacy from all the devout pilgrims, clergy, and lay, of my own acquaintance who saw him, including of course many American servicemen of World War II, for whom a visit to Rome and a public audience with the Pope was a rare oasis of peace in the midst of the violence of the time.

[71]So his advisor, Professor Robert Leiber, recalled: "Pius XII was very careful not to close any doors prematurely. He was energetic on this point and regretted that in the case of Galileo." Robert Leiber, *"Pius XII," Stimmen der Zeit*, Freiburg im Breisgau, 163 (1958–59), 81ff.

[72]Vatican website, http://www.vatican.va/holy_father/pius_xii/encyclicals/documents/hf_p-xii_enc_30091943_divino-afflante-spiritu_en.html, *Divino Afflante Spirito*, ENCYCLICAL OF POPE PIUS XII ON PROMOTING BIBLICAL STUDIES, COMMEMORATING THE FIFTIETH ANNIVERSARY OF *PROVIDENTISSIMUS DEUS*. Consulted 22 July 2012.

Deus,[73] but very timidly. He had meant both to relate the teaching of Scripture to scientific findings and to defend it against attacks, and for this purpose had founded the Pontifical Biblical Institute,[74] which was to adapt Catholic study of the Scripture to modern scholarship while defending its inerrancy. Any such opening was slammed shut again during Pius X's crusade against Modernism. For all the efforts Benedict XV made to lessen the rigors of anti-Modernism, this forbidding attitude toward Scripture study was deepened yet further by his 1920 Encyclical *Spiritus Paraclitus*,[75] which required acceptance of the most literal meaning of every word and verse of Scripture, down to asserting that Moses himself had written every word of the Pentateuch, including the account of his own death in Deuteronomy. Now Pius XII's new Encyclical would become the *magna carta* of Catholic scholars' study of the Scriptures.

His choice of the feast of St Jerome for its publication was significant because Jerome himself had done his translation from original languages, Hebrew and Greek. His Vulgate translation into Latin had become the only permitted text for Catholic study, since it had long been the version upon which doctrinal definitions were based in the Western Church, and the only permitted source for further Catholic translations into other languages. Even the redoubtable Ronald Knox had had to do his epochal translation from the Latin of the Vulgate. Pius XII now called on Catholics to prepare new translations from the original languages. He encouraged first textual criticism ("the lower criticism"), study of original sources and manuscripts, papyrus fragments and palimpsests to determine the accurate text of the Scriptures, but also the historical-critical method of reading ("the higher criticism"), investigating the historical circumstances in which the text was written, hypothesizing about authorship, dating, and similar concerns. The Encyclical called for study of the ancient languages themselves, Hebrew, Aramaic, and Greek, as well as the cognate languages which might have influenced

---

[73]Vatican website, *PROVIDENTISSIMUS DEUS*, ENCYCLICAL OF POPE LEO XIII ON THE STUDY OF HOLY SCRIPTURE, published 18 November 1893. Consulted 22 July 2012.
[74]"Biblical Commission." F. L. Cross ed., *The Oxford dictionary of the Christian church* (New York: Oxford University Press, 2005).
[75]Papal Encyclicals Online, http://www.papalencyclicals.net/Ben15/b15spiri.htm, *SPIRITUS PARACLITUS*, ENCYCLICAL OF POPE BENEDICT XV ON ST. JEROME 15 SEPTEMBER 1920. Consulted 22 July 2012.

the text. Catholic scholarship of the Bible would take off from this letting down of the barriers by Pius XII, a tremendous boon to the Church which soon realized that only so could it achieve a serious reading of the Scriptures. His principle: "We ought to explain the original text which was written by the inspired author himself and has more authority and greater weight than any, even the very best, translation whether ancient or modern. This can be done all the more easily and fruitfully if to the knowledge of languages be joined a real skill in literary criticism of the same text."[76]

That same year, 1943, the Pope issued another Encyclical *Mystici Corporis*,[77] which would lead into one of the main discussions of the Second Vatican Council and have decisive influence on its Constitution on the Church, *Lumen Gentium*. Pius, drawing on theological discussion that had gone on in the twenties and thirties of the twentieth century, a rediscovery of the Pauline image of the Church as Body of Christ, described the whole body of the faithful in his encyclical as the Mystical Body of Christ, giving authoritative weight to the concept.[78] At the Council this thinking would blossom into the definition of the Church not in terms of an institution but as the People of God, one of its main concepts.

The liberative character of Pius XII's magisterial teaching to the Church appeared again somewhat counterintuitively in his 1950 Encyclical *Humani Generis*,[79] seen at the time as a negative commentary on more liberal Catholic thought. The Pope presented it as a defense of magisterial authority in the Church against new forms of teaching seen as a recrudescence of Modernism, "a new intellectual current, a new public mood within the Church and new behavior patterns."[80] This was a time when many of the theologians who would

---

[76]*Divino Afflante Spiritu*, #16.

[77]Vatican website,http://www.vatican.va/holy_father/pius_xii/encyclicals/documents/hf_p-xii_enc_29061943_mystici-corporis-christi_en.html, *MYSTICI CORPORIS CHRISTI*, ENCYCLICAL OF POPE PIUS XII ON THE MYSTICAL BODY OF CHRIST, 29 June 1943. Consulted 22 July 2012.

[78]Sebastian Tromp, "Annotations ad enc Mystici Corporis," *Periodica* 32 (1943), 377–401.

[79]Vatican website, http://www.vatican.va/holy_father/pius_xii/encyclicals/documents/hf_p-xii_enc_12081950_humani-generis_en.html, ENCYCLICAL *HUMANI GENERIS* OF THE HOLY FATHER PIUS XII . . . CONCERNING SOME FALSE OPINIONS THREATENING TO UNDERMINE THE FOUNDATIONS OF CATHOLIC DOCTRINE published 12 August 1950. Consulted 22 July 2012.

[80]*Humani generis*, #15.

be the leading thinkers of the Second Vatican Council—Congar, Rahner, de Lubac, Chenu—were being prohibited from teaching by the action of the "Holy Office," successor to the Roman Inquisition that had carried on the interrogation of Galileo. Yet the Encyclical reinterpreted Modernism. A pillar of theological fundamentalism had been rejection of evolutionary theory, which the Encyclical describes as yet unproven, warning against "fictitious tenets . . . which repudiate all that is absolute, firm and immutable,"[81] yet opens the way to serious scholarly attention to evolution, acknowledging that it may accurately describe the biological origins of human life. And so with other bug-a-boos of Catholic attitudes to science. The language is caution, but the effect the opening up of otherwise closed doors. *Humanae Generis* represented a moment of panic during Pius XII's reign, but he handled it with characteristic restraint.

That same year, 1950, on 1 November, All Saints Day, the Pope solemnly proclaimed a new infallible dogma, the bodily Assumption of the Blessed Virgin Mary into heaven.

Pius IX, before him, had made the proclamation in 1854 of the Immaculate Conception of the Blessed Virgin Mary as an infallibly defined dogma. The earlier Pope had an eye to the infallibility definition that he would win from the Council, Vatican I, 16 years later, in 1870. His Immaculate Conception definition can be taken as a demonstration of his own papal capacity to define a doctrine infallibly as binding in faith. He had been anxious to do it on his own, not by prior consultation with the world's bishops, "*ex sese, not ex consensu Ecclesiae*," though in fact the concept has had wide popularity for many centuries, and numerous bishops had been asking for its definition since the time of Gregory XVI.[82] An Apostolic Constitution, *Ineffabilis Deus*,[83] attests the definition, but it was proclaimed on 8 December (providing the requisite 9 months before the birthday of the Virgin on 8 September) before a great assembly of bishops in the Vatican.

Pius XII's repeat of this doctrinal venture, the definition of the Assumption, came just a few months after his censorious Encyclical

---

[81]Ibid., #6.
[82]Mark Miravalle, *Introduction to Mary* (Santa Barbara, CA: Queenship Publishing, 1993), 64–70.
[83]Papal Encyclicals Online, http://www.papalencyclicals.net/Pius09/p9ineff.htm, issued 8 December 1854. Consulted 22 July 2012.

Humanae Generis, which, for all his customary care to open rather than close doctrinal possibilities, had demonstrated his anxiety in defense of papal prerogatives in the office of teaching. He had taken the pains Pius IX had not taken to consult bishops, requesting their opinion, by an Encyclical *Deiparae Virginis Mariae* of 1946,[84] on whether such a definition was opportune. As with the Immaculate Conception, there was no biblical narrative on which to base it. The argument in both cases was a simple *decet*: "it is fitting," a thing which, in the judgment of the popes, God ought appropriately to have done in virtue of Mary's high calling. Both had been popular pieties for a very long time, and occasion had been taken to exercise the power of infallibility as defined. Why did either Pope do this? They were infallibility demonstrations.

No other issue of Pius XII's time exceeded that of the raging Second World War. Like Benedict XV before him, the Pope recognized this as the primary field on which he needed to concentrate such influence as he could have. The world proved expected it of him and would attend to his voice more than it had to Benedict, but still refuse to bend to his pleadings. Like Benedict again, he tried to maintain a neutrality that would preserve his access to all sides, this though he was both the negotiator of the 1933 Reichskonkordat with Germany and one of the writers of Pope Pius XI's *Mit brennender Sorge* denunciation of the Nazis.

Right at the beginning of the war his refusal to issue a condemnation of the invasion of Poland offended the Catholic Poles.[85] Reports came in constantly of atrocities, sometimes committed against Catholics, sometimes by them, and the Vatican regularly took the position that its knowledge was incomplete.[86] That it was can be seen in the incident when the Pope wept on hearing that Polish Cardinal Hlond had prohibited the holding of Catholic liturgical services for German soldiers on Polish soil. Later, in his first Encyclical, *Summi*

---

[84]Vatican website, http://www.vatican.va/holy_father/pius_xii/encyclicals/documents/hf_p-xii_enc_01051946_deiparae-virginis-mariae_en.html, *DEIPARAE VIRGINIS MARIAE*, ENCYCLICAL OF POPE PIUS XII ON THE POSSIBILITY OF DEFINING THE ASSUMPTION OF THE BLESSED VIRGIN MARY AS A DOGMA OF FAITH. Consulted 22 July 2012.

[85]Michael Phayer, *Pius XII, The Holocaust, and the Cold War* (Indianapolis: Indiana University Press, 2008), 6.

[86]Phayer, 8.

Pontificatus,[87] 20 October 1939, the Pope did condemn the invasion, occupation, and partition of Poland under the Molotov-Ribbentrop pact. "The blood of countless human beings, even noncombatants, raises a piteous dirge over a nation such as Our dear Poland, which, for its fidelity to the Church, for its services in the defense of Christian civilization, written in indelible characters in the annals of history, has a right to the generous and brotherly sympathy of the whole world, while it awaits, relying on the powerful intercession of Mary, Help of Christians, the hour of a resurrection in harmony with the principles of justice and true peace."[88] By 18 January 1949, hearing of the slaughter of 15,000 Polish civilians, the Pope said on Vatican Radio, "The horror and inexcusable excesses committed on a helpless and a homeless people have been established by the unimpeachable testimony of eye-witnesses."[89] But not for him the confrontational style of Pius XI. Pius XII would soar serene above the travails of the world.

The Nazis murdered 2,500 monks and priests in Poland while sending others to concentration camps,[90] and the Dachau concentration camp in Germany listed 2,600 Catholic priest prisoners.[91]

The Vatican's independent and sovereign City State was in the eye of the storm and constantly endangered. The public neutrality ensured that it was never invaded not the Pope himself under threat. Instead the Vatican turned to providing aid from different parts of the world to victims of the war.[92] The Pope called on Giovanni Battista Montini, the future Pope Paul VI, then an Archbishop, one of the three main figures in the Secretariate of State and a man who saw the Pope every morning until 1954,[93] to organize an office for the assistance of prisoners of war and refugees which, between 1939

---

[87]Vatican website, http://www.vatican.va/holy_father/pius_xii/encyclicals/documents/hf_p-xii_enc_20101939_summi-pontificatus_en.html, *Summi Pontificatus,* Encyclical of Pope Pius XII On the Unity of Human Society. Consulted 23 July 2012.

[88]*Summi Pontificatus,* #106.

[89]Sir Martin Gilbert, *The Second World War* (New York: Macmillan, 1970), 40.

[90]Owen Chadwick, *A History of Christianity* (New York: Barnes and Noble, 1995), 254-f.

[91]John Vidmar, O.P., *The Catholic Church Through the Ages* (Mahwah, NJ: Paulist Press, July 2005), 327–31.

[92]Felicity O'Brien, *Pius XII* (London and Bristol: Burleigh Press, 2000), 8.

[93]Andrea Lazzarini, *Paolo VI, Profilo di Montini* (quoted from *Papst Paolo VI,* Herder Freiburg, 1964), 58.

and 1947, dealt with nearly ten million information requests and produced over 11 million reports on missing persons.[94] The Vatican surely did not lack for information as the war progressed.

What the Pope could do magisterially was to build up a Catholic teaching on war as it was practiced in this time. His Christmas addresses on peace were a main focus of these teachings. That of 1942 s-pole of "the hundreds of thousands of persons who, without any fault on their part, sometimes only because of their nationality or race, have been consigned to death or to a slow decline."[95] This outraged the Nazis, who claimed the speech was "one long attack on everything we stand for. . . . He is clearly speaking on behalf of the Jews. . . . He is virtually accusing the German people of injustice toward the Jews, and makes himself the mouthpiece of the Jewish war criminals," convincing *The New York Times* at that time that "The voice of Pius XII is a lonely voice in the silence and darkness enveloping Europe this Christmas. . . . In calling for a 'real new order' based on 'liberty, justice, and love,' . . . the pope put himself squarely against Hitlerism."[96] Other annual Christmas statements would follow, each protesting the dehumanization caused by the war. One of the first atomic weapons were on the scene, the Pope spoke unequivocally, expressing the traditional Catholic view that "every act of war directed to the indiscriminate destruction of whole cities or vast areas with their inhabitants is a crime against God and man," in a speech recorded in the Vatican newspaper *Osservatore Romano* on 7 August 1945. The newspaper, an official organ of the Vatican, commented: "This war provides a catastrophic conclusion. Incredibly this destructive weapon remains as a temptation for posterity, which, we know by bitter experience, learns so little from history."

But the great question aroused by Pope Pius XII's conduct during the war remains the *Shoah*, the Holocaust of the Jews. What leadership did he show?

Right at the beginning of his reign, the pope ostentatiously appointed to Vatican posts a number of prominent Jewish scholars who had been dismissed from Italian university positions under

---

[94]Corrado Pallenberg, *Inside the Vatican* (New York: Hawthorne Press, 1960), 58.
[95]Phayer, 53.
[96]David G. Dalin, "Pius XII and the Jews: A defense," *Weekly Standard*, 6, no. 23 (16 February 2001).

Mussolini's racial laws.[97] He quickly arranged a deal with the Brazilian President Getúlio Vargas, for thousands of visas to enable Jews to escape Europe, a deal that was then sabotaged by Brazilian diplomats colluding with the Nazis.[98] Informed in the Spring of 1940 of plans to deport Lithuanian Jews to Germany, he repeatedly called Ribbentrop on 11 March of that year, protesting this treatment of Jews.[99] In a widely distributed personal letter on Vatican letterhead, he exhorted Catholic clergy to do what they could on behalf of the Jews.[100]

One can cite many such incidents throughout the war. When deportations were scheduled in Italy and in Rome itself, the Vatican sheltered 477 Jews within its own precincts, while another 4,238 received protection in Roman monasteries and convents.[101] Eighty percent of Rome's Jews escaped the Holocaust, with help from some German diplomas who cooperated to this end with the Pope.[102]

But the Pope never issued a blanket condemnation of the genocidal program against the Jews as such. Partly this was a prudential decision after the Dutch bishops had such a statement read out in all their churches on 20 July 1942, the Nazis, in retaliation, ordered on July all Jewish converts to Catholicism, until then spared, to be rounded up and sent off to Auschwitz, where they were presumably gassed on 9 August . This included the famous Edith Stein, Carmelite nun, subsequently canonized a saint under her religious name Teresa Benedicta of the Cross, and her sister Rosa, also a convert.[103] His reticence on issuing such a condemnation may have kept the Vatican as institution alive to do the many things he did. The Pope also argued on several occasions that he could not issue such

---

[97]Dalin, 70.

[98]Jeffrey Lesser, *Welcoming the Undesirables: Brazil and the Jewish Question* (Berkeley, CA: University of California Press, 1995), 151–68.

[99]Ralph McInerney, *The Defamation of Pius XII* (South Bend, IN: St Augustine's Press, 2001), 49.

[100]Justin Ewers, "Sainthood on Hold," *U.S. News and World Report*, 17–24 November 2008.

[101]"Anti-Semitism in the Roman Catholic Church: The Church's ole in the Nazi Holocaust", *Religious Tolerance Network*, http://www.religioustolerance.org/vat_hol12.htm. Consulted 23 July 2012.

[102]Dalin, 82–5.

[103]María Ruiz Scaperlanda, "Edith Stein: St. Teresa Benedicta of the Cross" (Huntington, IN: Our Sunday Visitor, 2001), 154.

condemnations one-sidedly, without simultaneously condemning the Soviets.[104]

Nevertheless, the public picture was one of heroism. Throughout the war, public opinion maintained that he was that "lonely voice in the silence and darkness of Europe" defending the Jewish victims, as *The New York Times* had named him.[105] The Nazis had regarded him as adversary.[106] Not until after his death, when in 1963 the German playwright Rolf Hochhuth produced his play, *Der Stellvertreter: Ein christliches Trauerspiel*, as the Second Vatican Council was well under way, did this tide turn, and massively. Since that time he has been the whipping boy for all the world's indifference, and that of the Catholic Church, to the fate of the Jews.

But that goes beyond the purview of this chapter, which concerns the face of the Church as John XXIII found it when elected Pope in 1958. He perceived it as disengaged from the world it lived in, reduced largely to remaining cultural habits of Catholicism, far removed from vibrant contact with its own resources of tradition and faith, in need of waking up to the measure of its Gospel, its dust-encrusted windows thrown wide. Less than 3 months after his 28 October election he would issue the public call to an Ecumenical Council, on 25 January 1959. Cardinal Giovanni Battista Montini, who would inherit the running of the Council when elected Pope after its first year, remarked "the holy old boy doesn't realize what a hornet's nest he's stirring up."[107]

---

[104]Harold H. Tittmann, Jr., *Inside the Vatican of Pius XII: The Memoir of an American Diplomat During World War II*, cited in Raul Hilberg, *The Destruction of the European Jews* (2003), 3rd edn, 1204–5.

[105]Note 96 above.

[106]Note 97 above.

[107]George Weigel, "Thinking Through Vatican II," *First Things*, June/July 2001.

5

Vatican Council II:
Its first period, 1962

"Now I rejoice," writes St Paul, "in my sufferings for your sake, and in my flesh I am filling up what is lacking in Christ's afflictions for the sake of his body, that is, the church." Colossians 1, 24.

The verse expresses well the character and the task of Pope John XXIII, Angelo Giuseppe Roncalli, just short of 77 years old at the time of his election. The long reign of Pius XII had been epochal in the experience of the Church, its learned Pope teaching constantly through times of terror. The Cardinals who voted for Roncalli felt they were electing an "interim Pope," someone who would hold the chair briefly until they had more time to think what sort of Pope they wanted. The four and a half years of his papacy would surprise them all.

Pope John presented a transparently human personality, in great contrast to the hieratic figure of Pius XII. The accoutrements of office—elaborate vestments, triple crown, sedia gestatori, and waving flambelli—sat awkwardly on him as extraneous burdens, never able to conceal the humanity beneath.

Countless stories are told to illustrate this human character of the Pope. My own favorite from the time was of two wealthy, privileged, and ever censorious dowagers of my acquaintance, ever welcome in the entourage of bishops. They had a splendid ebony and ivory crucifix on their mantle, which, they always told their visitors, they had brought to Rome to be blessed by every pope of the century. On seeing Angelo Roncalli appear on the balcony, elected Pope, they declared: "This peasant will never bless our crucifix."

He took at once to making pastoral visits in his diocese of Rome, appearing on Christmas Day of 1958 among polio-stricken children at the Bambino Gesú hospital in Rome, proceeding from there to the Santo Spirito hospital and from there to the Regina Coeli prison, where he told the prisoners "You could not come to me so I came to you."[1] In his diary he recorded ". . . great astonishment in the Roman, Italian and international press. I was hemmed in on all sides: authorities, photographers, prisoners, wardens. . . ."[2] His habit of sneaking out of the Vatican to walk the streets of Rome at night earned him the nickname "Johnny Walker," after the popular whiskey of that name.

Early in his reign, Pope John assembled a Roman Synod, which met and promulgated its already formulated resolutions on 25–27 January 1960. Here were the Roman clerics who controlled the curial machinery of the Church, and the Pope gave them their head. They decreed enforcement of the strict separation of the clerical state from others in the full manner of the Council of Trent, prohibited women from setting foot in sanctuaries, required that all teaching in seminaries be done in Latin, ordered that Gregorian chant be the norm in all liturgical celebration, while new hymns would require prior approval by the bishops. They prohibited any relaxation of rubrical norms, particularly forbidding any altars at which the celebrating priest would face his congregation and, in general, called for a reversion of the Church to the most rigorous habits of clericalism.[3]

Consternation followed. Those of us who were watching (I at that time as a theology student in the Jesuit *Hochschule St Georgen*

---

[1] *L'Osservatore Romano, Weekly Edition in English*, 6 September 2000.

[2] Peter Hebblethwaite, *Pope John XXIII: Shepherd of the Modern World* (Garden City, NY: Image Books, 1987), 303.

[3] Romano Amerio, *Iota Unum: A Study of Changes in the Catholic Church in the 20th Century* (Kansas City: Sarto House, 1996), 54–6. The passage concludes: "Anybody can see that this massive reaffirmation of traditional discipline, which the synod wanted, was contradicted and negated in almost every detail by the effects of the council. And so the Roman synod, which was to have been an exemplary foreshadowing of the council, fell within a few years into the Erebus of oblivion, and is indeed *tanquam non fuerit*. As an instance of this nullification I may say that having searched for the texts of the Roman synod in diocesan curias and archives, I could not find them there and had to get them from secular public libraries."

in Frankfurt) described the Synod as "the great leap forward into the 11th century." Many of my classmates feared that the coming Council would follow the same impulses. My own observation of Pope John told me to have good hope: having given the synodal clerics their head, he would do the same with the Council Fathers, as, in fact, he did.

What was lacking in the Church as John XXIII found it? This genial man had a distinctive point of view, having certainly suffered much in the Church to fill up the afflictions of Christ. Already ordained a priest and teaching in a seminary, he was drafted into the Italian army in World War I and served as stretcher-bearer on the slaughter-fields of that war. A share-cropper's son, he rose slowly through several Church offices until reaching the diplomatic corps in 1935. Made Apostolic Delegate to Turkey and Greece from that year to 1944, he used his position on a massive scale, often at peril to himself, to rescue many thousands of Jewish refugees from the Holocaust, gaining them safe-conduct out of various European lands, providing where necessary fake baptismal certificates, making it possible for those who reached Istanbul to go on to Palestine or to other destinations of their choice.[4]

In 1944, General De Gaulle, returning with his Free French to Paris, made it clear that he would not receive the Vichy-leaning Papal Nuncio as head of the diplomatic corps for the New Year greeting. Pope Pius XII pulled Archbishop Roncalli suddenly out of his relative obscurity to become the new Nuncio to France.[5] Serving there during the period of doctrinal panic marked by the Encyclical *Humanae Generis* and the silencing of so many theologians in France and elsewhere, he picked up Yves Congar's heavily censured *Vrai et fausse réforme dans l'Église*, which he annotated extensively, asking a missionary friend who visited him in Paris whether true

---

[4]For biographical data, Hebblethwaite's *Pope John XXIII: Shepherd of the Modern World*, cited above, is a reliable source, also Peter and Margaret Hebblethwaite's *John XXIII: Pope of the Century* (Continuum International, 2000). The Pope's own personal diary is also available: *Journal of a Soul*, translation by Dorothy White of *Giovanni XXIII Il Giornale dell' Anima* (Geoffrey Chapman, 1965).

[5]John W. O'Malley, *What Happened at Vatican II* (Cambridge, MA: The Belknap Press of Harvard University Press, 2008), 103f. O'Malley's book is a treasure-house of knowledge about the Council, on which I will rely heavily in this and the following chapter.

reform were actually possible in the Church.[6] Only in 1953, when for his services in France he was made Patriarch of Venice, did he become a Cardinal, the customary award for one who had been Nuncio to a major Catholic country.

His election as Pope in his old age must have been an altogether unexpected surprise, but he knew at once what he had to do in the short time that would be given him. Congar had taught this man, a lover of the Church, that reform must be done IN the Church, the real Church as it is, and not TO it. What was lacking to the Church, the thing that needed to be filled up in the flesh of the Body of Christ was much of the love that Christ had assigned to his followers as their true task. John, having lived that love all his life, was determined to bring it to full blossom in the Church. In calling the Council he recognized that this must not come as a decree from on high but must result from consultation and the profound reflection of the whole Church.

The hallmarks of the Church had become insistence on disciplined uniformity and submission. Popes of the nineteenth and twentieth centuries, and not only those, had trembled at the thought of any loss of CONTROL over the thought or in the active life of Catholics, and had acted to suppress it. Jesus had told his disciples, "He that is not against us is for us." (Mk. 9, 40) For much of our history Church leadership had preferred the reading, "He that is not with me is against me" (Mt. 12, 30 and Lk. 11, 23), but when it came to the test and the impetuous "Sons of Thunder," James and John, wanted to call down fire from heaven, a favorite tactic of some ancient prophets, to consume a Samaritan village, which had rejected them for their Jewishness (Lk. 9, 54), Jesus turned and rebuked them. And when Peter, in the Garden of Gethsemane, drew his sword in defense of Jesus, he was told, "Put your sword into its sheath. Shall I not drink the cup which the Father has given me?", the cup of his sufferings, whose full measure the Church was to fill up.

The unloving and ignorant way that Christians had dealt with Jews throughout our common history stood out in his consciousness,

---

[6]Yves Congar, *True and False Reform in the Church*, translated by Paul Philibert, a 2011 reissue by The Liturgical Press, translating the 1968 revised edition of the 1950 *Vraie et fausse réforme dans l'Église*; Philbert's Preface, p. 2, n. 2. Subsequent references to Congar's *True and False Reform in the Church* will be to this edition.

a problem made more urgent than ever through the outrage of the *Shoah*, so evident to this man who had for years risked his own life and career for the rescue of its victims. Christians had, with great consistency through their history, done vast injustice to the Jews, which had to be addressed. Pope John paid close attention to the Jewish scholar, Jules Isaac,[7] sent to him by French President Vincent Auriol. Isaac, since the 1947 International Conference at Seelisberg, Switzerland, *Les Amitiés judéo-chrétiennes*, had been a leader in the thinking of Christians, including Catholics, on how to remedy their anti-Jewish teachings.[8] Pope John had already engaged German Jesuit Augustin Bea, whom he had made a Cardinal, to prepare and advance through the Council a declaration on the Jews and other religions.

Protestants too had been treated only as adversaries, "heretics," and hardly regarded as fellow Christians at all, as had the Orthodox, regarded as "schismatics" by Catholics for so many centuries, both of them estranged and treated as Christian cast-offs since the crises of the eleventh and sixteenth centuries. The Orthodox understandably questioned the ecumenicity of all the Councils of the second millennium, in which they had no part. John would invite observers, both Protestant and Orthodox, to the Council and they would be clearly heard at all stages of the deliberations, even though they would not have a vote.

And then there were the advocates of the "two swords" theory, who believed in the exclusive religious rights of Catholics and thought it the duty of the state, when possible, to acknowledge and foster those rights. Among the theologians who had been summarily silenced during the 1950s and forbidden to teach was New York Jesuit, John Courtney Murray, who had much to say of the separation of Church and State, religious liberty, and the rights of conscience.

In all these matters, Christians had offended and John intended the Council to set them right.

Liturgy, too, had become rather a black hole in the Church's practice. Pius XII had already pointed out, in *Mediator Dei*, the importance the Eucharist should have as the very font from which

---

[7]O'Malley, 219.
[8]Especially his *Jésus et Israël*, editions of 1948 and 1959.

Christian life would spring. A liturgical movement had striven through the twentieth century to rescue Catholic celebration of the Mass from its general unintelligibility. Movement away from the traditional Latin, not understood by most Catholics even though they tried to use missals with a vernacular translation on facing pages with the Latin, seemed too radical a step after all the centuries in which Latin had been enforced. The Mass could be done with a remote and majestic dignity, but became too often a hurried hugger-mugger mutter, where people said their rosaries in the pews while awaiting the moment of consecration and elevation. "Going to Mass," Sunday obligation under pain of hell, was duty, "Going to Communion" an individual privatized ritual hardly connected to the action of Christ in the whole Church. The bishops coming to the Council would understand that well and make it their first task to rescue the Mass from this morass.

But the real substance of the Council, what would make the Church itself intelligible to its people as a communion of its members in faith, would be an understanding of its collegial structure and a recognition of the People of God, the whole community and all its members, as constituting it.

Some 2,500 bishops would arrive for the opening of the Council, 11 October 1962, a grand spectacle watched by tens of thousands in the square and millions more worldwide on television. There were, besides, the *periti*, theological advisers brought by the various bishops, and observers from 17 Orthodox and Protestant churches as well as Jews and other religions.

Vatican Council I, by way of comparison, had 787 member participants.[9] Over the course of the Council's four periods, average attendance of bishops would range from 2,100 to 2,300.[10]

As first major event, the Pope gave them an address, *Gaudet Mater Ecclesia,*[11] "The Mother Church Rejoices," that would have tremendous influence in the shaping of the Council. It was of the

---

[9]Maureen Sullivan, *101 Questions and Answers on Vatican II* (New York: Paulist Press, 2002), 21.

[10]Faculty of Catholic University of America, "Vatican Council II," *New Catholic Encyclopedia*, XIV, 1st edn (New York: McGraw-Hill, 1967), 563f.

[11]http://www.saint-mike.org/library/papal_library/johnxxiii/opening_speech_vaticanii.html, "Opening Speech to the Vatican II Council, Pope John XXIII, 11 October 1962." Consulted 26 July 2012.

Pope's own writing, every word carefully pondered.[12] It would take a while to sink in, delivered as it was in Latin, which would be the language of the Council, and with the strange convolutions of papal language, at the end of a lengthy ceremony. *Osservatore Romano* headlined "Chief Duty of the Council: To Defend and Promote Doctrine," while *Le Monde* proclaimed "Pope Approves Research Methods in Modern Thought." The address would support both impressions, but there is much more.[13]

The joy of the title sprang simply from the presence of this massive representation of the Church. A Council, like the others of Christian history, said the Pope, would express the mind of the whole Church in genuine depth. All the resources of the Church's patrimony would guide it, but in meeting the many problems of the present it should turn away from the "prophets of gloom" who found no good in the Modern World. Instead, in their striving for evangelical perfection, they should "make themselves useful to society as it was, so that the highest and noblest in human society would take its strength and growth." Guarding the tradition in its full integrity, the Council should not involve itself in "a discussion of one article or another of the fundamental doctrine of the Church which has repeatedly been taught . . .," but take "a step forward toward a doctrinal penetration and a formation of consciousness in faithful and perfect conformity to the authentic doctrine, which, however, should be studied and expounded through the methods of research and through the literary forms of modern thought. The substance of the ancient doctrine of the deposit of faith is one thing, and the way in which it is presented is another."

In dealing with errors, the Church should "make use of the medicine of mercy rather than that of severity. She considers that she meets the needs of the present day by demonstrating the validity of her teaching rather than by condemnations." She should show herself as "the loving mother of all, benign, patient, full of mercy and goodness toward the brethren who are separated from her."

---

[12]A generous summary of the address is given in O'Malley, *What Happened at Vatican II*, 94–6. The most definitive analysis of its import is given by Giuseppe Alberigo and Alberto Melloni, "L'Allocutione *Gaudet Mater Ecclesia* di Giovanni XXIII (11 ottobre 1962): Sinossi critica dell'allocutione," in *Fede, tradizione, profezia: Studi su Giovanni XXIII* (Paideia: Brescia, 1984), 223–83.

[13]O'Malley, 94f.

She would make unity her objective, and at three levels: the unity of Catholics among themselves, the unity of prayers and ardent desires of those Christians separated from the Apostolic See, and "the unity in esteem and respect for the Catholic Church which animates those who follow non-Christian religions."

The Council was thus to offer, in positive terms, the loving message of Christ rather than condemnations. The ecumenical and inter-religious dimensions were integral to its plan, but in terms of welcome rather than as a quest for submission. This represented, in fact, a great change from attitudes that had predominated in the past, and that were normally taken for granted in the curial offices.

Pope John later confided to his trusted secretary, Fr Loris Capovilla, that as he delivered his address, "Every now and then I glanced at my friend on the right," Cardinal Alfredo Ottaviani, head of the Holy Office.[14] On the following days, the Pope would receive the observers, both Protestant and Orthodox, telling them, in French, of his earlier contacts with other Christian leaders. "Never, to my recollection, was there among us any muddling of principles, any disagreement at the level of charity on the joint work that circumstances required of us in aid of the suffering. We did not negotiate, we talked. We did not debate but loved one another."[15]

October 13 saw the first working session of the Council. It was brief. After an opening Mass, Archbishop Pericle Felici, Secretary General of the Council, presented the list prepared by Cardinal Ottaviani in the Curia of members he considered appropriate for the different working commissions. Felici announced that elections would be held immediately. Confusion followed as the bewildered bishops tried to fill out the 160 places on their ballots, 16 for each of the ten commissions, some calling out across the aisles to one another with advice, until Cardinal Achille Liénart of Lille, France, rose from the table where the ten Cardinal Presidents were seated to ask that the voting be postponed for a few days while the bishops got to know one another. His motion was seconded by another

---

[14]Ibid., 96.
[15]*Acta Synodalia Sacrosancti Concilii Vaticani II*, 32 volumes (Vatican City, Typis Polyglottis Vaticanis, 1970–99, henceforth *AS*), I, 1, 196–8. *AS* lists and identifies all these observers, 192–6.

of the presidents, Cardinal Josef Frings of Cologne, and with the agreement of all ten presidents the election was put off to the following Tuesday and the session adjourned.[16]

A die was cast by this action. Leading individuals would become important in the Council, and it was widely felt that Cardinal Ottaviani had tried to gain curial control over its deliberations by presenting his list of safe names. Cardinal Giuiseppe Siri of Genoa rushed to Ottaviani's office to complain that Liénart's action was "a maneuver directed . . . by a certain antipathy to the Curia, . . . the eternal inferiority-complex which the northerners have in their relation with Rome."[17] I can recall, as theology student in Frankfurt, how one of our professors, Fr Otto Semmelroth, who had been present not as a *peritus* himself but as an assistance to Karl Rahner, told us of the bishops standing at the doors of the basilica over the following days handing out suggestion lists, which were gleefully received like "*heisse Simmel*," (hot buns). He received from us students, for that, the nickname "Otto der heisse Simmelroth."

In the event, after the 2,500 bishops' lists, each of 160 names, had been counted by hand, the chosen commission members were largely the same as on the curial list, with only 64 additions. Asian and African bishops, not well known to the others, had poor representation, but Pope John balanced the lists in adding the additional members he was allowed by the "Regulations." Later, in November, 1963, the second year of the Council, Pope Paul VI, at the request of the members, who by now had learned to know each other quite well, asked the fathers to vote new members to bring each commission up to 30. This made them far more representative of the will of the assembly.[18] In addition, on 22 October 1962, after the elections were finished, Pope John raised Cardinal Bea's Secretariat for Christian Unity to the status of an eleventh commission, thus ensuring that Bea's team would remain intact as the membership.

Those "Regulations" had been promulgated by the pope himself back on 6 August 1962. They represented him, not the Council.

[16]O'Malley, 97.
[17]Quoted in Andrea Riccardi, "The Tumultuous Opening Days of the Council," in Giuseppe Alberigo and Joseph Komonchak (eds), *History of Vatican II*, 5 volumes (New York: Orbis Press, 1995–2006, henceforth Alberigo/Komonchak, *History*), 2, 29, n. 12.
[18]O'Malley, 98f.

The could be and were changed, in minor ways, both by John himself and by his successor, Paul VI, but never by the act of the Council.[19]

The bishops next met in working session on 20 October, to take up the document "On the Sacred Liturgy." But first they would issue a brief "Message to the World," suggested from within the French delegation to the Council, particularly by theologian Marie-Domenique Chenu, O.P., one of the many who had been silenced during the panic of the 1950s, and who now feared that the Council might close itself off from the real issues of the world and lose itself in theological and doctrinal abstractions.[20]

The statement was brief, and little noticed in the press at the time, but it committed the bishops to a message of mercy, kindness, and compassion along the lines of the Pope's opening address. "We urgently turn our thoughts to the problems by which human beings are afflicted today. Hence, our concern goes out to the lowly, poor and powerless. Like Christ, we would have pity on the multitude heavily burdened by hunger, misery, and lack of knowledge. . . . As we undertake our work, therefore, we would emphasize whatever concerns the dignity of the human person, whatever contributes to a genuine community of peoples."[21] Christianity would seem to be breaking out.

That message absorbed the whole of the 20 October session. Before they got to their first work on an actual decree, on 22 October, the bishops had now spent a week and a half since the 11 October opening of the Council. They had begun to wonder how long they would be there, away from the pressing concerns of their dioceses. No one seems to have expected that the Council would take 4 years. Texts, *schemata*, for decrees on various matters had been presented to them by the Preparatory Commissions, headed in almost all cases by the Cardinal Prefect of a Roman Congregation, with the expectation that these, already presented to the Pope, would simply get the approval, perhaps with minor emendations, of the Council. It did not happen so.

---

[19]Ibid., 100.
[20]On this development and the influence of outstanding theologians, see Giovanni Turbanti, *Un concilio per il mondo modern: La redazione della constituzione pastorale "Gaudium et Dpes: del Vaticano II* (Bolgna: Il Mulino, 2000), 119–35.
[21]*AS* I, 1, 230–2.

That the Council discussed the document on the liturgy first arose partly from the bishops' sense that this had priority, but also from the fact that, among the seven *schemata* prepared in advance for their consideration this one was most ready. Renewal, adaptation of the liturgy had already happened, though on quite a timid scale, in the restoration by Pope Pius XII of the Easter Vigil and other parts of the Holy Week triduum, with some further editing in John XXIII's Missal of 1962 which had been edited somewhat earlier in the year, before the opening of the Council.[22] Hence, revision did not appear a prohibited thing. The *schema* provided derived largely from principles enunciated in Pius XII's Encyclical *Mediator Dei*. Fr Annibale Bugnini, professor of liturgy at the Lateran and Urbaniana universities in Rome, who had guided Pius XII in his liturgical changes, had the largest hand in its composition. But in February 1962, a new Prefect of the Congregation of Rites, Cardinal Arcadio Larraone, a very conservative opponent of any change, saw to it that Bugnini was excluded from the preparatory commission and even dismissed from his teaching posts, to be replaced by Fr Ferdinando Antonelli, whom Larraone considered more of his own thinking. This created among the Council fathers a perception of manipulation. But when it came to a presentation of the already approved *schema*, Antonelli provided a pretty straightforward presentation of the Bugnini document, including its very strong insistence on the active participation of the congregation.

Everyone had been very reticent about proposing changes in the liturgy, and preservation of the tradition had figured high on the list of requirements. But Bugnini's proposal included the admission of the laity to the chalice on some occasions, the great hurdle over which John Hus had been burned at the stake in the fifteenth century, and while upholding the virtues of Latin it had quoted from *Mediator Dei* Pius XII's observation that "in some rites it is clear that the vernacular has proved very useful for the people," suggesting it might be used for readings, announcements, certain prayers, and music. The Council of Trent had, in fact, left open both practices, the cup and the vernacular,[23] but in the sixteenth century either cup or vernacular sounded too Protestant.

---

[22]It is to this 1962 Missal of John XXIII that the present-day advocates of the Latin-language "Tridentine Mass" return.

[23]John W. O'Malley, "Trent and Vernacular Liturgy," *America*, 29 January 2007.

All this whetted the bishops' appetite. Cardinal Joseph Frings of Cologne opened the discussion by describing the *schema* as the legacy of Pope Pius XII. Other bishops came in with suggestions for and against the proposals and the discussion opened the way to so many interventions that, over the 3 weeks from 22 October to 13 November, 328 had been presented on the floor and another 197 in writing. Cardinal Ottaviani wanted the issue to be submitted to his Doctrinal Commission for approval, but the bishops voted 2,162-46, a 97 percent approval, to send it instead to the Liturgical Commission, which would sort through the recommendations and present a final text for the Council's own acceptance. When it was finally presented the following year, 4 December 1963, it received a landslide 2,147-4 endorsement, and was promulgated by the new Pope Paul VI as the Constitution *Sancrosanctum Concilium*.[24]

This treatment of the liturgical constitution set the precedent for how other *schemata* would be handled. The bishops had taken the process into their full assembly and Pope John's intention to make the Council a true consultation of the whole Church had found its concrete form.

The process, unexpectedly clumsy, required amounts of time that no one had anticipated. It had become clear that the Council would not finish that year, 1962. Liturgical practice would continue to develop. Within 2 years the Mass would begin to be said in people's own languages, perhaps the most perceptible change made by the Council. A commission to oversee these developments, appointed by Paul VI on 4 January 1964, restored the discarded Fr Bugnini as its secretary. Cardinal Larraone, still Prefect of the Congregation of Rites, would serve as a member but the chairmanship went to Cardinal Giacomo Lercaro of Bologna.[25]

These events also solidified several important hallmarks of the Council, as Pope John had designed it. *Aggiornamento* first. The bishops had understood that the Church should be opened up to the actual life of its own time, but along with this and as its engine, the *ressourcement*, the close attention and faithful return to its origins in its scriptural roots and in its long tradition of teaching and practice. Liturgists would return to these sources, not to

---

[24]O'Malley, *What Happened*, 136–9. My account of the Council sessions will consistently follow O'Malley's text.
[25]O'Malley, 139.

"modernize" the Mass but to bring it closer to those fundamental and traditional sources.[26]

As important in principle would be the realization that the Church must adapt itself to local circumstances. "The Church does not wish to impose a rigid uniformity in matters that do not involve the faith or the good of the whole community," important in a Church which would embrace all the cultural differences of the world and not consist of Europeans only. Third would be the practical demonstration of Episcopal collegiality. The entire episcopate had reflected on these matters and not simply taken them from the curial center. This fundamental principle would need formal statement later in the Doctrinal Constitution on the Church, the *Lumen Gentium*, but the bishops had just done it in fact. And finally, the liturgy had been taken out of the hands of clergy alone and handed over for the full and active participation of the entire Church. This amounted to a demonstration of the other most fundamental principle of the Council, that the entire communion of faith, the Church in all its members, is People of God.

Resistance would sometimes take vehement form. One of my own memories, from the Spring of 1965 when I was a Jesuit "Tertian,"[27] is of driving out to a Connecticut parish to say Mass on a Sunday, the week before the Scripture readings were to go into English. The Pastor told me I should sit down after the Gospel reading and he would give the homily. Stepping to the microphone he announced: "Next week, everything is going to be confused! I'm going to be confused! You're going to be confused! I'm not going to like it! You're not going to like it! But they tell us we have to do the readings in English." He went on in tones of outrage, all those exclamation points audible, while I sat white-knuckled at the chair. He was not the only one of what I came to call the "non-survivors of the Council," many of them excellent priests and people who simply could not stomach the change.

More than a month had gone by now since the opening of the Council, as it came, on the very day of the vote on liturgy, 13 November, to its second task. Commentators sometimes suggest

---

[26]Ibid., 140.
[27]Jesuits, after completing their formal studies, have a "third year of formation," which brings them back to the ascetical training of their 2-year Novitiate. I was back from theology studies in Germany for the tertian year at Pomfret, Connecticut.

that, from the beginning, the Council had turned away from the preparatory *schemata* that the Curia had presented to them, but with the liturgy proposal they had simply taken their cue from the possibilities the Bugnini *schema* had offered them and expanded on them. Now, as they turned to the proposed document on "The Sources of Revelation," they came to the real turning point of the Council.

Cardinal Ottaviani, head of the Doctrinal Commission, which had prepared the document, humiliated already at what the Council had done with the liturgy over his objections, introduced it, taking only 5 minutes to state that, though alternative proposals existed, this one had the approval of the Pope and, under terms of Canon 222 of the Code of Canon Law, could not be rejected by the Council. The bishops could discuss only this text.[28]

Here was one of the main issues over which the Reformation had been fought in the sixteenth century: were there two distinct sources of the Revelation of God in Christ, Scripture and a Tradition which was in the hands of the Church's *Magisterium*, or, as the Protestants said, one source only, "*sola Scriptura?*" The bishops were aware that much new theological discussion had dealt with this subject.

Ottaviani, in his introduction, had said: "You have heard many people speak about the lack of pastoral tone in this *schema*. Well, I say that the first and most fundamental pastoral task is to provide correct doctrine. 'Teach!' The Lord's greatest commandment is precisely that: 'Teach all peoples.' Teaching correctly is what is fundamental to being pastoral. Those who are concerned with a pastoral style can later give the Church's teaching a fuller pastoral expression. But take notice: councils speak in a style that is orderly, lucid, concise, and not in the style of a sermon or a pastoral letter of some bishop or other, not even in the style of an encyclical of the Supreme Pontiff. This style of council discourse is sanctioned by its use through the ages."[29]

Fr Salvatore Garofalo then spelled the way through the chapters of the *schema*. The first of its five chapters gave the familiar account

---

[28]Discussed by Riccardo Burigana, "La Commissione 'De Divina Revelatione,'" in M. Lamberigts, Cl. Soetens and J. Grootaers (eds), *Les Commissions conciliaires à Vatican II* (Leuven: Biblioteeek van de Fakulteit Godgeleerdheid, 1996), henceforth Lamberigts, *Commissions conciliaires*, 27–61, at 27.
[29]*AS* I/3, 27–8.

of revelation coming from two distinct sources: the Scripture and a Tradition that contained truths that the scriptural authors had not set down in writing. A second chapter, on inspiration, inerrancy, and literary composition, saw every part of Scripture, down to the last detail, as inspired by God and entirely free from error in matters religious or secular *"in qualibet re religiosa vel profana."* A third chapter, on the Old Testament, allowed it no other meaning than its momentum toward the New. The theme of the fourth chapter was the New Testament itself. It permitted no inaccuracy in the Gospel account of Jesus' words and deeds and condemned, in particular, any questioning of the infancy narrative in Matthew and Luke. A fifth and final chapter gave authority to St Jerome's Latin Vulgate version of the Scripture, paid reverence to the Greek Septuagint version of the Old Testament but made no mention at all of the Hebrew original.[30]

When this presentation was finished, Cardinal Liénart stood, among the ten Presidents of the Council, to say *"Non placet."* The entire *schema* had to be rejected. It misconstrued what the Council of Trent had said about the relation between Scripture and Tradition, and was "frigid" in its language, without the warmth proper to a document about Scripture. Faith was not based on "Scholastic arguments" but on the Word of God.[31]

Liénart's *"Non placet"* was followed by another, as severe, from Cardinal Frings.[32] He was followed by Cardinal Ernesto Ruffini of Palermo and Siri, both pleading for consideration of the *schema* as reinstating the condemnations of Modernism by Pius X, whose Oath against Modernism still circulated in the Church.[33] But Cardinal Paul-Émile Léger of Montreal demanded that the whole document be revised, as based on the fear of error and consequently having a negative tone that would discourage exegetes and inhibit scholarship.[34] Cardinal Franz König of Vienna added his *"non placet,"* appealing to the teaching of Pius XII's great Encyclical *Divino Afflante Spirito.*[35] Next, Cardinal

---

[30]Summarized in O'Malley, 143f.
[31]*AS* I, 3, 32–4.
[32]Ibid., 34–6.
[33]Ibid., 37–9.
[34]Ibid., 41f.
[35]Ibid., 43f.

Bernhard Alfrink of Utrecht, rejecting the *schema*, called for an entirely new document.[36]

Now an American was heard from. The whole American delegation had until then proven very docile to the lead of the Curia, but now Cardinal Elmer Ritter of St Louis broke with the pro-Curia leadership of Cardinals Spellman and McIntyre to cast his "*Non Placet*," characterizing the document as full of negativity and pessimism and casting suspicion on the work of Catholic exegetes.[37] The curial conservatives had, in fact, mounted a massive campaign against the Pontifical Biblical Institute, trying to have it shut down.[38] As the last nail in the coffin of the *schema*, Cardinal Augustin Bea, former Rector of the Biblicum, the most learned Scripture scholar among the cardinals and the Pope's chosen man to deal with these questions, added his rejection: if they could not have an entirely new *schema*, he said, the existing one must be most radically revised, so that the study of Scripture might not be based wholly on fear of error.[39]

The course of the Council had changed. The "*De Fontibus*" *schema* had circulated enough among leading figures of the Council and their *periti* that the bishops were ready for it. Cardinal König had shown it to Karl Rahner and received a damning review of it. Cardinal Alfrinck had gathered Dutch bishops together a month before to discuss Edward Schillibeeck's critique of the *schema*. Cardinal Bea had held a discussion of it in the Secretariat for Christian Unity, whose members were already frustrated at the refusal of Cardinal Ottaviani to meet with them to discuss Scripture, so important an element in ecumenical dialogue.[40] As one American Protestant observer remarked, "The dam broke."[41]

---

[36]Ibid., 43–5.

[37]Ibid., 47f.

[38]I heard personal testimony to this from the redoubtable exegete, Fr Norbert Lohfink, who returned to us at the Jesuit Theologate, Hochschule Sankt Georgen in Frankfurt, to describe how at his doctoral defense the chamber was packed with bishops, archbishops, and cardinals from the Council whose presence at the Biblicum that day witnessed to their defense of the institution against this attack.

[39]*AS* I, 3, 48–51.

[40]These details in O'Malley, 145ff.

[41]Douglas Horton, *Vatican Diary 1962: A Protestant Observes the First Session of Vatican Council II* (Philadelphia: United Church Press, 1964), 111.

Debate would not carry on as long as for the liturgical *schema*. Eighty-five comments accumulated over the next 6 days, most of them negative, before a vote was taken, on 20 November, on whether to continue the discussion or discard the proposal. It turned out to be a confusing vote, because the phrasing, "Should the discussion be interrupted?" left the bishops uncertain whether to vote "*Placet*," which would mean "No," or "*Non placet*," which would mean "Yes." This gave an unclear result; 2,209 votes were cast (a few hundred bishops had gone home by now), of which 1,368 were for discontinuing, 822 for continuing, an evident enough sign that the bishops wanted to discard the proposal, but short, by 105, of the two-thirds majority required for such a decision by the "Regulations." Now the Pope, who had never before made a personal intervention but had written privately in his journal, on 14 November, that "the schema does not take into account the specific intentions of the Pope,"[42] had a message read to the Council after Mass on the following day, resolving the impasse. "Yielding to the wishes of many" he would not require the bishops to continue debating a proposal they did not want, but referred it again to a "mixed commission," made up of members of both the Doctrinal Commission and the Secretariat for Christian Unity, who were to "emend the schema, shorten it, and make it more suitable."[43] Early in the third period of the Council, on 30 September 1964, a far different proposal "On Divine Revelation," would be introduced.

Debate on every aspect of Vatican Council II continues to this day. Other than for the schismatic followers of Archbishop Marcel Lefebvre in the Society of Saint Pius X, it never seems right to those who still take alarm at the Council to reject it outright. Instead they argue that others have over-interpreted it. George Weigel, reviewing the great Alberigo/Komonchak *History*, objects to the "Cowboys and Indians" version of the Council, "in which a small, hardy band of courageous liberals is finally vindicated when it crushes its intransigent, Curia-led conservative opposition and launches the

---

[42] Angelo Giuseppe Roncalli – Giovanni XXIII, *Pater Amabilis: Agende del pontefice, 1958-1963*, ed. Mauro Velati, Edizione natzionale dei diari di Angelo Giuseppe Roncalli – Giovanni XXIII (Bologna: Istituto per le scienze religiosi, 2007), 454: "la stesura della proposta non tenne conto delle precise intenzione del Pape nei suoi discorsi ufficiali."

[43] *AS* I, 3, 259.

Catholic Church into a new dialogue with the modern world."[44] But we cannot overlook the fact that the bishop/representatives of the entire Church, in union with the Pope, had undertaken a thorough and reformative rethinking of the Church, a rethinking based firmly on its original sources and fundamental Christian principles of love and compassion, much as had been envisioned by Yves Congar a dozen years before.

John XXIII had carefully constructed for them the freedom to undertake that task, and he refused consistently to preempt any question or determine it by decree. When, in our own time, after all the retraction from the great insights of the Council, we hear it argued that Pope John would not have done the things that were done by decision of the Council, as if the legitimization of anything that was done would be its coming as decree from the Pope, we should recognize this truth, that governing the Church by decree would have gone counter to his whole instinct for its reform through the collegial action of all its representatives of the people of God.

This first period of the Council had now only 2 weeks to go before its planned closing on 8 December, and it had become clear that the bishops would have to return next year. Very hurriedly, in 3 days' discussion, the bishops approved a document on the Mass Media and referred it to a commission that would produce its final form. Then at last they came to the important document "On the Unity of the Church," *De Unitate*, dealing with relations to the other Christian churches, of particular concern to the Oriental Catholics, but getting minimal attention now as the closing date approached. On 30 November, the presiding officer asked the bishops to indicate simply by standing in their places to vote a termination of this discussion. It was practically unanimous and the following day a vote was taken, 2,068-36, to refer its contents to be incorporated instead into other documents.[45]

The most outspoken figure of the eastern churches, Melkite Patriarch Maximos IV Saigh, who always addressed the Council in French to distance himself from the prevalent Latin, had already intervened during the Scripture debate to ask when they would get to the heart of the matter with a discussion of the Church itself and

---

[44]"Thinking Through Vatican II," *First Things*, June–July 2001.
[45]O'Malley, 152f.

the relation, left unaddressed by Vatican I, between its papal head and its members. He complained that the Doctrinal Commission had not yet released its intended text.[46]

At last on 30 November Cardinal Ottaviani rose to introduce the *schema* "On the Church," *De Ecclesia*. Clearly humiliated by the reception of the liturgical and revelation document, he informed the assembly that this new schema was the work of 70 commission members, that it had the approval of the Central Preparatory Commission and the Pope himself had ordered that it be presented to them. He added:

> The concern of those who prepared the *schema* was that it should be as pastoral and biblical as possible, not academic (*scholasticum*), and that it be done in a form comprehensible by everybody. I say this because I expect to hear the usual litany from the fathers of the Council – its academic, it's not ecumenical, it's negative, and other things like that.
>
> Further, I'll tell you what I really think. I believe that I and the speaker for the commission are wasting our words because the outcome has already been decided. Those whose constant cry is "Take it away! Take it away! Give us a new schema!" are now ready to open fire. I'll tell you something you may not know: even before this *schema* was distributed – Listen to me! Listen to me! – even before it was distributed, an alternative *schema* had already been produced. Yes, even before the merits of the *schema* have been looked at the jury has rendered its verdict. I have no choice now but to say no more because, as Scripture teaches, when nobody is listening words are a waste of time.[47]

The disgruntled Cardinal was correct. An alternative schema had been prepared by theologian Gérard Philips, a more moderate member of his own commission, at the prompting of Cardinal Léon-Joseph Suenens, Archbishop of Malines-Brussels, and that at the suggestion of the Secretary of State and Chairman of the Council's Secretariat for Extraordinary Affairs, Cardinal Amleto Cicognani, longtime Apostolic Delegate to the United States.

---

[46]*AS* I, 3, 53f.
[47]*AS* I, 4, 121.

Bishop Frane Franić of Split-Makaraska in Croatia then presented the 11 chapters of the 82-page document: on "the nature of the Church Militant," on the episcopacy, on religious orders, on the laity, on the Magisterium, on authority and obedience (its main preoccupation throughout), on Church-state relations and finally on ecumenism.

It did not get the same fire-storm of rejection as the scriptural schema had received.[48] Instead Cardinal Liénart, as first respondent, treated the *schema* as a given, but his observations differed to the point of incongruity from the way the *schema* had dealt with the same topics. Eventually he "dared" to make some suggestions, "not led," he said, "by a spirit of contention or opposition but out of love for the truth. 'Friend of Plato, but more a friend of truth.'"[49]

Cardinal Ruffini was happy with the text,[50] but Cardinal König had a number of issues. Cardinal Alfrink, after a few criticisms, said: "I should like to request that before the next period of the Council the schema be reworked by a missed commission appointed by His Holiness."[51]

Cardinal Ritter, who since his critique of the Scripture schema had become recognized as lead voice in the American delegation, replacing Spellman and McIntyre, offered a number of criticisms and, like Alfrink, called for a reworking.[52] Then came the heavy criticism, from Émile-Joseph de Smedt, Bishop of Bruges and Vice President of Cardinal Bea's Secretariat for Christian Unity. He denounced the schema for its triumphalism, clericalism, and juridicism. Its pompous and romantic style, he said rendered it triumphalistic. It conceived the Church in pyramidal style, everything flowing from the top. The People of God, he intoned, is more fundamental to the Church than its hierarchy. This would be recognized as major

---

[48]*AS* I, 4, 122–5. A detailed analysis of this text, compared with the eventual Dogmatic Constitution *Lumen Gentium* approved by the Council, Antonio Acerbi, *Due eccelesiologie: Ecclesiologia giuridica ed ecclesiologgis di communion nella "Lumen Gentium"* (Bologna: Edizioni Dehoniane, 1975), 107–49. See also Richard Gaillardetz, *The Church in the Making: Lumen Gentium, Christus Dominuis, Orientalium Ecclesiarum* (New York: Paulist Press, 2006).
[49]*AS* I, 4, 126f.
[50]Ibid., 127–9.
[51]Ibid., 134–6.
[52]Ibid., 136–8.

theme of the entire Council. And the Church must show itself more a mother than a juridical institution.[53]

This debate went on three more days, until on 3 December Cardinal Frings, speaking this time on behalf of the entire German episcopate, decried the *schema* as "not catholic." It cited hardly any Fathers of the Church, Greek or Latin, nor even the medieval theologians. "I ask: is this the right way to proceed? Is it scientific, is it universal (*oecumenicus*), is it catholic – in the sense of the Greek *Katholon*, which means what embraces the whole and looks to the good of the whole? Thus I ask: is such a way of proceeding genuinely catholic?"[54] Frings had brought the discussion back to the basic aim of the Council, *ressourcement*, the return to the ancient sources of tradition rather than to rely only on the nineteenth century or even the sixteenth.

The bishops knew that they were now at the core issue of the Council, the nature of the Church. Only 3 days remained before the closing of the first period, and the document *De Ecclesia* was in deep trouble. Cardinal Suenens now rose to break the tension and show a way forward,[55] in a speech that reflected the Pope's 11 September radio address about the Council to all the world.[56]

Suenens, in his Lenten address to his diocese, had contrasted the Church looking inward (*ad intra*) to one looking outward to the world (*ad extra*). His speech had drawn the attention of Pope John, who adopted that language in his radio address. Suenens had further emphasized that the Council should emphasize what unites Catholics with others, not what separates them, language also adopted by Pope John. John had then asked Suenens to draw up a plan that would bring order and focus into the Council. Cicognani had forward this plan to a group of Cardinals who met in May at the Belgian College in Rome: Cardinal Julius Döpfner of Munich, Montini, Siri, Liénart, and Suenens himself. The speech Suenens delivered on 4 December, then, reflected all this preparation. The Pope had seen a draft and made suggestions which Suenens

---

[53]Ibid., 142–4.

[54]Ibid., 218–20.

[55]*AS* I, 4, 222–7.

[56]That address can be found in *Acta et Documenta Concilio Vaticano Apparanda Series secunda (Praeparatoria)*, 7 volumes (Vatican City: Typis Polyglotta Vaticanis, 1964–69), I, 1, 248–355. (Suenens' inward/outward reference at 350.) Henceforth *ADP*.

incorporated, so Suenens was actually speaking for the Pope, who in turn had his ideas from Suenens.[57]

The Council, Suenens asserted, needed a central theme, which should be, in the Pope's words of 11 September, "the Church of Christ, Light of the World," *Ecclesia Christi, Lumen Gentium*. The first part of the phrase looked to the inner reality of the Church, "What do you say of yourself?" The second part looked to the Church's relation to the world outside it: the human person, social justice, evangelization of the poor, world peace. The Council would engage in three dialogues: one with its own membership, a second ecumenical one "with brothers and sisters not now united with it," and finally a dialogue "with the modern world." In this he sowed the seed of what would eventually become the most distinctive document of the Council, *Gaudium et Spes*, "The Church and the Modern World."

"Let us hope that this plan that I propose will open a way for a better hearing of the Church and understanding of it by the world today and that Christ may be for the men and women of our times ever more the way, the truth and the light."

Suenens' speech was greeted with grand applause. The following day Cardinal Montini, who within 6 months would be Pope Paul VI, gave his endorsement.[58] The Pope, on 6 December, recommended that the bishops dedicate themselves during the intersession to preparing next year's period. He established a Coordinating Commission under Secretary of State Cicognani. Everyone recognized, without having to take a formal vote, that the *De Ecclesia* text would undergo massive revision in the new commission.[59] The Pope addressed them then, after a concluding Mass on 8 December, the last time most would see or hear him again.

---

[57]O'Malley, 157f.
[58]*AS* I, 4, 291–4.
[59]*AS* V, 1, 34–7.

6

The Council without Pope John

The Council's first year had engendered a renewed sense of life in the Church. Bishops returned to their homelands determined to make good use of their "intersession" time preparing for the next year. In Germany they met for much of the Spring of 1963 in Mainz, where theologians of the stature of Karl Rahner assisted them.[1] The Coordinating Commission under Cicognani, first announced on 6 December, worked through the comments made from the floor in the light of Suenens' overall plan for the Council and the Pope's opening address of 11 October, and selected from the many drafts in circulation 17 texts which, though they would undergo change, remained a master plan from that time on. The Scripture and *De Ecclesia* texts received special attention. Some lay figures were invited to participate in preparing documents on the Lay Apostolate and what was still called the mysterious "*Schema* 17," building on the Suenens reference to the Church and the Modern World.[2]

Everyone knew that the Pope was ailing. He had published his Encyclical *Pacem in Terris*[3] on Holy Thursday, 11 April, a great

---

[1] This provided a great benefit to us Jesuits studying for ordination at the Hochschule Sankt Georgen in nearby Frankfurt, as Rahner stayed with us and would lecture, extempore, every evening for us, giving us a bird's eye view of this first of the preparations.

[2] O'Malley, 161–4.

[3] Vatican website, http://www.vatican.va/holy_father/john_xxiii/encyclicals/documents/hf_j-xxiii_enc_11041963_pacem_en.html, *Pacem in Terris*, Encyclical of Pope John XXIII on Established Universal Peace in Truth, Justice, Charity, and Liberty, 11 April 1963.

advance on the many appeals in times of crisis by Benedict XV, Pius XI, and Pius XII. This offered a comprehensive approach to a world of peace and justice, fully engaged with the world as it was. But on 3 June, after intense suffering from a perforated stomach cancer, Pope John died, his last words, as the Papal Sacristan Petrus Canisius Van Lierde anointed him: "I had the great grace to be born into a Christian family, modest and poor, but with the fear of the Lord. My time on earth is drawing to a close. But Christ lives on and continues his work in the Church. Souls, souls, *Ut omnes unum sint.*"[4]

The conclave that met to choose his successor saw a contest between the curial types and those mostly Northern cardinals who had led the massive majorities in the Council, but who could not produce a two-thirds majority among the 80 cardinals, 29 of them Italians. A Lercaro who would have voted with the Council majority was balanced by a Spellman and a McIntyre who would vote with the curial leadership. Continuation of the Council was not in doubt after all that the Church had invested in it. The question was what character a new Pope would give it. The conclave settled on Cardinal Giovanni Battista Enrico Antonio Maria Montini, well known and respected among the Curia, where he had served in the Secretariat of State from 1922 to 1954, he and his colleague Domenico Tardini regarded as the closest and most influential counselors to Pope Pius XII. Pius made him Archbishop of Milan in 1954 without naming him a cardinal, as was usual for the head of the largest diocese in Italy, but the post made him automatically Secretary to the Italian Bishops Conference. He won a strong reputation there for commitment to the social teaching which had been growing in the Church since Leo XIII.

Pope John made him a cardinal in 1958, relying on him often as one who knew the ways of the Curia better than himself. He rather foresaw that Montini would be his successor, and was known to have regarded him as indecisive. A persistent rumor has it that he conferred on him the nickname *Amleto*, "Our Hamlet." Montini kept his counsel during the first period of the Council, hardly heard from before his endorsement of Suenens' plan for the Council in the very last days.[5]

---

[4]Peter Hebblethwaite, *John XXIII, Pope of the Council*, Rev. edn (Glasgow: Harper Collins, 1994), 502.
[5]Peter Hebblethwaite, *Paul VI: The First Modern Pope* (Mahwah, NJ: Paulist Press, 1993), 322f.

John XXIII had created a realm of freedom for bishops in which they could reflect uninhibitedly on the future and the deep traditions of the Church they loved. The Pope would enable them and confirm their findings, as when he referred the Revelation document to a special mixed commission after the inconclusive vote,[6] but not interfere or muzzle them. This made the new Pope, Paul VI, very nervous. Subsequent events would show his anxiety about the Council, and at key points he would take decisions out of the bishops' hands and reserve them to himself.

Members of the Council had complained always of the slow pace of proceedings, often blamed on the ten Presidents who had presided over sessions in turn. Paul VI's first order of business was to alter the "Regulations," which were entirely in the Pope's hands, by appointing four "Moderators" who would take turns moderating the sessions, three of them chosen from the majority—Döpfner, Lercaro, and Suenens—while the fourth, Cardinal Grégoire-Pierre Agagianian, Prefect of the Congregation of the Propagation of the Faith (*Propaganda Fidei*) would be a curial counterpoise to them. None of them was chairman of the entire group, so they would have to function as a team. Archbishop Felici remained Secretary General of the Council.[7]

The Pope's opening address to the Council when it reconvened on 29 September 1963, reaffirmed its pastoral character, the *aggiornamento*, citing extensively Pope John's *Gaudet Mater Ecclesia* of the previous year, and promising that it's central theme, as Suenens had recommended, would be the Church. He was in the process of writing an encyclical on the Church, he told his hearers, and would tell them now of its content. When it was published,[8] therefore, the following year, it would represent his own teaching on the subject, parallel to but independent of the Council's Dogmatic Constitution *Lumen Gentium*. The matter of the reform of the Curia, which he had already announced, a matter of great interest to the Council, he would reserve to himself.[9]

---

[6]See *supra*, Chapter 5, p. 9.
[7]O'Malley, 167–71.
[8]Vatican website, http://www.vatican.va/holy_father/paul_vi/encyclicals/documents/ hf_p-vi_enc_06081964_ecclesiam_en.html, Eccleciam Suam, Encyclical of Pope Paul VI On the Church, 6 August 1964.
[9]O'Malley, 172.

The Council went immediately to the document on the Church, much transformed and still largely the revised text of Gérard Philips, which Cardinals Ottaviani and Browne[10] found themselves constrained to introduce. It had acquired now, from its opening words, the title *Lumen Gentium*, which it would retain through all subsequent revision. It altered the earlier text most fundamentally by its assertion that the work of the Church was the fostering of holiness in its members. With that the juridicism of the earlier draft was overcome.[11]

Every word would receive much scrutiny and revision as the discussion went on, but the opening question, in the first chapter, was whether the Catholic Church, and it alone, was "the Church of Christ." The language propagated in the late 1940s by Leonard Feeney, so extreme that Pius XII had to condemn it, led the Council to this question.[12] Like the first draft of the document, this version would answer yes, but with the qualification that baptized Christians of other confessions are, in fact, joined to "the Church of Christ." A final version, the result of the full discussion in the Council (approved 21 November 1964), would say: "This Church, set up and organized in this world as a society, *subsists in* the Catholic Church, governed by the successor of Peter and the bishops in communion with him, although *outside its structure many elements of sanctification and of truth are to be found which, as proper gifts of the Church, impel towards Catholic unity.*"[13]

This sentence, with its key term "subsists in" (*subsistet in*) rather than a simple "is" to describe the Catholic Church's relation to the Church of Christ, has been disputed in subsequent years. That the Council included that term, along with the following clause italicized here, has since carried the sense that other Christian bodies may also claim participation in the one Church of Christ, and indeed there appears to be no other reason for it. Two prominent Jesuit professors

---

[10]Cardinal Michael Brown, O.P., from Ireland but firmly entrenched in the curial minority, former Master General of the Dominican Order.

[11]O'Malley, 174f.

[12]Cf. above, previous reference to Feeney, Chapter 1, p. 3, n. 3.

[13]*Lumen Gentium*, ch. 1, #8, Tanner II, 854. Tanner gives, on facing pages, both the Latin original and an English translation. In the Latin version the lines are numbered on each page, in this citation lines 26–30. Subsequent references will cite these lines after the page and number of a section.

at the Gregorian University in Rome have written extensively of it, Karl Josef Becker, S.J. (subsequently created Cardinal, 23 February 2012), disputing that the passage carries such a meaning, and Francis A. Sullivan, S.J., defending the interpretation.[14] The ecumenical discussion among churches, less lively today than it was at the time of the Council, has relied heavily on this passage.

Chapter 2 of this eventual Dogmatic Constitution carried the title *De populo Dei*, "The People of God." It brought that concept, a principal outcome of the Council, into sharp relief. A third chapter, "On the hierarchical constitution of the Church and in particular the episcopate," introduced, as a surprise decision, a restoration of the diaconate, no longer as only a transitional office before ordination to the priesthood but as a permanent sacramental office in itself, and furthermore provided that married men could become "permanent deacons," the first time that the question of clerical celibacy came before the Council.[15] It clarified, moreover, an old question, asserting that a bishop was actually ordained to a new order in the priesthood, "the fullness of the sacrament of order,"[16] not simply raised to an honorific dignity, and for that reason possessed true and inalienable authority, not to be exercised other than in communion with the Pope but by virtue of their ordination. It cited Leo XIII to the effect that bishops were "not to be considered vicars of the Roman Pontiff, because they exercise a power that is proper to themselves and most truly are said to be presidents (*antistites*, "overseers") of the people they govern."[17]

A fourth and final chapter, on the laity, develops further the full participation of all its members in the one Body of Christ, the Church, and their calling to holiness. But the initial naming of the whole membership as the Church, clerics, and lay, People of God, had already taken its place as the lead concept of the Constitution

---

[14]Fr Karl Josef Becker, S.J., "An Examination of Subsistit in: A Profound Theological Perspective," 14 December 2005, www.ewtn.com/library/Theology/subsistitin.htm. Consulted 11 August 2012. Francis A. Sullivan S.J., "A Response to Karl Becker, S.J. on the Meaning of *Subsistit in*," *Theological Studies* 67 (2006), 395–409. Sullivan, "Quaestio Disputata: Further Thoughts on the meaning of *Subsistet In*," *Theological Studies*, 1 March 2010, http://www.readperiodicals.com/201003/1979521561.html. Consulted 11 August 2012.

[15]Tanner II, p. 874, *Lumen Gentium* #29.

[16]Ibid., p. 870, *Lumen Gentium* #26, line 17.

[17]Ibid., p. 871, *Lumen Gentium* #27, lines 28–30. And cf. the appended note 59.

as a whole. This, and the collegiality concept, generated considerable debate on the floor of the Council, but the majority held firm.

We should make it our task, now, not to follow the deliberations with the same attention to detail as we have for the first period, but to see what changed with the new papacy. Bishops, the vast majority of them, had formed their sense of new directions the Church should take and would continue to follow that course. The question became whether that course met with trust, in the public and from the highest echelons of Church governance.

A portion of the Catholic public reacted very negatively to the changes from the start,[18] people one can see as the non-survivors of the Council who remain frightened and disappointed by its consequences. They have continued so. One should take it for granted that the curial party would resist, and they did. That left the attitude of the new Pope himself as the key variable. He had expressed himself, when Pope John first announced the Council, in terms of seeing it as a "hornets' nest."[19] But he would inherit the responsibility now for carrying the task through.

Cardinal Browne, concluding, as Vice President of the Doctrinal Commission, discussion of Chapter 2 in the *Lumen Gentium* text on 15 October, had insisted: "Now that we have heard everything the Council Fathers have said in the General Congregation, it is evident that our first care in revising chapter two is to make sure that in every single phrase the doctrine of the primacy of jurisdiction of the Roman Pontiff is not only protected but made to shine forth more brightly."[20] But the bishops found next morning that the expected ballots had not been handed to them to vote on the chapter. It turned out that the already printed ballots had, the previous evening, been burned on the Pope's instructions. Someone apparently had gotten to him, sounding an alarm, and the terms "conspiracy" and "treachery" were heard in the aula. Cardinal Ottaviani let it be known that he resented the moderators having referred the chapter to the Council for a vote without first clearing it with his Doctrinal Commission.

---

[18]Mark S. Massa, S.J., develops this surprising discovery, that the Church, so long seen as unchanging monolith, could actually change, as the central datum of his book, *The American Catholic Revolution: How the '60s Changed the Church Forever* (New York: Oxford University Press, 2010).

[19]Cf. above, Chapter 4, p. 20, n. 107.

[20]*AS* II, 2, 601.

The next several days saw pleas from either side to the Pope to decide the question. He eventually referred it to an *ad hoc* group consisting of the ten Presidents and Archbishop Felici's Secretariat but headed by Cardinal Eugène Tisserant, the Dean of the College of Cardinals. Pope Paul reviewed the text at length, and on 28 October Cardinal Suenens was able to announce that the vote would finally take place 2 days later. This met strong applause, but Felici still, in Ottoviani's name, asked for further postponement. Tisserant's commission voted against this. The voting then on Chapter 2, in five parts, showed overwhelming approval: (1) on the assertion that Episcopal ordination conferred a supreme grade in the priesthood, 2,125-34; (2) on the recognition of all bishops, including auxiliaries, as members of that College, in communion with the Pope and the College of bishops, 2,154-104; (3) that the bishops, always in communion with the pope, enjoyed full and supreme power over the universal Church, 2,148-336; (4) that this power was by divine ordinance and therefore not by delegation of the Pope, 2,148-408; and (5) that the Council recommended restoration of the permanent diaconate, 2,120-525.[21]

This landslide result marked another turning point for the Council. The assembly knew what it wanted for the Church. Without detracting from Vatican I's assertion of the primacy of the Pope, it had balanced it with a definition of the role of bishops, who also had care of the universal Church.

Was it done in union with the pope? It turned out that the Pope Paul was, in fact, pleased with the outcome.[22] That he had acted in a way so last-minute, public and embarrassing to the moderators, and why he had had the ballots burned rather than simply put under lock and key remained puzzling. Complaints about procedure had never ceased since the beginning of the Council, and now the underlying procedural issue had become the role of the Pope himself and what influences would most easily get to him.[23] His procedures differed from those of Pope John. On 29 October, the day before the vote, Cardinal Ottaviani had clashed with Suenens, asking him: "Why are you constantly going to the Pope?" Suenens' response: "Because you too go to the Pope. Furthermore, I am a member of the Council

---

[21]For this entire episode, O'Malley, 182–4.
[22]Article "Procedure" in Alberto Melloni et al., eds. *Cristianesimo nella stori: Saggi in onore di Giuseppe Alberigo* (Bologna: Il Mulino, 1996), 383-f.
[23]O'Malley, 184f.

of Presidents, a member of the Coordinating Committee, and I am the Moderator."[24]

The rest of the discussion of *Lumen Gentium* went more smoothly, with some protests from Cardinals Ruffini, Siri, and others of the curial party to the references to the laity's share in the priestly mission of Christ.[25] Cardinal Bacci wanted an insert saying that the priesthood of the laity was "not priesthood in the true and proper sense."[26] Much discussion followed on whether reference to the role of Mary should be the subject of a separate document or should be added as a new chapter to *Lumen Gentium*. A close vote, with a majority of only 40, decided this on 29 October, the day before the landslide votes on the five questions in Chapter 2, and a new Marian chapter was included, largely the work of Gérard Philips.[27]

A document on the office of bishops introduced the next major transitional moment in the Council. At its introduction on 5 November it received criticisms of a by-now familiar kind—too juridical, not pastoral enough, but in particular it took no account of collegiality, and treated the rights and privileges of bishops as concessions from the Holy See rather than by virtue of their episcopal ordination. It identified the authority of the curial Congregations with the authority of the pope himself, making them superior to the bishops.[28] Cardinal Browne defended this position at great length, warning of the danger of episcopal conferences encroaching on the authority of the Holy See, and asserting that it was premature for the *schema* to deal at all with the question of collegiality, as that doctrine was still under study by the Doctoral Commission, of which he was vice president. "We must wait, therefore," he challenged, "until the Commission makes its report to the Council before this schema deals with anything concerning episcopal collegiality."[29]

---

[24]Article by Melloni, "Beginning of the Second Period," in Alberigo/Komonchak, *History*, 3: 99.

[25]Tanner II, 875, *Lumen Gentium* #31, lines 12–17.

[26]*AS* II, 3, 278f.

[27]O'Malley.

[28]*AS* II, 4, 366, for the passage: "In the exercise of his full and supreme jurisdictional power over the universal Church, the Roman Pontiff makes use of the Congregations of the Roman Curia, which thus in his name and with his authority bring his office to fulfillment for the good of all the churches and in service to the same sacred pastors [i.e., the bishops]."

[29]*AS* II, 4, 476–8, 486.

This was too much for Cardinal Frings. In an address 2 days later, written in part by his theological councilor Josef Ratzinger, he expressed his amazed rejection of Cardinal Browne's intervention. Commissions, like Browne's Doctrinal Commission, had no authority to render judgment on an issue approved after long discussion by the Council Fathers. They had no access to truths hidden from the Council, but were the Council's instruments. Their task was to carry out the will of the Council.

Frings went much further. An appendix to the *schema* contained rules according to which the Congregations should henceforth operate. They should be moved from the appendix to the main text, and should apply to all the Congregations, "even to the Supreme Congregation of the Holy Office, whose procedures in many respects are inappropriate to the times in which we live, harm the Church, and are for many a scandal." These were such words as were seldom heard in a public forum and they were greeted, according to the records, with applause from the bishops—*plausus in aula*. Not even by that Congregation, said Frings, should anyone be judged and condemned without being heard.[30]

Ottaviani, the next scheduled speaker, responded angrily to these unaccustomed words again the Holy Office, whose president, he reminded them, was the Pope himself. Ottaviani, Antonianni, and Siri were rumored to be demanding an apology from Frings, but both the Melkite Patriarch Maximos V Saigh and Cardinal Lercaro had already been exploring practical ways to implement this surprise discovery of the collegiality of bishops. By the end of two more days of debate, the Council referred the *schema* back to its originating commission for revision. What reappeared in the next years was not a revision but a wholly new schema, which went on to become the Decree *Christus Dominus*,[31] a strong assertion of the collegiality of bishops.

---

[30]*AS* II, 5, 72–5. For the role of Josef Ratzinger in this, cf. Jared Wicks' lecture, "Prof. Ratzinger at Vatican II: A Chapter in the Life of Pope Benedict XVI" (New Orleans: Loyola University, 2006), 12. Wicks goes on: "Actually, Cardinal Frings added his own seven lines of sharper criticism beyond Joseph Ratzinger's draft. They concerned the right of persons accused of doctrinal error to be presumed innocent and to make a defense against the accusation. The episode is also dealt with in Norbert Trippen, *Josef Kardinal Frings (1887–1978)*, 2 volumes (Paderborn: Ferdinand Schöningh, 2003–05), 2: 383–8. O'Malley covers this, 192.

[31]Tanner II, 921–39, Decree on the Pastoral Office of Bishops in the Church, approved 28 October 1965.

Ecumenism, another word dreaded in the Curia, came next. Pius XI, in a 1928 Encyclical, *Mortalium Animos*,[32] had roundly condemned the ecumenical aspirations of Protestant churches as "dangerous fallacies," "this evil." True, the Holy Office had issued an Instruction, *Ecclesia Catholica*, in 1949, the year after the establishment of the World Council of Churches, which recognized action of the Holy Spirit in the Ecumenical Movement and gave permission for Catholics to recite the Lord's Prayer with Protestants.[33] But no one would have imagined, before the election of Pope John XXIII, that this topic would be the subject of a Catholic Council.

It had originally been a chapter in the Doctrinal Commission's original document on the Church, which had been so roundly rejected in the first year of the Council. Now it reappeared as an independent *schema* firmly in the hands of Cardinal Bea's Secretariat for Christian Unity. It had five chapters, on (1) Catholic Principles of Ecumenism," (2) "The Practice of Ecumenism," (3) "Christians Separated from the Catholic Church," (4) "Catholic Attitude toward Non-Christians, Especially the Jews," and (5) "On Religious Liberty." Those last two would eventually, after much anguished discussion, become separate decrees. Yet when the first three chapters were presented by Cardinal Cicognani[34] and Bishop Joseph Martin of Rouen, they were received with heartfelt emotion by the bishops, who by now had become familiar with the many Observers.[35] Absent from the text was the familiar call to the other Christian communities "to return," which had figured prominently in both *Mortalium Animos* and *Ecclesia Catholica*.

While these three chapters would ultimately make their way through the Council with comparative ease, the one on the Jews,

---

[32]Vatican website, http://www.vatican.va/holy_father/pius_xi/encyclicals/documents/hf_p-xi_enc_19280106_mortalium-animos_en.html, *Mortalium Animos*, Encyclical Letter of Pope Pius XI on Religious Unity.

[33]I can testify myself to the shocked dismay among my professors at the Jesuit Novitiate, Shadowbrook, Lenox, Massachusetts, when in these years I began talking, respectfully, with the local Protestant pastors.

[34]He rather than Bea, because he was Prefect of the Congregation for the Oriental Church and President of the Council's Commission on the oriental Churches, and the topic of the Eastern Churches was taken up first.

[35]As witnessed by Yves Congar, *Mon journal du concile*, ed. Eric Mahieu, 2 volumes (Paris: Éditions du Cerf, 2002), 1: 539. See also *AS* II, 5, 472–9.

presented by the German Cardinal Bea with reference to the tradition of anti-Semitism that had culminated in the Nazi tragedy, met instant alarm from the oriental churches, living among Arabs, who feared it would be read as an endorsement of the State of Israel and Zionism. In later versions in the following years, and as a separate Decree, the momentous *Nostra Aetate*, it would include sections on Islam and other religions. Bishop De Smedt introduced the chapter on religious liberty, which would have a long course of discussion and would also become a separate Declaration, *Dignitatis Humanae*. But the first three chapters, after 4 days of discussion, and despite strenuous objection from Cardinal Ruffini,[36] were approved as a base text by another overwhelming majority, with only 86 votes against. The chapters on the Jews and religious liberty would have a much longer course to go.

And by now the second period, frustrating to the bishops by comparison with the first, had run its course. On its last day, 4 December, the Council solemnly and with much celebration approved its first two completed documents: the Constitution on the Liturgy, *Sacrosanctum Concilium*; and the Decree *Inter Mirifica* on the Means of Social Communication.

But Pope Paul had a surprise in store at the end of his lengthy address at the concluding Public Session, in which he summarized the accomplishments and remaining tasks of the Council. In January (1964), he would go on pilgrimage to the Holy Land. Soon it became known that he meet there with the Ecumenical Patriarch Athenagoras. His trip would be seen as ratifying the ecumenical spirit of the Council and forecasting full reconciliation among the Christian churches.

That meeting, when it came on 5 and 6 January, captured the world imagination, energized the work on the ecumenism document at the Council and would lead to the declaration of mutual forgiveness that came at the conclusion of the Council 2 years later.[37]

The intersession again saw much activity, especially in the commissions tasked with preparing final documents. The chapter "On the Hierarchical Structure of the Church" proved difficult, as a small but determined minority argued that the collegiality concept violated

---

[36] *AS* II, 5, 339f.
[37] O'Malley, 199f.

the primacy decision of Vatican I and curtailed papal authority. By mid-May the document seemed ready, but the Pope stepped in on 19 May with 13 suggestions (*suggerimenti*) on collegiality which he wanted the commissions to consider,[38] explaining that these were "to prevent, as far as possible, future misinterpretations of the text."[39] This was the first of many interventions the Pope would make through the rest of the Council, spoken of as "the red pencil of the Pope."[40] The commission, considering the Pope's suggestions at great length, in fact, modified several of them. Where the Pope suggested that the bishops' authority be exercised only "according to the prescriptions of the head [the Pope]", the commission restored its formula that it "never be exercised independently of the Roman Pontiff." Where Pope Paul had described himself as "the head of the Church," the commission preferred "visible head" or "Supreme pastor," since Christ alone was head of the Church. And where the Pope wanted to say that he was "responsible only to the Lord," *uni Domino devinctus*, the commission insisted that he was "responsible to revelation, to the fundamental structure of the Church, to the sacraments, to the definitions of previous councils" and more.[41]

Still on the evening, 13 September, before the Council reopened, 25 cardinals, 16 of them of the Curia, one of the nine non-curials Cardinal McIntyre of Los Angeles, presented a lengthy memorial to the Pope asking that he effectively quash the whole of Chapter 3 and suspend the Council at the end of this period, until he could have a new commission of theologians of his own choosing draw up a new document. Paul VI reacted angrily to this effort, rebuking Cardinal Larraone, the instigator of this move, declaring it would be disastrous for the Council and for the Church. In some consternation he consulted now with Secretary General of the Council Felici, so often an opponent of the Council majority, but Felici concluded his own memo: "In the end it is necessary to have faith in the conscience

[38]Documents on this development are in Jan Grootaers, *Primauté et collegialité: Le dossier de Gérard Philips sure la Nota Explicativa praevia (Lumen Gentium, Chap. III)* (Leuven: Leuven University Press, 1986), 30f., 125–39.

[39]*AS* V, 2, 507–9, at 508.

[40]Article by Jan Grootaers, "Le crayon rouge de Paul VI: Les interventions du pape dans le travail des commissions conciliaires," in Mathijs Lamberigts (ed.), *Commissions conciliaires* (Leuven: Center for the Study of the Second Vatican Council, 1996), pp. 316–51.

[41]O'Malley, 202.

of the Council Fathers, in the force of truth, and above all in the help of the Holy Spirit."[42]

In the meantime, on 6 August, the Pope had issued his own Encyclical on the Church, his first and one written entirely by himself, *Ecclesiam Suam*,[43] as he had promised at the opening of the second period. He avoids any reference, positive or negative, to collegiality, and refers only once, and in an unimportant context, to "the people of God," the two main concepts the Council was wrestling with.

The document would have one important influence on the Council, due to its frequent use of the term "dialogue," which occurs 77 times, becoming the principal topic of the Encyclical. It thus entered into the Council's own vocabulary so regularly, especially in the eventual Pastoral Constitution on the Church in the Modern World, *Gaudium et Spes*, that we often identify the concept of dialogue as "the spirit of Vatican II."[44]

That text had, on 13 June, emerged in the commission as a *schema 13*, the germ of *Gaudium et Spes*, which would occupy much of the Council's attention through the two concluding annual periods.

Pope Paul opened the third period with a something new made possible by the previous year's decisions on liturgy: a Mass celebrated by himself as Principal Celebrant with 24 concelebrants from 19 countries. No one had seen the rite of concelebration in the Western Church other than at ordinations for many centuries, though it was common in the Eastern churches. In his long discourse, the Pope conceded to the bishops a role in the governance of the Church while insisting most on the prerogatives of the pope, but as in his Encyclical he avoided any mention of the People of God.[45]

The bishops then set to on the document *Lumen Gentium*. What had been the first three chapters of the previous year, already discussed at length, had now become several more, the chapter on the call to

---

[42]O'Malley, 202f. The whole episode is treated at length in *Paolo VI e i problemi ecclesiologici al Concilio: Colloquio internazionale di studio* (Rome and Brescia: Edizioni Studium and Istituto Paolo VI, 1989), 595–604. The same dossier has all the crucial memoranda and other documents leading to the "Nota praevia" on Chapter 3, edited by Giovanni Caprile, 587–697.

[43]Vatican website, www.vatican.va/holy_father/paul_vi/encyclicals/documents/hf_p-vi_enc_06081964_ecclesiam_en.html, Ecclesiam Suam, Encyclical Letter of Pope Paul VI, On The Church, 6 August 1964.

[44]O'Malley, 203f.

[45]*AS* III, 1, 140–51. O'Malley, 206f.

holiness had become two, on religious and on the laity. A new chapter had been added on the eschatological character of the Church, and the added chapter on the Virgin Mary. Only the chapter on the hierarchical structure remained controversial. When those who had subscribed to the 13 September memorandum found that they had failed to halt the process altogether, they argued for a new debate, which Pope, moderators, and the vast majority refused. But on the morning of 15 September, Felici announced that this chapter, unlike the others which would be voted on more simply, would receive 39 separate votes on alternative wordings. To these the members could respond not only "Yes" or "No," *placet* or *non placet*, but also "Yes, with qualification," *placet iuxta modum*, which would thereby introduce a further emendation. Four addresses on the chapter would first take place, one opposed, Cardinal Franc Franić, then three in favor: König; Archbishop Pietro Parente, the Assessor of the Holy Office and long a critic of "la nouvelle théologie" during those years of panic in which so many now prominent theologians had been suppressed, but now become an advocate of collegiality; and Bishop Luis E. Henríques Jiménez, auxiliary of Caracas, Venezuela. Voting on all the now 40 variant wordings took the next 8 days, but negative votes on specific sections about collegiality never exceeded 322 out of 2,245, or 15 percent. The proposal on restoring the permanent diaconate met more opposition, 702, though only 629 opposed ordaining married men to the diaconate. A proposal that unmarried men be so ordained and not bound thereafter by celibacy was defeated by a vote of 1,364. A final vote on the chapter as a whole was then divided into two votes, one on collegiality and the other on the diaconate. Collegiality passed easily with 1,624 *placet*, 572 *placet iuxta modum*, and only 42 *non placet*. The diaconate got only slightly more negative votes, 53, and fewer *placet iuxta modum* than had been cast on collegiality.

All those emendations, *placet iuxta modum*, would now have to have the consideration of the commission and submitted to another comprehensive vote, but the Constitution *Lumen Gentium*, one of the most important documents of the Council, was now as good as passed. It would finally be solemnly proclaimed by the Pope only at the end of next year's final period, 7 December 1965.[46]

Looming on the agenda now were two of the most contentious topics, separated from the original document on the Church to become

---

[46]For this whole proceeding, O'Malley, 206–11.

separate Declarations on their own: Religious Liberty and the Jews. Much changed from the year before, the declaration On Religious Liberty came to the floor on 16 September, facing heavy opposition, more than there had ever been for collegiality. This would affect the Church's relation to governments and the making of concordats, and was thus of vital concern to the Secretariat of State.

The Church, since the time of Constantine, had assumed a kind of comfortable marriage of throne and altar, calling often for "the secular arm" to implement, drastically, its judgments of condemnation. The militantly secular state emerged only in the nineteenth century and was massively condemned then by the Church. Christians of all denominations had become used to the formula of the 1555 Peace of Augsburg, *cujus regio, eius religio*, which saw it as the prerogative of any king or ruler to determine what religion his subjects must adhere to—or be punished! The Catholic Church, as much as any, expected this support from a Catholic State, though insistent on freedom for itself if the state were not Catholic. That tolerance need not be extended, however, to other religions, because "Error has no rights."[47] The sixteenth-century Mennonites, who rejected outright any right of the state to determine their religious faith, were regarded for that reason as the radical left wing of the Reformation and persecuted equally by Catholic or Protestant.

What the proposed Declaration on Religious Liberty would contain seemed to citizens of the United States only the natural outcome of their Constitution and they tended to be shocked if they heard the actual position of the Church, unmindful of the condemnation of "Americanism" by Pope Leo XIII.[48] Yet theologians such as Msgr Joseph Clifford Fenton and Fr Francis Jeremiah Connell, C.S.S.R., both professors at the Catholic University of America and both *periti* at the Council, defended it stoutly. Along with Fr John Shea of the Immaculate Conception Seminary in Darlington, New Jersey, they had carried on an aggressive dispute with Jesuit Fr John Courtney Murray in the 1950s.[49] Murray, Professor at Woodstock College and editor of the Jesuit journal *Theological Studies* from

---

[47]This position had been iterated by Gregory XIII in his 1832 *Mirari* Vos (above, Chapter 3, p. 5, n. 19), by Leo XIII both in *Rerum Novarum* and in his condemnation of "Americanism," and by Pius XI in *Mortalium Animos* (above, p. 6, n. 32).

[48]Cf. above, Chapter 4, p. 3.

[49]P. Granfield, "Fenton, Joseph Clifford," *New Catholic Encyclopedia*, vol. 5, 2nd edn (Gale: Detroit, 2003), 684–5.

1941 to his death in 1967, had come to advocate religious freedom as defined by the First Amendment to the U.S. Constitution. He regarded the traditional Catholic teaching on church-state relations as inadequate to the moral insights of contemporary peoples. The American model, he argued, was truer to the truth of human dignity than was control by paternalistic states.[50]

As head of the Holy Office, Cardinal Ottaviani had attacked Murray's ideas, without naming him, in a speech at the Lateran University on 2 March 1953, on the duties of a Catholic state regarding religion.[51] Pope Pius XII had entered the lists himself on 6 December that year in a radio address that reaffirmed the traditional teaching.[52] And in 1955, under pressure from the Holy Office, Murray's Jesuit superiors prohibited him from publishing further on the subject.

The topic had come to the fore, however, in 1960, when John F. Kennedy ran for President of the United States and this was a principal argument against him, that as a Catholic he would have to obey his Church and work to suppress all other religions. When the Council came, so soon afterward, the American bishops arrived convinced that the Council had to take action on this matter. Cardinal Spellman of New York, himself a conservative in agreement with the curial party on most other subjects, brought Murray with him as a *peritus*, the appointment confirmed by Pope John himself who, in the same month as he appointed Murray, issued his Encyclical *Pacem in Terris*, which taught the right of every human being "to worship God according to his own conscience."[53] Yet even as the Council was at work Archbishop Egidio Vagnozzi, the Apostolic Delegate to the United States, strove to have Murray silenced.[54]

---

[50]*American National Biography*, edited by John A. Garraty and Mark C. Carnes (New York: Oxford University Press, 1999) contains a good summary biography of Murray by Leon Hooper, S.J.

[51]Published as Alfredo Ottaviani, *Doveri dello stato cattolico verso la religione* (Rome: Pontificio Ateneo Lateranense, 1953), 9f.

[52]Pius XII, "Ci riesce," in *Discorsi e radiomessaggi di Sua Santità Pio XII* (Vatican City: Typografia Poliglotta Vaticana, n.d.), 15: 483–9, at 486–9.

[53]*Pacem in Terris*, #14.

[54]Reported by Daniel Callahan, "America's Catholic Bishops," in *The Atlantic Monthly*, April 1967.

Cardinal Bea had had seen to it that there was a chapter in the second-period draft of *Lumen Gentium* on religious liberty, and now on 23 September Bishop De Smedt once more introduced a revised draft, as a brief separate Declaration, "On Religious Liberty, that is, on the Right of the Individual and of Communities to Liberty in Religious Matters." The title began with the words *De libertate religiosa*. Only in its final version would it acquire, as its title, the opening word *Dignitatis Humanae*.

In the floor debate, opposed by Cardinal Ruffini, Cardinal Fernando Quiroga y Palacios of Santiago de Compostella and, of course, Ottaviani, the declaration turned out to have the support of the otherwise conservative bishops from behind the Iron Curtain, even the somewhat skeptical Cardinal Carol Wojtila of Kraków, of the British and of the French. It was seen as not yet ready for a vote and referred back to the Secretariat for Christian Unity, where Murray now set to work revising it in light of the debate, in close collaboration with Pietro Pavan, who had been principal author of Pope John's Encyclical *Pacem in Terris*.[55]

That set the stage for consideration of the other much contested declaration On the Jews and Non-Christians, for which Pope John had given a special mandate to Cardinal Bea as early as 1960. Opposition here centered on political fears about the effect reconciliation with the Jews might have for Christians of the Middle East, but the still recent success of the Rolf Hochhuth play *Der Stellvertreter*, accusing Pope Pius XII of temporizing about the Holocaust of the Jews, deeply offended people in the Vatican, most particularly Pope Paul VI himself who had been among Pius XII's closest assistants during the war. But a conciliar document on the Jews would have to thread the line between recognition that Christians had mistreated Jews and the many passages in the New Testament, especially in the Gospel of John, that treated "the Jews" as the enemies of Christ, as well as the fierce line in St Matthew's Gospel (27:25), "His blood be upon us and upon our children." Christians had treated the Jews as Christ-killers and had felt bound to work for their conversion.

By the end of the first period of the Council it had become clear that a document on the Jews would also have to treat other religions,

---

[55]O'Malley, 214–18.

especially Islam as an Abrahamic faith, and the declaration would gradually expand to include them all. Still, the version Bea presented to the Council in September 1964 had as yet only a single sentence after the portion on the Jews, about Muslims and the love for all human beings.[56]

As the text went through revision after revision through the spring and summer of 1964, deep division became evident between Bea and Pope Paul. Bea wanted to absolve, of the crime of Christ's death, not only contemporary Jews but also the Jews of Christ's own time, restricting the blame only to certain leaders, but the Pope prevailed, and the text Bea presented to the Council contained only the sentence: "Let everyone take care not to impute to the Jews of our time what happened during the Passion of Christ."[57]

Representatives of the Oriental Rite churches took immediate alarm at the schema, seeing it as complicating their relations with the Arab nations among whom they lived. Cardinal Ignace Tappouni, Patriarch of Antioch in the Syrian rite spoke for them all in calling the initiative "inopportune" and begging that it simply be removed from the agenda.[58]

Cardinal Ruffini spoke for the curial minority in complaining about this panegyric to Jews. He would not accuse the Jews of deicide, because no one can kill God, but he expected their apology for unjustly condemning Jesus to death. Rather than call on Christians to love Jews Christians should be calling on Jews to love them.[59] Most speakers, though, spoke in favor, many of them asking for the earlier text with its stronger statement on deicide rather than the weaker one Bea had introduced.[60]

On 9 October, though, Cardinal Bea read to the assembly two letters signed by Felici in instruction from the Pope, one about the declaration on religious liberty, the other on this declaration about the Jews. The one on religious liberty was to be replaced by a new text, to be written by a mixed commission with equal numbers of members from Bea's secretariat and from the Doctrinal Commission,

---

[56]O'Malley, 218–21.
[57]AS III, 2, 328. "*Caveant praeterea ne Iudaeis nostrorum temporum quae in Passione Christi perpetrata sunt imputentur.*"
[58]AS III, 2, 582.
[59]Ibid., 585–7.
[60]O'Malley, 223f.

with names suggested from among the most vehement opponents of the idea: Cardinal Browne, Archbishop Marcel Lefebvre, and the master General of the Dominican order, Fr Aniceto Fernandez.[61] The declaration on the Jews should be abandoned in favor of a mention inserted into *Lumen Gentium*. This too would be composed by a mixed subcommission, with members from Bea's secretariat and the rest from the Doctrinal Commission, to be named by Ottaviani.[62] Both declarations were thus taken out of the hands of Bea's Secretariat for the Unity of Christians.

That the Pope had intervened so drastically, and against what was clearly the will of the majority in the Council, raised a firestorm in the media, which learned of it immediately, as well as consternation in the Council itself. The Pope had certainly come under colossal pressure both from within the Council and from Arab governments, some of whom had apparently threatened to close down their embassies to the Holy See.[63]

Next day, 10 October, Bea wrote a letter in Italian to Pope Paul, in which he said Felici's letters seemed not to reflect the understanding he had received from the Pope in a private meeting on 5 October. He questioned therefore whether Felici had accurately conveyed the mind of the Pope. While they had spoken of submitting the text of the declarations to the Doctrinal Commission to see that they were orthodox, a procedure, which was acceptable both to Bea and Ottaviani, there had been no talk of mixed commissions. Bea wrote of the serious consequences this action would have for the Council and "for the authority of Your Holiness." The mixed commissions would be read as a vote of non-confidence in the Secretariat. Bea asked for clarification from the Pope.[64]

His was not the only letter the Pope received. Another came from 13 leading figures of the Council including Frings, Liénart, König, Döpfner. Meyer, and Ritter, which spoke of the "great distress" with which they had learned that the religious liberty declaration was to be sent to a new commission, some of whose members opposed the clear sentiments of the majority. Agreed procedure, they felt, had been violated.[65]

---

[61]*AS* V, 2, 773.
[62]Ibid., 764f.
[63]O'Malley, 224f.
[64]*AS* V, 2, 778f.
[65]*AS* VI, 3, 440f.

After a few days the situation returned to what it had been before the two Felici letters. No one apologized, nothing was explicitly disowned, but Bea had the two texts again firmly in the hands of his Secretariat. The episode passed like a bad dream, but it was clear that the opponents of the two declarations would fight again before they returned in the next period.[66]

This third period of the Council would see other significant clashes and significant new insights as well. The document on revelation returned, its opening chapter no longer dealing with a list of revealed truths but rather with the action of God in Christ, who is himself the revelation. Its transmission to us is through the witness of the Apostolic Church, which we have enshrined in the Scriptures, a more fundamental meaning of Tradition than that of the teachings of Church authority through Christian history. The *magisterium* of the Church is thus "not above the Word of God but acts as its servant."[67]

The argument on the floor, though, concerned more the second chapter, on the question whether Tradition contained truths not dealt with in the Scripture, a matter of great worry to those most concerned for papal infallibility and therefore for the two Marian definitions proclaimed by Pius IX and Pius XII. The chapter's paragraph 8 saw Tradition as experienced by the Church, and not indeed by the *magisterium* only but in the whole being of the Church, in its worship and its whole experience of spiritual realities—"*ex intima spiritualium rerum experientia.*" Thus, Tradition can "progress" (*proficit*) as the Church grows in its understanding through reflection and experience.[68] Debate lasted through 6 October, by which time the subcommission of the Doctrinal Commission that had prepared the text realized they were on the right track and needed only to refine it.[69]

Documents On the Lay Apostolate, prepared at John XXIII's insistence with participation of lay commission members including

---

[66]O'Malley, 226.
[67]Ibid., 226f.
[68]O'Malley, in his footnote 68 to p. 228, sets out a comparison of the three texts: that of the original 1962 version, this proposed version prepared in 1963, and the final version in the Constitution, which by then had acquired the title *Dei Verbum* of 1965.
[69]O'Malley, 228f.

women, On the Life and Ministry of Priests, and on the Eastern Catholic churches (*Orientalium Ecclesiarum*) had relatively easy initial passage,[70] until on 20 October the Council finally came to the promised "schema 13," which now bore the title "On the Church in the Modern World," *De Ecclesia in Mundo Huius Temporis*. This touched new ground, unaccustomed in Church documents: human dignity themes, solidarity across ethnic and racial, but also religious lines, safety and justice for peoples, the Church as servant to the world in its basic concerns.

The curial minority had, of course, their usual range of objections, worried that concern with the world might obscure the Church's supernatural mission. But this schema brought up a division between the German-speaking and French-speaking contingents, the Germans, with Ratzinger and Rahner as their theological counsel, taking a more pessimistic outlook on human society, a more Augustinian view, the French a more optimistic one, drawing more on Thomas.[71]

Discussion continued for three full weeks, to 10 November, with over 150 speeches from the floor, bringing the time close to 21 November, which Paul VI has set as the final day of this year's sessions. Issues of nuclear warfare received attention, with the Americans defensive but Cardinal Alfrink complaining that the statement was less forceful than John XXIII's in *Pacem in Terris*.[72] But the real fireworks came when discussion turned to birth control, the topic that would convulse the Church a few years later.

John XXIII, at the suggestion of Cardinal Suenens, had established a Papal Commission to study the subject, as had been announced to the cardinals by Pope Paul on 23 June.[73] The previous year John Rock, a Catholic physician who had taken part in the development of the oral contraceptive, "the pill," had published his widely reviewed book, *The Time Has Come*.[74] Several Council members had reminded the Fathers that, since this was the subject of a Papal

---

[70]Ibid., 229–32.

[71]Ibid., 233–6.

[72]*AS* III, 6, 459–61.

[73]*Acta Apostolicae Sedis: Commentarium officiale* (Vatican City: Typis Polyglottis Vaticanis, published regularly since 1909, henceforth *AAS*), vol. 56 (1964), 581–9, at 588f.

[74]John Rock, *The Time has Come: A Catholic Doctor's Proposals to End the Battle over Birth Control* (New York: Alfred A. Knopf, 1963).

Commission, they were not to debate it. Yet, it was too important to keep it off the floor. Cardinals Léger and Alfrink, Bishop Josef Reuss (Auxiliary of Mainz), speaking for 145 bishops "from various countries and parts of the world," and Bishop Rudolf Staverman of Sukarnopura, Indonesia, spoke in favor of modifying the traditional teaching, as embodied in Pius XI's Encyclical *Casti Connubii*.[75] Staverman spoke of marriage as an evolving historical reality on which the Church could not simply repeat old formulas.[76] Patriarch Maximos IV Saigh, speaking as always in French, spoke of the gulf between the Church's official teaching on the subject and the actual practice in most families, and of the population explosion in various parts of the world which condemned hundreds of millions of people to misery without hope. This required of the Church, he said, to revise its official positions in the light of modern research, theological, psychological, and sociological as well as medical.[77] Suenens, though, speaking of the development of doctrine and the population explosion, made a dramatic appeal: "I plead with you, brothers. We must avoid another 'Galileo Case.' One is enough or the Church." And he asked that the Pope make public the names of the members of the Papal Commission so that the Council should have the fullest information on the subject and the whole People of God be represented in the discussion.[78]

It was Suenens' speech, calling for what sounded like a plebiscite, and receiving applause in the Council, that so angered Pope Paul that he called Suenens in for an audience in which he reproached him for lacking in judgment.[79] In a subsequent speech in the Council, the Cardinal backed away from his call for publication of the names and conceded that the issue was in the hands of the "supreme *magisterium*."[80]

---

[75]Vatican website, www.vatican.va/holy_father/pius_xi/encyclicals/documents/hf_p-xi_enc_31121930_casti-connubii_en.html, *Casti Conubii*, Encyclical of Pope Pius XI On Christian Marriage, 31 December 1930.

[76]*AS* III, 6, 71–3.

[77]Ibid., 59–62.

[78]Ibid., 57–9.

[79]See Leo Declerck and Toon Osaer, "Les relations entre le cardinal Montini/Paul VI (1897-1978) et le cardinal Suenens (1904-1996) pendant le Concile Vatican II," in *Notiziario* 51 (2006), 49–77.

[80]*AS* III, 6, 379–81, at 381.

The end of this third period of the Council would see some of its most rocky moments, initiated by this dissension over the Declaration on Religious Freedom and the topic of birth control. On 16 November, Archbishop Felici introduced a "Preliminary Note of Explanation," *Nota explicative praevia*, to Chapter 3 of *Lumen Gentium*, the Dogmatic Constitution on the Church, which dealt with the collegiality concept.[81]

A substantial minority of the Council, 322 members, had voted against any mention of a "college" of bishops in the document, and among the assents "with reservation," *placet iuxta modum* votes, 47 amendments had been suggested. The *Nota praevia*, it became clear, was a direct intervention by Pope Paul, as Felici announced it dramatically as coming "from a higher authority," *Superiore denique Auctoritate*, though it had been written in the Doctrinal Commission, but on direct orders from the Pope, who was never seen in the *aula* other than for the "Public Session" on 21 November, when final votes would be taken and he would promulgate the year's results. Principal author was, as usual, Gérard Philips.[82] The burden of the note was to affirm that the bishops' collegiality would be exercised only with the assent of the Pope, so as to safeguard the primacy and pastoral independence of the Pope, as defined by Vatican I.

Why had the Pope acted so? His motive seems to have been to promote acceptance of the collegiality principle by obviating some of the objections of that uneasy minority, and in this he succeeded, as the number of *non placet* votes for Chapter 1 dropped to 46 the following day, 17 November, and when a final vote was taken on the whole Constitution on 18 November it had only 5 negative votes among the 2,156 cast. Still, an impression remained that somehow the concept of collegiality had been weakened, despite the fact that these reservations had already been carefully written into the text even before the *Nota praevia*.[83]

The Fathers expected then that the Declaration on Religious Liberty would come up for voting on its separate chapters, the votes again to be recorded as *placet*, *non placet*, or *placet iuxta modum*.

---

[81]Ibid., 8, 10–13.
[82]Philips gave his own account of this episode in his *Carnets conciliaires* (Leuven, Centre for the Study of the Second Vatican Council, Archives), 134–41.
[83]O'Malley, 244f.

But in three separate letters to the Council of Presidents a small group of bishops, mostly Spanish or Portuguese but with the names Ottaviani and Lefebvre among them, argued that the text had so changed from its first introduction that it should be treated as an entirely new text, for which much more time should be given.[84] Bishop Luigi Carli of Segni then wrote, on 19 November, to Cardinal Francisco Roberti, the Secretary of the Congregation of the Council, arguing that a vote now would violate the "Regulations." His arguments prompted Cardinal Tisserant to announce, as one of the ten Presidents, that the vote would be postponed to the following year.[85]

Coming so close to the announced final date for the year's work, this shocked the Council. American bishops, especially, who had a stake in the matter, led a petition to Pope Paul, asking "urgently, most urgently, and with the greatest possible urgency" that he reverse the decision.[86] It would mean that, next year, the whole case would have to be argued anew.

The Pope had not made this decision, but under siege from both sides of the argument, by the next day, he let it stand. The day stands out in the memory of the participants as the "Black Thursday" of the Council, creating a suspicion that a small number of members were able to use the Pope to achieve results they could never get from the Council itself.[87]

Pope Paul, in fact, promised that the Declaration would return in the next period, "if possible, before any other."[88] Later commentators have tended to credit the Pope's decision as just. Even Yves Congar had noted a month earlier that the new text, twice as long as the original, was really new, and felt that the redactors, especially Pavan and Murray, had tried to put it across too easily.[89]

On that same last working day of the period, 20 October, the Pope sent 17 emendations to the text On Ecumenism, "kind suggestions expressed with authority" (*suggestiones benvolas auctoritative*

---

[84]*AS* V, 3, 79–82.

[85]*AS* III, 8, 415.

[86]*AS* V, 3, 89–91. ". . . *instanter, instantius, instantissime. . . .*"

[87]Albert Prignon writes of the minority using "a kind of blackmail" on the Pope, "une sorte de chantage." *Journal conciliaire de la 4e Session*, ed. L. Declerck and A. Haquin (Louvain-la-Neuve: Publications de la Faculté de Théologie, 2003), 78.

[88]*AS* III, 8, 554f.

[89]Congar, *Mon journal*, 2: 202.

expressas),[90] letting it be known that he considered refusing to promulgate the Decree if the suggestions were not accepted.[91] It fell to Johannes Willebrands, future Cardinal who would be successor to Cardinal Bea at the Secretariat for Christian Unity, at this point secretary to the secretariat, to plead against this to the Pope, but to no avail. Protestant observer Douglas Horton, in fact, with his strong interest in the decree, regarded the changes the Pope asked for as "trifling but interesting."[92] But the Council, which would vote favorably the next day, 20 November, for the decree, 2,054-64, found itself required at the last moment to ratify changes they had never seen or discussed.[93]

The year's work concluded with the Public Session of 21 November, at which Pope Paul solemnly promulgated three new documents: *Lumen Gentium*, the Dogmatic Constitution on the Church, a central pillar of the Council's work; Orientalium Ecclesiarum, the Decree On the Oriental Churches; and *Unitatis Redintegratio*, the Decree on Ecumenism, the three of them a solid product for the year's work. In his address, the Pope celebrated the Constitution On the Church as a great accomplishment, adding: "The most important thing to be said about that promulgation is that through it no change is made in traditional teaching."[94] He described the Church as "both monarchical and hierarchical," "both primatial and collegial."[95] Use of the term "monarchical" sounded foreign to the Council, which had sedulously avoided it. It appears nowhere in this Constitution nor in any document of the Council. There had been discussion, regarding the chapter on the Virgin Mary, of declaring her "the Mother of the Church," a title many bishops wished to confer on her after this century and more of new declarations of attributes of the Virgin, but the Council had declined to do so because it appeared to place Mary above the Church rather than within it as a preeminent model for Christians. The Pope, nevertheless, in his allocution, now conferred it upon her himself, as if

---

[90]*AS* III, 8, 422f.

[91]*AS* V, 3, 68, 71f.

[92]Douglas Horton, *Vatican Diary 1964: A Protestant Observes the Third Session of Vatican Council II* (Philadelphia: United Church Press, 1965), 179.

[93]O'Malley, 243. And see Pierre Duprey, "Paul VI et le decret sur l'Oecuménisme," in *Paolo VI e i problemi ecclesiologici al Concilio: Colloquio internazionale di studio* (Rome and Brescia: Edizioni Studium and Istituto Paolo VI, 1989), 225–48.

[94]*AS* III, 8, 909–18, at 911.

[95]*AS* III, 8, 913.

to assert his personal *magisterium* in distinction to that of the Council acting with him.[96]

The session thus ended on a sour note. As a grim-faced Paul VI was carried from the basilica on his *sedia gestatoria*, past the rows of bishops, applause was muted.[97] The bishops wondered whether a fourth period would be as hard as the third.[98] They had a Pope conscious of the great inheritance he had from his predecessor, John XXIII, conscientious in his determination to help the Council bring all the benefits that a true reforming consultation of the Church could accomplish, but consumed by his fears and anxieties, which the "prophets of doom" and the resistors to any change could play upon at will.

---

[96]*AS* III, 8, 916. Carbone, solicitous to defend the action of the Pope, narrates the events leading up to this declaration of Mary as Mother of the Church, in *Paolo VI e i problemi ecclesiologici al Concilio: Colloquio internazionale di studio* (Rome and Brescia: Edizioni Studium and Istituto Paolo VI, 1989), 91–5. A lengthy doctrinal analysis follows by René Laurentin, La proclamation de Marie; Mater ecclesiae. Par Paul VI: *Extra concilium* mais *in concilio* (21 November 1964), ibid., 310–75.

[97]This was the description of Xavier Rynne, the popular pseudonymous chronicler of the Council, *Vatican Council II* (Maryknoll, NY: Orbis Press, 1999), 426.

[98]O'Malley, 147.

7

Bringing the Council to its conclusion

The gloom that had surrounded the conclusion of the third period of the Council in these late days of 1964 cleared significantly as the Pope undertook another spectacular overseas journey. Air travel had opened the world to the former Prisoner of the Vatican and Paul VI leaped at the opportunity. On the evening of 2 December, he arrived at the Bombay airport for a 3-day visit, having informed Cardinal Valerian Gratias, Archbishop of the city, that he wished to come in complete simplicity, in the manner of Mohandas Ghandi, meeting with the poor, regardless of religion or caste, rather than with the rich or powerful.[1]

His visit constituted an illustration of some of the most contested aspirations of the Council: respectful of the many religious traditions of India, as the yet-to-be-passed Declaration on Non-Christian Religions would have it; urging upon the great powers of the world that they spend their money not on the arms race but on addressing "the many problems of nutrition, clothing, shelter and medical care that afflict so many peoples,"[2] in keeping with the teachings of what would be the Council's Pastoral Constitution on the Church in the Modern World. Television and other media were alive with moving scenes of the Pope among the destitute and orphans, often with tears in his eyes. The world's press echoed to the

---

[1]As so often, I rely on the narrative in John W. O'Malley, S.J., *What Happened at Vatican II*, here pp. 247ff.
[2]Paul VI, *Insegnamenti di Paolo VI*, 17 volumes (Vatican City: Libreria Editrice Vaticana, 1965–79), 2, 716, the original language English.

plaudits of this "pilgrim of peace, joy, serenity and love,"[3] dispelling the unfavorable impressions of the "black week" in November. He had become the embodiment of the spirit of the Council.

Bothered still by the harsh coverage of November after he returned to the Vatican, the Pope, on 11 January, called upon the Jesuit editor of *La Civiltà Cattolica* to see that his journal and those of the "other religious orders" publish articles making known the positive results of the third period and reassuring the readers that some lacunae would be filled in the next period (Jews, religious liberty)."[4]

Clearly enough there would be a further session of the Council, but it remained in doubt whether it would be in the Spring of 1965, in the latter part of the year as before, or postponed for a year or even 2 years. That left the commissions charged with revision of the 11 remaining *schemata* in doubt whether they had 2 months or 2 years to complete their work until, on 6 January, the Pope announced that the Council would reconvene on 14 September. In the meantime, the Pope would begin celebrating Mass, beginning 7 March, in various parishes of Rome *in Italian*, thus throwing his full weight behind the liturgical reform already determined by the Constitution *Sacrosanctum Concilium*.

Four of the *schemata* faced serious trouble. In the document on Revelation, the minority who were now describing themselves as the "International Group" wanted to restore what they saw as the teaching of the Council of Trent on Scripture and Tradition, two sources, with the emphasis falling on Tradition. The same people stood adamantly opposed to the Declaration on Religious Liberty, as contradicting statements of recent popes. With regard to the document on The Church in the Modern World, the German and the French bishops still opposed each other on whether it was too optimistic or too pessimistic in its view of humanity, the Germans now joined vigorously by the young Polish Archbishop of Kraków,

---

[3]Paul VI, *Insegnamenti*, 2, 687.

[4]Giovanni Caprile, "Contributo alla storia della 'Nota Explicativa Praevia,'" in *Paolo VI, problem ecclesiologici*, 589–697, at 589. Caprile explains that the Holy See sent documentation to the journal, which he prints here, to help it fulfill the Pope's wish. Included is his correspondence between September and November, 1964, with Larraone, Ruffini, Ottaviani, Carli, and others, illustrating the pressure brought to bear on the Pope. The resultant article in *Civiltà Cattolica* is reproduced, 681–97.

still a relative unknown, Karol Wojtila. The troubling questions of birth control (though the Pope had formally removed it from the agenda) and the stockpiling of nuclear weapons loomed large.

Nothing more worried Paul VI, though, than the document on the Jews and the Non-Christian Religions. In opposition to Bea, the Pope wanted to reinstate the mention of deicide, which had been removed from the text, fearing that its omission might imply denial of the divinity of Christ, as Bishop Carli, now a principal spokesman for "the Group," insisted.[5]

On 25 June, Carli addressed a letter to the Pope, signed by himself, the future schismatic Marcel Lefbvre and Archbishop Geraldo de Proença Sigaud (of Diamantina, Brazil), but in the name of the Group, asking for a change in the debate procedures of the Council. The letter was channeled through Cardinal Cicognani, Chairman of the Secretariat for Extraordinary Questions and President of the Coordinating Commission. The Pope's reply, in a letter from Cicognani to Carli, on 11 August, was a sharp rebuke, telling him that the "alliance" (*alleanza*) as such was highly inappropriate for an ecumenical Council, and that it would give rise to other such factions, doing grave damage to the work of the Council at a time when everyone should be striving to promote unity and serenity of judgment.[6] As O'Malley comments, the response shows how irksome the maneuvers of the Group had become and how deeply they were resented.[7]

On 14 September, as he reopened the Council, Pope Paul issued a *motu proprio*, a document "on his own initiative," titled *Apostolica Sollicitudo*, by which he established as an institution the Synod of Bishops.[8] Received immediately as the practical instrument through which the bishops as a body would exercise their role in

---

[5]He had published two articles in an Italian journal for the clergy, which others in The Group circulated widely: Luigi Carli, "La questione giudaica davanti al Concilio Vaticano II," *Palestra del Clero*, 44 (1965), 185–203; and Carli, "È possible discutere serenamente della questione giudaica?" ibid., 465–76.

[6]All of this is printed in Giovanni Caprile, ed., *Il Concilio Vaticano II: Cronache del Concilio Vaticano II*, 5 volumes (Rome: Edizione "La Civiltà Cattolica", 1966–69), 5: 53–4.

[7]O'Malley, 251f.

[8]Vatican website, www.vatican.va/holy_father/paul_vi/motu_proprio/documents/hf_p-vi_motu-proprio_19650915_apostolica-sollicitudo_en.html.

the governing of the Church, it was soon seen by the advocates of collegiality as rigorously limiting that role, everything about it subjected so "immediately and directly subject to the power" of the Pope that it would be strictly an advisory body with no authority beyond what the Pope might give it.[9] In future years, it would show itself a broken staff for the expression of the bishops' thoughts, nothing like the central consultative body of bishops for which Cardinal Lercaro and Maximos V Saigh had been calling for the previous 2 years.

The bishops listened rather apprehensively to the Pope's lengthy address for the reopening of the Council. Most had not seen him since the abrasive days of late November. Pope Paul had spent the summer warning, in sermons and allocutions, of a "crisis of authority" and "crisis of obedience" in the Church, complaining that "truths that stand outside time because they are divine are being subjected to a historicism that strips them of their content and unchangeable character."[10] The address, however, was altogether different,[11] thanking God for the great grace of the Council. Repeatedly he exclaimed "*Grande quiddam hoc est Concilium!*" and with the note: We are *one people, the People of God.* We are the Catholic Church."[12]

Much in the spirit of the proposed Pastoral Constitution *Gaudium et Spes*, he spoke of love for the world and of the Church's concern for it. He concluded with two surprise announcements: one that of creating the Synod of Bishops, the other that he would, during the time the bishops were in session, travel to New York to address the United Nations, carrying the voice of the Council in proclaiming "concord, justice, fraternal love, and peace among all human beings, who are loved by God and gifted with good will."[13]

The Fathers applauded enthusiastically, feeling the address was a vote of confidence in the Council, giving it a welcome shot of energy and renewing its determination to carry on to the end. When the Pope had finished, Felici rose to announce that debate would

---

[9]*AAS* 57 (1965), 776: "*Nostrae potestate directe atque immediate subiectum;*" "*consilia dandi.*"
[10]Typically, *Insegnamenti*, 3: 1008.
[11]*AS* IV, 1, 125–35.
[12]Ibid., 129. "*Unus populous sumus, videlicet populus Dei. Nos efficimus Ecclesiam Catholicam.*"
[13]Ibid., 135.

begin next day on the *schema* "On Religious Liberty." This won more applause. The Pope had kept his promise that this *schema* would not disappear but would stand at the top of the agenda.[14]

Contradictory opinions came much more to the fore when Bishop De Smedt introduced this schema, further revised, the next day. Not only the curial party but, in near unanimity, the Spanish bishops rejected the concept altogether. Americans, Cardinal Spellman, and Cushing to the fore, and Canadians endorsed it wholeheartedly. Cardinals Siri and Ruffini cited multiple condemnations by Popes from Gregory XVI, who saw it as "madness" to think that liberty could ever be separated from truth, that truth which the Catholic Church alone possessed, to Pius IX in the Syllabus of Errors, and even Leo XIII, Pius XI and Pius XII.[15] Such curial rejection was expected, but Spanish Cardinal Benjamin de Arriba y Castro, Archbishop of Tarragona, stated bluntly that "The fundamental principle in this matter, which must be held without dilution, is this, only the Catholic Church has the right and the duty of preaching the Gospel. Therefore, proselytism of Catholics by non-Catholics is illicit and, insofar as the common good allows, must be impeded not simply by the Church but also by the state."[16] Was this to be a difference of teaching between those from predominantly Catholic countries and the rest?

At this point, Cardinal Giovanni Urbani, the new Patriarch of Venice who had replaced Angelo Roncalli there, speaking for 32 Italian bishops, came up with his own learned citations of Gregory XVI, Pius IX, Leo XIII, Pius XI, and Pius XII to support a certain "progress" (*progressio*) in their teachings. "The doctrine of civil liberty in religion," he declared, "is rooted in that progress." Some concerns and misgivings he had about the *schema*, but his verdict was: "the civil right to religious liberty is for certain inscribed in the teaching that the holy Church must now and in future proclaim to the world, not only because it is timely but because it is true."[17]

"The Group" continued its assaults for the next 3 days, through 17 September, in speeches by Carli, Lefebvre and others, despite

---

[14]O'Malley, 123f.
[15]Pius XII had condemned the proposition that Church and State could be separate as recently as 6 December 1953, in an address to Catholic lawyers: *AAS* 45 (1953), 794–802.
[16]*AS* IV, 1, 209f.
[17]Ibid., 211–15.

the rebuke they had had from Cicognani on behalf of the Pope. Bea, resisting qualms from within his Secretariat, wanted a vote after Monday, 20 September, when the debate was supposed to be concluded. Those fearful of a negative vote argued over the weekend for sending the schema back to the Commission for further revision before voting on a text later. On the day, Cardinal Joseph Lefebvre, Archbishop of Bourges (a very different Lefebvre from Archbishop Marcel Lefebvre of Dakar) led off with a systematic analysis and refutation of the six objections of the opposition.[18] His support was followed by that of Cardinal Stefan Wyszyński of Warsaw, Primate of Poland and commanding authority because of his resistance to Communism.[19] Then came Cardinal Josef Beran, Archbishop of Prague, only recently released from Communist prison and house arrest and speaking now for the first time to the Council. He argued that the fourteenth-century burning of John Hus at the Council of Constance and the forced conversion of the people of Bohemia to Catholicism in the seventeenth century had done vast harm to the Church. He called for the Council to adopt the *schema*, demanding of all governments that they desist from impeding the free exercise of religion and free from prison all clergy and laity held there unjustly for their religious beliefs.[20] The avalanche of support concluded with Cardinal Agnelo Rossi, Archbishop of Sao Paolo, who had his suggestions but spoke positively for 82 bishops from Brazil, the largest Catholic population in the world.[21]

Cardinal Bea went again to the Pope and the Moderators, asking for a vote. Ruffini did the same, asking the opposite.[22] The Moderators inclined not to hold the vote. Next day in the Council, the Fathers noted that Felici, Tisserant, and Agagianian arrived late, after the Mass. Had they a message from the Pope? After a few more speeches, Agagianian asked whether they wanted to terminate discussion of the schema, having heard 62 interventions. By a large majority they did. Then to everyone's astonishment Felici rose to announce an immediate vote on the *schema*, as basis for a definitive version. This decision had been made in the papal apartments that morning. The vote was 1,997 in favor, only 224 opposed, far less

---

[18]Ibid., 1, 384–6.
[19]Ibid., 1, 387–90.
[20]Ibid., 393f.
[21]Ibid., 399–403.
[22]*AS* V, 3, 357, 365.

than it had seemed. With nearly 90 percent approval a critical milestone had been passed for the Council.[23]

This one question had truly great centrality for Christian faith. If, in fact, the profession of Christianity could be privileged or required as an adjunct of civil society, then it was reduced in its essence to an instrument of civil control. Its appeal, at the same time, would be so powerful that both civil and religious authority would contest that power as a means of bending society to their will. That had been a weakness of the Church all the time since Constantine first saw Christianity as an effective instrument to help him govern his empire. To renounce that concept would be a most powerful way to return the Church to the Gospel of Christ.

Mennonites had discovered this in the sixteenth century, teaching that kings and governments had no authority to decide the religion of their subjects, and for that reason had been regarded as the "radical Left Wing of the Reformation," targeted by Catholic and Protestant alike.[24] The whole Christian world at this stage, Protestant and Catholic alike, and the Orthodox too, who had had to defend the freedom to practice their faith in a region turned Muslim, was now recognizing its essential rightness. The Declaration would yet be subject, after more fine-tuning, to a final vote, but the essential work had now been done.

That much accomplished, the Council could now turn its attention to the *schema* on the Church in the Modern World. Since the early nineteenth century, pope after pope had repudiated any relation to this modern world. The *schema* had grown in scope since the previous year's sessions, and contained, in its second chapter, contentious matter on the ends of marriage and birth control. But the great task was to reconcile the difference between the Germans and the French. Both Karl Rahner and Josef Ratzinger regarded its view of human society as too optimistic. Debate on the *schema* would go from 21 September to 8 October, and as everyone knew, if it were not approved in the short remaining time that year, there would be no coming back.

A meeting of the French and German theologians had taken place on 17 September to seek rapprochement among them. Over the succeeding days, three German Jesuit theologians, Alois Grillmeier,

---

[23]For this whole discussion, O'Malley, 254–7.
[24]Cf. Prof John D. Roth, Mennonite Church History, http://history.mennonite.net/.

Otto Semmelroth, and Johann Baptist Hirschmann (all of them my own teachers from Frankfurt) made it their business to deal with all the objections, *modi*, their colleagues raised.[25] By 22 September, French Dominican theologian Marie-Dominique Chenu, who had been part of these discussions, defended the schema fervently in a lecture at the Centro di Documentazione Olandese in Rome. His lecture was widely read by the Fathers of the Council and did much to win their support.[26]

In the debate on the floor, the negative comments of Group members Ruffini,[27] Siri,[28] and the Brazilian Archbishop Sigaud of Diamantina,[29] portraying a world of demonic corruption, had an effect contrary to their intention, actually turning the opinion of the Fathers away from a pessimistic understanding of the modern world and its possibilities. The German bishops were moderating their criticism, warming to the *schema*.

Discussion of marriage in part II of the *schema* brought a *contretemps* when Archbishop Elias Zhogby, the Melkite patriarchal vicar for Egypt, asked that a way be found to allow remarriage for innocent spouses abandoned by their partners.[30] On direct orders from the Pope[31] the newly made Cardinal Charles Journet, a Swiss

---

[25]Discussed by Joseph A. Komonchak, "Augustine, Aquinas or the Gospel *sine glossa*? Divisions over *Gaudium et Spes*," in Austin Ivereigh (ed.), *Unfinished Journey: The Church Forty Years after Vatican II, Essays for John Wilkins* (New York: Continuum, 2003). He gives a longer version in "Le valutazioni sulla Gaudium et Spes: Chenu, Dossetti, Ratzionger," in Joseph Doré and Alberto Melloni (eds), *Volti di fine concilio: Studi di storia e teologia sulla conclusione del Vaticano II* (Bologna: Il Mulino, 2000), 115–53.

[26]Giovanni Turbanti, *Un concilio per il mondo modern: La redazione della costituzione pastorale "Gaudium et Spes" del Vaticano II* (Bologna: Il Mulino, 2000), 643–51; also Turbanti, "Il ruolo del P.D. Chenu nell'elaborazione della costituzione *Gaudium et Spes*," in *Marie-Dominique Chenu: Moyen-Age et modernité* (Paris: Le centre d'études du Saulchoir, 1997), 173–212.

[27]*AS* IV, 2, 21–3.

[28]Ibid., 24f.

[29]Ibid., 47–50.

[30]*AS* IV, 3, 45–8.

[31]Albert Prignon, *Journal conciliaire de la 4e Session*, ed. L. Declerck and A. Haquin (Louvain-la-Neuve: Publications de la Faculté de Théologie, 2003), 141; also Gilles Routhier, "Finishing the Work Begun: The Trying Experience of the Fourth Period," in Giuseppe Alberigo and Joseph Komonchak (eds), *History of Vatican II*, 5 volumes (Maryknoll, NY: Orbis Press, 1995–2006), 5, 159, n. 440.

theologian, was set ahead of a scheduled speaker to respond, bluntly: "The doctrine of the Catholic Church on the indissolubility of sacramental matrimony is the very same doctrine that Jesus Christ revealed to us and that the Church has always preserved and proclaimed."[32] Zoghby's response, delivered only some days later, was that he did not attack the indissolubility of marriage but thought in terms of a dispensation like that of the Petrine Privilege.[33]

Yet despite the novelty of the whole content of the schema, the discussion moved on surprisingly smoothly. Archbishop Michele Pellegrino of Turin, just promoted from a professorship, raised very realistic concerns about the way Vatican nervousness had hindered serious research in the ecclesiastical disciplines, citing the punitive excesses of the anti-Modernist crisis. That this came from an Italian bishop signaled a break in the conservative mentality of that hierarchy. Pellegrino wanted the document to contain explicit recognition of the needs of freedom for theologians in their fundamental research, especially in the area of history.[34]

As the Fathers moved on to consider issues of war and nuclear armaments, their attention and that of the press and media crossed to New York, where, on 4 October, the twentieth anniversary of the organization, Pope Paul made his historic visit to the headquarters of the United Nations. The Pope chose not to be met at the airport by President Lyndon Johnson, because he preferred his visit to be that of a pastor, rather than a Head of State, solicitous for the welfare of the world. He introduced himself to the General Assembly as "a man like you, a brother," wishing "to serve you to the best of Our abilities, with disinterest, humility and love." His visit was an endorsement of the whole concept of the United Nations, "the road we must travel in the interests of modern civilization and world peace," the very things the Council was seeking in trying to relate the Church to the Modern World. His address contained a ringing affirmation of "the rights and fundamental duties of human beings – their dignity, their liberty, and above all their religious liberty,"

---

[32]*AS* IV, 3, 58f.
[33]Ibid., 257f.
[34]Ibid., 135–7.

things that so recently had been the centers of such controversy in the Council itself.[35]

With that striking papal accolade to its work, the Council proceeded on 6 October to the chapter "On the Community of Peoples and the Promotion of Peace." In view of the dangers of nuclear weapons, was the classic distinction of just and unjust wars now obsolete? The Fathers tended toward that conclusion, and this time no one was more vehement in promoting this shift in perspective than Cardinal Ottaviani, a life-long opponent of war who, in fact, had been the author behind Pope Pius XII's constant peace statements throughout the course of World War II. He began his intervention by saying "War must be completely outlawed."[36] Ottaviani's speech was warmly applauded by the Fathers, but others of "The Group" dissented strongly, Carli insisting that war could be justified "even in our atomic age," and arguing that conscientious objection on the part of citizens, when called to military service by their governments, was illegitimate.[37]

Discussion of the Modern World *schema* concluded on 8 October, its main lines now settled and approved by the Council. Rahner and Ratzinger, the Germans who had from the start wanted a less optimistic Augustinian cast to the document were included in the commission to sort out all the *modi* in the 160 speeches and many written comments that had been devoted to it, but as the conclusion of the Council neared so closely they would move with great dispatch.

The most difficult section would be that on marriage. The majority opinion would go against ranking the "ends of marriage" in terms of their priority. The text would, however, state that God had endowed the marriage state "with various benefits and

---

[35]His speech, in its original elegant French, appears among the Council's Acta themselves, as *AS* IV, 1, 28–36. All the world's newspapers carried translation into many languages, but an English translation can be found in Henri Fesquet, *The Drama of Vatican II: The Ecumenical Council, June 1962-December 1965*, trans. Bernard Murchland (New York: Random House, 1967), 662–70.

[36]*AS* IV, 3, 642f., opening: "*Bellum omnino interdicendum!*" The history of Ottaviani's antiwar convictions and activity has been researched by French Worker Priest Jean Goss, and is reported by Tom Cornell in the Claretian publication *Salt of the Earth*, 1999, salt.claretianpubs.org/issues/peace/tcorn.html.

[37]*AS* IV, 3, 657–60.

with various ends in view." It developed especially "the intimate partnership of life and the love that constituted the married state," asserted "the equal personal dignity that must be accorded to man and wife in mutual and unreserved affection." Without giving it rank of priority among ends, it asserted that "marriage and married love are by nature ordered to the procreation and education of children," whom the spouses should welcome as gifts of God. But it left out any mention of the traditional concept that marriage was an honest remedy for concupiscence, and instead put its emphasis on love and partnership.[38]

And then there was birth control, the issue that would convulse the Church just a few years later. Invention of the birth-control pill, oral contraception, had been as recent as 1960. Despite a long tradition opposing limitation on births, Pius XI's Encyclical *Casti Connibii* (1930) had recognized prudential reasons for controlling the number of children so long as it was done "in accordance with nature," which was understood as keeping intercourse to the infertile times of the woman's cycle: the "rhythm method." In view of sentiment in favor of permitting use of the oral contraceptives to Catholics, John XXIII had in 1963 appointed a commission of six European experts, non-theologians, to study this, paying attention to the alarming growth of world population.[39] Paul VI, later that year after John XXIII's death, had added theologians to the commission and expanded it to 72 members from 5 continents, including 16 theologians, 13 physicians, and 5 women without medical credentials, with an executive committee of 16 bishops, including 7 cardinals.[40] The conciliar commission responsible for the Modern World document well understood the authority of that special commission, and that the Pope had reserved this question to himself.

The document, therefore, confined itself to a generic statement, recognizing that there were circumstances in which spouses could

---

[38]O'Malley, 265.

[39]Cf. William Henry Shannon, "The Papal Commission on Birth Control," ch. VII in *The lively debate: response to Humanae vitae* (New York: Sheed & Ward, 1970), 76–104.

[40]Robert McClory, *Turning point: The inside story of the Papal Birth Control Commission, and how Humanae vitae changed the life of Patty Crowley and the future of the church* (New York: Crossroad, 1995).

legitimately limit the number of their children, provided it were done in conformity with the law of God and the teaching of the Church. Nothing went beyond what theologians had been saying before the Council.[41]

The questions of war and armaments remained to be voted. In the last week of the Council, the Americans would become very defensive on their nuclear deterrence. The newly appointed Archbishop of New Orleans, Philip M. Hannon, allied with Cardinal Spellman, would circulate a petition to reject the chapter that dealt with them, arguing that these weapons had been beneficial in protecting the freedom of much of the world. The Group sided with him but most of the Fathers resented that effort as dangerous to the very viability of what had by then come to be known as the Pastoral Constitution *Gaudium et Spes*.[42] The text allowed for conscientious objection by Catholics, called on the wealthy nations to convert their expenditures on armaments to helping the poor, and called on Catholics to cooperate in the international organizations, which worked for peace and justice.

In every way, the text represented a change in orientation of the Church to the world. It had been Pope Paul's wish, most welcome to the Council, that the text focus on *dialogue*. Even its initial address is "not only to the sons and daughters of the Church and all who call upon the name of Christ but the whole of humanity as well." It was extraordinary for this Church, which for so long had treated everything to do with change and modernity in the world with suspicion and even rejection, to open itself now to a respectful and cooperative relation with all of humanity. The very term "humanism" had acquired, practically since the Enlightenment period, an overtone of atheism or overt hostility to religious claims or authority, but now "Christian Humanism" could once again become an intelligible term, as it had been during the most fruitful periods of the Church's life. O'Malley can speak of it as a view of "a human nature created by God, infused with the Holy Spirit, and destined for God." Speaking of Christians as partners in the Paschal Mystery, configured by the death of Christ but moving forward

---

[41]O'Malley, 265f.
[42]These testy exchanges are detailed by Peter Hünermann, "The Final Weeks of the Council," in the Alberigo/Komonchak, *History*, 5, 386–427, esp, 419–21; also in Ralph M. Wiltgen, *The Rhine Flows into the Tiber: The Unknown Council* (New York: Hawthorn Books, 1967), 278–82.

strengthened by the hope of the resurrection, he quotes the text: "All this holds true not only for Christians but also for all people of good will in whose hearts grace is active invisibly. For, since Christ died for everyone, and since all are, in fact, called to one and the same destiny, which is divine, we must hold that the Holy Spirit offers to all the possibility of being made partners, in a way known to God, in the Paschal Mystery."[43]

Concluding its discussion of *Gaudium et Spes* on 7 October, the Council was energized now, to spend its final weeks on a variety of further documents. A Decree On the Mission Activity of the Church, *Ad Gentes Divinus*, came first, replacing one that had been rejected the year before. It addressed the need to separate the mission enterprise from the era of colonialism and imperialism with its assumptions of European superiority, accommodating itself to local cultures and circumstances. The text shows signs of hurried preparation and discussion, given that a third of the bishops present came from mission territories facing unprecedented political, economic, and cultural challenges in their countries. It recognized, though, that Christian faith must now be explained "in terms of the philosophy and wisdom of the people," which would mean "a more profound adaptation [to local cultures] in the whole sphere of Christian life."[44]

Next, in the sessions of 13 and 14 October, a declaration On Christian Education, *Gravissimum Educationis*, a document never before having the central attention of the Council but much discussed and revised in its commission, was agreed through votes on its *modi* and the document as a whole. This had been a difficult task because of the vast differences in systems of education in different countries and cultures.[45]

Most important was the declaration on Non-Christian Religions, *Nostra Aetate*, which returned to the floor on 14 and 15 October, after having been so long contested both by The Group and by the Oriental churches. It received approval in votes on its revision and the text as a whole.

A transformation of the Catholic and Christian outlook on Judaism and Jews, after all the centuries of contempt, had been among the

---

[43]O'Malley, 267.
[44]Ibid., 268f.
[45]Ibid.

dearest wishes of Pope John XXIII in calling the Council, the purpose for which he had enlisted the help of Cardinal Bea. As the text went through heavy revision during the session of 1964, Pope Paul himself had had reservations about the "deicide" question, but the heaviest trepidations came from the churches of Eastern rites. They had to live among Arab and Muslim peoples who would connect any rapprochement with Jews with the territorial claims of Israel. This was a document initially concerned basically with Jews, containing a single sentence with regard to Muslims and, in conclusion, a simple statement of good will to all peoples. As it came back to the floor in these concluding days, the word "Jews" had disappeared from its title, which was "On the Relation to Non-Christian Religions." After an introductory chapter and two chapters on Judaism, a chapter had been added on Islam and the faith of Muslims and another on the other faiths. The *schema* as a whole now met a strong consensus in the Council, but 243 negative votes remained, a worrying number given the overwhelming votes on other documents.

That the opposition had diminished so much resulted from Bea's action in sending his assistants, Willebrands, De Smedt, and Pierre Duprey, to visit and consult with every one of the patriarchs. That action had brought back the votes of the Eastern Catholic bishops. The ever-articulate Patriarch Maximos IV Saigh had been particularly helpful, proposing four changes in the document that were accepted with no problem. Bea's Secretariat then prepared an Arabic translation, which Willebrands and De Smedt personally delivered to the embassies of all the Arab states in Rome. Only The Group, the curia-based *Coetus* of International Fathers remained opposed, making up the bulk of those 243 negative votes. Full denial of a guilt for the crime of deicide, as Bea had wanted, had not been achieved. Instead a weaker statement said: "Although the Jewish authorities with their followers pressed for the death of Jesus, still the things perpetrated during the passion cannot be ascribed indiscriminately to all Jews living at the time nor to the Jews of today. . . . Moreover, the Church, which condemns all persecutions against any people . . . deplores feelings of hatred, persecutions, and demonstrations of anti-Semitism directed against the Jews at whatever time and by whomsoever."[46]

---

[46]O'Malley, 275f.

Already on 13 October, François Marty, Archbishop of Rheims, had introduced a statement On the Ministry and Life of Presbyters. Its discussion would last into the 16th, after which the Council took a recess of a week. An earlier text had met rejection the previous year, but it seemed necessary to say something of the priests.

The theme had first come up in 1962, Pope John XXIII's time and before the Council, when on 16 June the Central preparatory Commission had dealt with a text De sacerdotibus lapsis, On Lapsed Priests, those who had abandoned the priesthood. This early text had worked to the assumption that such defections always had to do with celibacy. It had consequently opened with a ringing reaffirmation of the discipline of clerical celibacy.[47] The question, therefore, was not one of celibacy, but about defections, a problem with which every bishop had to deal. Future leaders of the Council had taken part in this discussion, among them Bea, Suenens, Frings, Léger, but none had questioned the appropriateness of the discipline for priests of the Latin rite. Instead, they wanted to ease the situation of priests who, in many cases, had married and had been excommunicated automatically. Should they be given post factum dispensations and, if so, how should it be handled?

Consensus among these bishops was that the Council should not take up the question as it entailed complicated canonical procedures which were better not made part of a public discussion. The matter was left instead to the Holy See, and Pope John, when he was informed of the results, confirmed this consensus as binding in a letter to the Central Preparatory Commission. Consequently, it did not come up on the agenda of the Council.[48]

In the 3 years between 1962 and the final period in 1965, celibacy itself had become a question for a small group of Brazilian bishops, who had begun talking of the advisability of modifying the discipline for some regions. They had asked Cardinal Suenens to help them introduce it on the floor.[49] Hearing of this, Pope Paul intervened to

---

[47]Acta et Documenta Concilio Oecumenico Vatican0, Series secunda (Praeparatoria), 7 volumes (Vatican City: Typis Polyglottis Vaticanis, 1964–69), II, 4, 403–12 (text) and 412–33 (comments).

[48]Pericle Felici had important comments on this development in Giovanni Caprile, Il Concilio Vaticano II: Cronache del Concilio Vaticano II, 5 vols, in 6 (Rome: Edizioni "La Civiltà Cattolica"), 5, 706–9, which contains the substance of Felici's Il Vaticano II e il celibato sacerdotale (Vatican City: Tipografia Poliglotta Vaticana, 1969).

[49]Prignon, Journal conciliaire, 149f.

withhold celibacy from the agenda. In a letter to Cardinal Tisserant read to the Assembly on 11 October, the Pope called the discussion inappropriate and asserted his intention to safeguard and maintain the ancient discipline of the Latin Church with regard to celibacy of the clergy. He conceded, though, that if bishops wished they could send their concerns to the Council of Presidents, who would convey them to him.[50]

The bishops, even those who had asked for a change in the discipline, received this decision with applause, apparently fearing that to raise the question in public discussion would let loose a frenzy in the media at a time, in these closing days of the Council, when they would hardly be able to give it adequate treatment.[51] Lacking such a decision, the *Presbyterorum Ordinis* decree remained a minor document among the Council's achievements. It did, after revision in the light of many *modi*, succeed in commending the celibacy of Latin rite priests without casting the married state as something inferior.

The ever-articulate Patriarch Maximos IV had prepared a speech critical of this Latin practice and comparing it with the different discipline of the Eastern rites. Hearing, before 11 October, of the Pope's action, he did not deliver the speech, but sent it, with a covering letter, to the Pope on 13 October.[52] The problems of the Latin church, he argued, should not be treated as taboo but confronted head-on. "Most Holy Father, this problem exists and is daily becoming more difficult. It cries out for a solution. . . . Your Holiness knows well that repressed truths turn poisonous."[53] Celibacy, he admitted, is a beautiful ideal, but should not be imposed as an indispensable condition for ordination.

---

[50]*AS* IV, 1, 40, for the Pope's letter, with Tisserant's reply, 41. Because the question would become so important, there has been a considerable subsequent literature on it. Mauro Velati "Completing the Conciliar Agenda," in Alberigo/Komonchak, *History*, 5: 194f.; 231–7; John W. O'Malley, "Celibacy: Decisive Moments in Its History," in *Sexuality and the U.S. Catholic Church: Crisis and Renewal*, ed. Lisa Sowle Cahill et al. (New York: Crossroad, 2006), 94–106; on John XXIII and Paul VI, Georg Denzler, *Das Papsttum und der Amtszölibat*, 2 volumes (Anton Hiersemann: Stuttgart, 1973–76), 2, 325–70; more generally, William Bassett and Peter Huizing, (eds), *Celibacy in the Church*, Concilium 78 (New York: Herder and Herder, 1972).
[51]O'Malley, 271.
[52]*AS* VI, 4, 550f., 551–4.
[53]Quoted in O'Malley, 272.

Other speakers, most from Asia and Africa, but including Cardinal Bea, also criticized the *schema* as too Western-oriented over the course of five sessions devoted to it. Questions of clericalism, always a corrosive element in the Church but bound to become more troubling in subsequent years, arose in the discussion. Should the priest be seen basically as a cultic figure, or should a more activist role be expected with regard to society. Cardinal Ruffino and Tarragona's cardinal Archbishop Benjamin de Arriba y Castro vigorously defended the more clerical option.[54]

Two years later, after the Council, Pope Paul would fulfill his promise to provide, on his own, a robust defense of the discipline of celibacy with his Encyclical, *Sacerdotalis Caelibatus*, of 24 June 1967.[55] The Encyclical gives a quite knowledgeable summation of the arguments brought against the discipline and the difficulties of celibacy, recognizes that it was not a requirement of Christ for his own disciples and Apostles, but argues that its symbolic and traditional values are "a brilliant jewel," guarded by the Church for centuries, which "retains its value undiminished even in our time when the outlook of men and the state of the world have undergone such profound changes."[56] Since making his promise to the Council, the Pope says, ". . . We have, over a considerable period of time earnestly implored the enlightenment and assistance of the Holy Spirit and have examined before God opinions and petitions which have come to Us from all over the world, notably from many pastors of God's Church."

That such a decision had been withheld from the Council and made instead by the Pope himself, after private consultation open only to himself, would have fateful consequences in subsequent years. Yet, even as the Pope upheld the law of celibacy for the Latin rite, he also announced what has become known since as the Pastoral Provision, allowing married ministers from other churches to be ordained and function as Catholic priests while remaining with their spouses.[57]

---

[54]*AS* IV, 4, 686–8, and 688f.
[55]Vatican website, *Sacerdotalis Caelibatus*, Encyclical Letter of Pope Paul VI on the Celibacy of the Priest, 24 June 1967, www.vatican.va/holy_father/paul_vi/encyclicals/documents/hf_p-vi_enc_24061967_sacerdotalis_en.html.
[56]The opening lines of the Encyclical.
[57]*Sacerdotalis Caelibatus*, ##42f.

The Council, though, on 16 October, took a much needed break for a week. Numbers of bishops had declined so much that, when the vote on the priesthood document as a whole was held that day, only 1,521 were present. The Fathers reconvened on 25 October, heard a few remaining speeches on *Sacerdotalis Caelibatus*, but then took another break, this one filled, for many of them in the commissions and their *periti*, with intense work revising and polishing the documents for final votes and their proclamation by the Pope. At a Public Session on 28 October, the Fathers took final votes on five documents, which were then promulgated by the Pope: On the Pastoral Office of Bishops, *Christus Dominus*; On the Renewal of Religious Life, *Perfectae Caritatis*; On the Training of Priests, *Optatum Totius*; On Christian Education, *Gravissimum Educationis*, and the long-fought On the Relation of the Church to Non-Christian Religions, *Nostra Aetate*. Numbers had grown again, to 2,322, and while the first three of these documents received only one to three negative votes, *Gravissimum Educationis* received thirty five and *Nostra Aetate* eighty eight from the hard-core opposition.[58] Ten of the eventual sixteen documents of the Council had now come to their final status.

The document on Revelation, which had now acquired the name *Dei Verbum*, The Word of God, had been so much revised that the whole day, 29 October, was invested in voting the many amendments suggested by the various *modi*. The document, an outright replacement for the one presented in the first year on The Sources of Revelation, which had sharply distinguished Scripture and Tradition as separate sources, placed its emphasis fully on the centrality of the Bible. But the hardcore opponents in the *Coetus* remained determined to treat Tradition as an alternative source containing truths not found in Scripture. Their concept of Tradition was practically synonymous with Magisterium, especially papal Magisterium. They worried about defending such doctrinal definitions as that of Pius IX on the Immaculate Conception and of Pius XII on the Assumption. In this they appeared to have the support of the Pope, who had written to the Commission asking clarification of the text and suggesting alternative formulas.

---

[58]O'Malley, 276f.

The Commission reached a compromise acceptable to the Pope, saying; "The Church does not draw her certainty for all revealed truths from Scripture alone."[59] Cardinal Ermenegildo Florit of Florence, explaining these last-minute changes on 29 October, told the Assembly: "Sacred Tradition is not presented as a quantitative supplement to Sacred Scripture, nor is Sacred Scripture presented as codification of all of revelation. It is clear, therefore, that the text of the *schema* is unchanged in its substance but has been perfected in its mode of expression."[60] Votes were then taken on each of the six chapters and on the whole, with only 27 negative votes on the entire *schema*. The next day, Paul VI gave approval to the printing of the text, which would then be ready for a ceremonial vote at the next Public Session.

Another recess followed until Monday, 9 November. The days were occupied with voting on the *modi* to various documents, including *Gaudium et Spes*. The Council, running short of time by now, then received a document on Indulgences. The Pope, as long ago as July, 1963, had requested such a document, prepared by the canonists of the Sacred Penitentiary. It was introduced by Cardinal Fernando Cento, long a nuncio to Belgium but since 1953 back in Rome as colleague to the curial cardinals. Indulgences had been the very occasion of Luther's first blow in the Protestant Reformation and the Fathers were highly conscious of the close attention among the Protestant observers. Their use had been challenged at the Council of Trent, but after very little discussion that Council had reaffirmed their legitimacy just before it ended, providing some measures to lessen abuse of them. In reward for certain good practices recommended by the Church, particularly by popes, individuals were supposed to get time off from their sentences to Purgatory. Many popes had added to the number of these indulgences, and in particular Pius XII had granted so many that it was easy to get several plenary indulgences (full remission of any punishment in Purgatory) in a single day.

Maximos IV Saigh led off, on behalf of all the Melkite bishops, roundly rejecting the entire practice. There was no connection, he

[59]*AS* IV, 5, 705.

[60]Ibid., 741. The episode is treated at length by a *peritus* deeply involved in it, Umberto Betti, *La Rivilazione divina nella Chiesa: La Trasmissione della rivelzione nel capitulo II della costitutione dommatica Dei Verbum* (Rome: Città Nuova Editrice, 1970).

said, between the intercession of the Church and the full or partial remission of temporal punishment due to sin. Nor had any such claims been made during the eleven centuries in which there was union between the churches of East and West.[61] Alfrink followed, speaking for all the Dutch bishops, then König speaking for the Austrians and Döpfner for the Germans, highly critical of the whole document, Döpfner critical not only of the underlying theology but of the misleading way the drafter had dealt with the history.[62] The document was effectively dead, and Felici, next morning, announced that there would be no more reports on it from groups of bishops, but if they wished they could submit them in writing.[63] Many episcopal conferences did: Belgium, England and Wales, Scandinavia, Brazil, Chile, Congo, Rwanda, Burundi, Dahomey, Japan, and Laos, all dissatisfied with the document and several calling for the abolition of the whole concept of indulgences.[64]

More than a year later, on 1 January 1967, Paul VI would issue on his own an Apostolic Constitution, *Indulgentiarum Doctrina*, only slightly modifying the traditional teaching in the matter. He attributed any change from the practice of the early or medieval Church to "progress" (*profectus*) of doctrine, and effectively restored the *status quo* that had existed before all those objections at the Council.[65]

At another Public Session, on 18 November, as final ceremonial votes were taken on the great Dogmatic Constitution on Scripture, *Dei Verbum* (2,344 in favor, 6 opposed) and the Laity Decree, *Apostolicam Actuositatem* (2,305 in favor, 2 opposed), after which the Pope solemnly promulgated them and delivered an allocution. The work of the Council was approaching completion, and he reminded the Fathers that they had only 20 days left. He had appointed three new bodies to implement the changes the Council

---

[61]*AS* IV, 6, 292–4.
[62]Ibid., 317–19, 323–35.
[63]Ibid., 415.
[64]Peter Hünerman records all this in his essay "The Final Weeks of the Council" (Albreigo/Komonchak, *History*, 5), 384.
[65]Vatican website, www.vatican.va/holy_father/paul_vi/apost_constitutions/documents/hf_p-vi_apc_19670101_indulgentiarum-doctrina_en.html, Apostolic Constitution of Pope Paul VI, *Indulgentiarum Doctrina*, whereby the Revision of Sacred Indulgences is Promulgated. Consulted 20 October 2012.

had enacted: one for the liturgy, one for the revision of Canon law, and one for the communication media. Three new Secretariats (later to become Pontifical Councils) would take their place in the curia: on Christian Unity, on Non-Christian Religions and on Non-Believers. He announced that the first Synod of Bishops would take place in 1967. Some changes, he said, had already been made in the Roman Curia, and more would soon be made in "the principal Congregation" (described as *prima* rather than the usual *suprema*), the Holy Office.

The Pope went on to warn against exaggerations that would twist the *aggiornamento* proclaimed by John XXII into *"relativism"*— first use of a term that would become, in subsequent years, a basic part of the vocabulary of those who would want to restrict the meaning of the Council. "Henceforth [*aggiornamento*] will mean for us an enlightened grasp of the intentions of the Council and the faithful implementation of its directives. . . . The time for debate is over."[66]

The Pope concluded by announcing three initiatives. He would open the process of beatification for his two predecessors, Pius XII and John XXIII. He would construct in Rome, as memorial of the Council, a new church dedicated to Mary under the title "Mother of the Church" (the title the Council had declined to endorse in a separate document. And finally, from 8 December, which would be the last day of the Council, a special Jubilee would begin, extending to Pentecost.

In retrospect, this address brings into focus several things that would become complaints after the Council. Putting those two very different popes together into one process leading to canonization obscured the differences between them. Much as we would experience years later, at the death of Pope John Paul II, there had been an immediate popular call for John XXIII to be canonized by acclamation. That would now be heard no more. Memorializing the work of the Council with an affirmation of what it had decided not to do, the proclamation of Mary as Mother of the Church, had the feeling of an override by the Pope. And the reform promised of the Holy Office, it was evident, would be designed to leave it essentially intact.

---

[66]*AS* IV, 6, 689–95.

A last bit of turbulence remained before the Council was over. On 20 November, as the final revision were being made to the Pastoral Constitution on the Church in the Modern World, *Gaudium et Spes*, a subcommittee led by Archbishop John Dearden of Detroit reported its revised form of the section on marriage and the family, on which it had consulted the special Papal Commission on birth control. Two individual theologians, Italian Franciscan Ermenigildo Leo, who was a *consultor* to the Holy Office, and American Jesuit John Ford, a member of the Papal Commission that had studied the subject, objected strongly and urged the Pope, directly and through others, to make a change in the text so that it would clearly reject the use of contraceptives. Otherwise, they argued, the Council would be questioning the teaching of previous popes, implying that a change in teaching was possible in the matter. The Pope's personal theological adviser, Carlo Colombo, a priest of Milan, inclined to agree with them.[67]

On 24 November, the Pope intervened. Ottaviani received a letter from Cicognani indicating changes that the Pope demanded should be made in the text. An open and clear rejection of contraceptives was among them, and the Pope insisted that reference should be made to the condemnation in the Encyclical *Casti Connubii*. The press immediately got word of the Pope's action and for some days angry irruptions dominated the news of the Council.

As O'Malley expressed it, the Council was left with a series of problems of a sort that had by now become familiar.

> How could the council make a pronouncement on an issue that the pope had removed from its competence? How could it make a pronouncement on an issue it had not discussed? How could it make a pronouncement when another body appointed by the pope himself was examining the matter? How could a subcommittee at this last minute present for a final vote a text in which such radical change had been made? Why did the letter come on at this late date, the last minute? If the council made a statement, would that not render the Papal Commission superfluous?[68]

---

[67]Eric Marcelo O. Genilo, *John Cuthbert Ford, S.J., Moral Theologian at the End of the Manualist Era* (Washington, DC: Georgetown University Press, 2007) discusses John Ford's opposition activities throughout the birth control discussion, esp. 47–59. On Colombo, rf. Prignon, *Journal conciliaire*, 222, 225, and 248.

[68]O'Malley, 284f.

As with other papal interventions, the Fathers scrambled to find a compromise, asking whether the Pope's *modi* were commands in virtue of his office or were to be voted on like the *modi* of other bishops. The Pope insisted, to Felici, Tisserant, and Cicognani, that he would brook no change in his points, though he would accept alternative wordings. Felici reported him saying, if others had their conscience, he too had his.[69] The next day, however, 26 November, Cicognani sent a letter to the Council saying the *modi* were to be regarded as "counsels" (*consigli*) of the Pope, and should be treated like the *modi* of any other bishop.

The Commission took him at his word. The final text contained no explicit condemnation of artificial means of birth control. It stated that Catholics were forbidden to use methods the Church had condemned. A footnote referred to *Casti Connubii* and two other papal documents and to the Pope's address to the cardinals on 23 June 1964, in which he announced the Papal Commission and said the matter needed thorough investigation.[70] A disgruntled Ottaviani presented a transcript of the discussion to the Pope, who signed on it that he accepted the judgment of the Council. When this fifth chapter of *Gaudium et Spes* come up for a final vote, it had only 155 negative votes.

The Council had received a warning now. The Papal Commission would continue its studies for another year and a half, before reporting back to the Pope with a majority favoring a change in the Church's position, but the Pope would then issue the encyclical that would electrify the Church and be a source of massive dissonance to this day.

After 2 days now of final voting on elements of the four remaining documents yet to be promulgated and a few days of no session, concluding ceremonials for the Council began on 4 December.[71] Pope Paul held an ecumenical prayer service for the more than a hundred non-Catholic observers in the basilica of St Paul Outside the Walls, where, in 1959, Pope John had announced his intention to hold a Council. Up to the beginning of the Council 4 years

---

[69]Ibid., 285.

[70]This entire episode is narrated in detail in Prignon, *Journal conciliaire*, 219–60.

[71]Hünemann's "Final Weeks," in Alberigo/Komonchak, *History*, 5, gives a full description of these final ceremonies, 465–83; also Giovanni Caprile, *Il Concilio Vaticano II: Cronache del Concilio Vaticano II*, 5 volumes (Rome: Edizione "La Civiltà Cattolica", 1966–69), 5, 499–526, and O'Malley, 586–9.

before, such a service would have been unthinkable. At the end, in the Benedictine monastery adjacent to the basilica, Cardinal Bea presented each of the observers to Pope Paul, who had a gift for each: a small bronze bell adorned with symbols of the four evangelists and the monogram of Christ.

The Fathers of the Council received their gifts on 6 December at a wrap-up business session in St Peter's: gold rings and an apostolic blessing. That done, Felici promulgated the Pope's bull announcing the Jubilee, complete with a plenary indulgence for all the faithful who completed the usual conditions.[72] The City of Rome had a gift to present as well: silver medals, each engraved with the name of the Council Father to whom it was given. After Cardinal Suenens finished the session with thanks from the four moderators to all who had taken part, the bishops emerging from the basilica found copies of the *Osservatore Romano* containing the document *Integrae Servandae*, which presented the reform the Pope had promised of the Supreme Congregation of the Holy Office. It would, henceforth, be called the Congregation for the Doctrine of the Faith.

The renamed Congregation would have a mandate essentially the same as before, "to protect the teaching on faith and morals throughout the entire Catholic world." But it was given a more positive function as well, of "investigating new teachings and new opinions . . . and promoting study of such matters and scholarly meetings."[73]

On the following day, 7 December, the ceremonies ran to a formal Public Session, all the bishops in full vestments and miters in the presence of the Pope. Final votes were taken on the four documents about to be promulgated. For the Decree on Religious Liberty, *Dignitatis Humanae*, it was 2,308 in favor, 70 opposed. The Decree on the Mission Activity of the Church, *Ad Gentes Divinitus*, received 2,394 votes in favor, only 5 opposed; the Decree on the Ministry and Life of Priests, *Presbyterorus Ordinis*, had 2,390 in favor, 4 opposed; for the Pastoral Constitution On the church in

---

[72]*AS* IV, 7, 635–40.
[73]Vatican website, www.vatican.va/holy_father/paul_vi/motu_proprio/documents/hf_p-vi_motu-proprio_19651207_integrae-servandae_en.html, Pope Paul VI, Apostolic Letter Given Motu Proprio Integrae Servandae. Consulted 20 October 2012.

the Modern World, *Gaudium et Spes*, 2,309 voted in favor, 75 opposed. The opposition on the Religious Liberty document and *Gaudium et Spes*, sign of the last holdouts from the *Coetus*, was still minuscule.

Then, in a moving ceremony, Bishop Willebrands read from the pulpit, in French, the Joint Declaration of Paul VI and Patriarch Athenagoras regretting the mutual excommunications that had passed between Greeks and Latins in 1054, each side accepting responsibility for that tragedy, and pledging to work for full communion between the two churches. As Pope and Patriarch had embraced at their meeting in Jerusalem, so now Willebrands and Meliton, the Orthodox Metropolitan of Heliopolis, embraced before the Council, to the hearty applause of the Fathers.

Mass followed, with a lengthy homily from the Pope, basically on the holiness of the Church amid the sinfulness of the world, notably a one-way street relation with little trace of the reciprocity taught in *Gaudium et Spes*, but professing, like the Good Shepherd, a loving attitude toward the world.[74]

The Pope then formally promulgated the four last documents, and Cardinal Bea rose to read the Pope's Apostolic Letter formally lifting the 1054 excommunication of the Greeks.

The Council concluded with a public Mass in St Peter's Square, attended by 300,000 people, televised worldwide, the long procession of bishop in their green vestments and miters emerging from the "Bronze Gate" of the Vatican to march into the square, the Pope on his *sedia gestatoria*.

The feast was that of the Immaculate Conception of the Virgin Mary. After the Mass, the Pope blessed the cornerstone of the new church to be built in honor of Mary as Mother of the Church. His farewell was addressed to those in the square, to those who followed on radio and television and "to all humanity," which he could address "because, for the Church, no one is a stranger, no one is excluded, no one is distant."[75] Messages of greeting were then sent to many categories of people: heads of governments, intellectuals and scientists, artists, women, the poor, the sick, youth, all read in French by cardinals. In conclusion Archbishop Felici read an

---

[74] *AS* IV, 7, 654–62.
[75] Ibid., 868–71.

Apostolic Letter, *In Spirito Sancto*, in which the Pope declared the Council concluded, enjoining that "everything the Council decreed be religiously and devoutly observed by all the faithful."[76] His final dismissal was "In the Name of our Lord Jesus Christ, go in peace," to which all answered "*Deo Gratias*."

---

[76]Ibid., 885.

8

Why was the Council
so important?

What then had really been accomplished by the Council?

Pope John XXIII had sought, in his language of *ressourcement* and *aggiornamento*, that the Church should regain access to its deepest sources and that it should join the world people actually lived in. Even as it had begun, Cardinal Léger of Montreal had said: "To grasp fully what will happen at the next Council, it is necessary to consider it in terms of the modern world." In the face of a changing world, the Canadian prelate predicted: "The Council will affirm that it is the will of the Church to meet new needs so that it may fulfill its mission of salvation."[1] As the Council's effects spread through the Church, one could now measure how far Pope John's vision had been fulfilled.

To understand those sources, one had to look back into the historical experience of the Church, seeing what had been lost, what had been gained in its growth. While it seemed in many ways that the whole public face of the Church was changed, this was not the first time such a thing had happened. Far greater changes had occurred several times in our history, some of which had meant actual disfigurement. The return to sources meant that much had to be restored.

Christians of the earliest centuries had a very distinctive sense of the meaning of their community of faith and its life. For them their

---

[1]Quoted in an *America magazine* editorial, "The World and the Council," 20 September 1962, reprinted as an archived article, 23 October 2012.

community itself was the effective sign—that is, a sign that actually brings about what it signifies—of God's presence and action in the world: what we would call a sacrament, though that was a word they did not use. Even prior to this sense of the community, they understood that the primary sign of God's presence and action in human life and history was Christ himself, the Word become flesh, Son of God incarnate. The Christian communion was sign of God's presence and action in the world because its life of faith revealed, to all the rest of the world that did not share it, that the Kingdom of God was already present among them. This meant that every aspect of the Christians' life, individually and corporately, was sign in this sense. Faith in God's presence and action permeated all they did. It was their vocation to manifest it in everything. The Pauline Epistles expressed this in the image of the Church as Body of Christ.

They had, of course, particular moments and practices in their lives that specially manifested God's presence and action among them, as primarily the Eucharist, the sharing of Christ's Body and Blood as food and drink that they habitually practiced whenever they met together as an assembly. But this was not thought of in terms of its being separate from the rest of the actions of their life, but rather as a sign of what the rest of their life actually meant.

Above all, they did not think of themselves as having periods of time that were irrelevant to their life as witnesses of faith, or contrary to it. They were a holy people, "the saints," always witnesses, whatever they were doing, to this presence and action of God in the world, yet conscious of themselves as sinners. Their attitude can be summed up as one of *sacramentality* (i.e., a sense that their life was "sacrament," even though the term "sacrament" is itself a later coinage).[2]

As time went on, this understanding of the whole of life as witness of faith faded. Being a member of the Christian community was no longer a constant risk of life itself and counter to the culture

---

[2]For this expression and the discussion of the progression, over a long range of the Church's history, from sacramentality to ritualism, and, with the Council, an effort to recover the outlook of sacramentality, I am indebted to Raymond Vaillancourt, *Toward a Renewal of Sacramental Theology* (Collegeville, MN: The Liturgical Press, 1979; a translation by Matthew J. O'Connell of *Vers un renouveau de la theologie sacramentaire*), 11–27.

of the society the Christians lived in, but instead an easy way of being a member of the general culture and of getting ahead in the world. Other things then seemed equally or more important, and the religious or faith-charged moments of life were understood as being something different from the rest. "Going to church" took the place of "being Church" (faith community, living its witness in all things). Hence, the particular moments or rituals of that part of life that was set apart as "in church" came to be explained and understood as "sacraments": ritual procedures that were the signs, as distinct from other elements of people's lives, of God's presence and action in the world.

This was a gradual process, but by some time in the Middle Ages (say, quite arbitrarily, by 1000 A.D.) the concept of *sacramental rite*, an isolated moment in the person's or community's life that carried the burden of religious expression, took the place of that earlier sense of the sacramentality of the whole of the Church's life of faith. The rest of life was about other things, and religion was now about these ritual actions that took place in church. The familiar definitions of sacraments, their matter and form, etc., accommodated themselves to this outlook. These particular actions were sacraments; those others were not.

That meant a practical secularization of most of life, a far vaster change in Christian consciousness than any of the things we have seen change in the years since Vatican Council II. But since it happened so gradually it was hardly noticed. There remained a residual sense that religious faith ought, somehow, to occupy more of a person's life than this, and various stratagems were tried to give it that importance in some alternative way. I have always had a suspicion that this is a part of the reason for the strong development of hierarchical ranking in the Christian community, the substitution of submission to authority for the pervasiveness of faith. But we will see that more sharply in another context a bit further on.

It is only in quite recent times that this enormous earlier transformation can now be recognized as such, and that because it has been addressed by Vatican II as a matter of the life of the Church. Some conscious effort (far from complete!) has been made to recover the early Church's sense of itself as sign to the rest of the world, in everything that the faith community is and does, of the presence and action of God in human life and history. We may tend nowadays to spend less of our lives thinking deliberately of faith and religion than many other generations have done, but can yet let our faith conviction permeate our lives, individual and corporate, in such a way that they express the sense of *the Church as sacramental sign*.

As one way of summarizing, then, this long-range view of the Church's history, we may divide it into three periods: (1) a period of *sacramentality*, the sense of the entire life of the Christian faith community as essentially a sign of God's presence and action in the world, to which it was counter-cultural; (2) a period of the *sacramental rite*, replacing that earlier sense of sacramentality of the whole of life, from some time in the Middle Ages; and (3) a new period, initiated in this Council, of an attempted return to sources, in which we find a renewed quest for a sense of *the Church as sacramental sign*.

Accompanying these momentous changes, there was a development of the Church's sense of its role in the world. If we read our way into the dialogue that today begins to take place between Christians and Muslims, we soon hear about one great supposed difference: that for Christians, Church and State are separate, while for Muslims, religious and civil society are one. I have never believed that this dichotomy has been as clear or as absolute, for either community, as that observation indicates, but it is true that in its beginnings, the Islamic faith community, gathered about the Prophet Mohammed in Medina and then in Mecca, did simultaneously govern civil society. The Christian community in contrast was, for its first three centuries, an outsider group, barely if at all tolerated by the Roman imperial State, alien and marginalized to its culture.

For as long as, and to the extent that this was true, the Christian community had neither power in nor responsibility for the State. The Christians were not all, as they are sometimes presented, the poor and enslaved, fringe citizens in Roman society. Prominent people, even some members of the senatorial class and imperial family, came into it from early on. But it was not until the opening years of the fourth century that the weight of the Christian community was such that the power class of the Empire felt they had need of it.

Diocletian (Emperor from 284 A.D., retired 305, died 313) was the last who believed he could get rid of the Christians by a renewal of the sporadic persecution that had been waged against them by authority. He tried harder, massacring more Christians, in the early 300s, than any of his predecessors, having to proceed often against his own trusted officers. He rather proved that it was a losing tactic.

He had also tried to rationalize the administration of the vast territory of the Empire by dividing it into Eastern and Western spheres, he ruling from the East and appointing a secondary Emperor of the West to rule from Rome, each of them with a subordinate who was titled "Caesar."

At Diocletian's retirement, this administrative division resulted in rivalry among these four officers and eventually war for the succession. Constantine, Trier-born son of the Caesar Constantius Chlorus, who had ruled in Northwestern Europe, was the eventual winner. First proclaimed Caesar by the legions in Britain in 306, he established his power in the Province of Gaul in 307, in Germany in 310, crossing the Alps into Italy in 312, and in 313 defeating his Western rival, Maxentius, at the battle of the Milvian Bridge outside Rome.[3]

According to legend, Constantine had a vision, seeing in the sun, as he first crossed the Alps: a luminous cross, with the words "*In hoc signo vinces*" (in this sign you will conquer), and consequently took the Christian cross as the standard of his legions. He subsequently professed himself a Christian. Having defeated Maxentius, Constantine issued, in 313, the Edict of Milan, granting equal rights to Christianity and all other religions in the Empire, much to the outrage of the Emperor of the East, Licinius, who renewed the persecution of Christians in his region. It took 10 more years of war before Constantine defeated Licinius, had him strangled in 323, and set up his new capitol, as ruler of the whole Empire, far in the East at Constantinople, which he caused to be built, beginning in 325, on the site of the ancient city of Byzantium.

Like Diocletian before him, Constantine divided the Empire administratively, leaving weak subordinates to govern in the West, the prelude to the eventual collapse of the Western part of the Empire before the assault of the barbarian invaders.

By the time Constantine had consolidated his hold on the whole Empire, the general religious toleration announced by the Edict of Milan had receded to the point that the old polytheistic tradition got as little tolerance as Constantine could manage to give it, and

---

[3]I won't attempt to footnote all this history, on which I am not an authority. A helpful treatment of the whole context can be found in Timothy David Barnes, *The New Empire of Diocletian and Constantine* (Cambridge, MA: Harvard University Press, 1982).

Christianity was to be the official religion of the State. The Christianity of the Empire, however, was to be at the service of the State, a pillar of public order and support for the Emperor, who did not himself take the trouble to be baptized until on his deathbed in 337. His new capital, Byzantium changing its name to Constantinople, the "new Rome," got a Patriarch of its own, claiming foundation by the Apostle Andrew. While Constantine built sumptuous basilicas in Rome at the tombs of the Apostles Peter and Paul, he paid little enough regard to the Bishop of Rome. In 325, the same year he began the building of Constantinople, he convened all the bishops who could conveniently be assembled (i.e., mostly those from the Eastern parts of the Empire) to his summer palace at Nicaea for what became known as the First Ecumenical Council. The Emperor presided, not in a church but in the audience hall of his palace, and had no hesitation about telling the bishops what they should decide.

All this made a tremendous difference in what it meant to be a Christian. Where before it had been risk, something one undertook only out of deep conviction, and which involved everything in one's life, now it was the smart thing to do, one of the conditions of worldly advancement. The Emperor had need of the bishops and the community they could vouch for. The bishops understood that they had attained their position of privilege for reasons other than solely for the advancement of Christian faith, but chose nonetheless to give unqualified adulation to the Emperor and treat him and his intervention on their behalf as the direct act of God, while giving him the assent and moral support he sought from them. It was politic.[4]

We can describe this as the Constantinian order in the Church. Church and State were to be two parallel bodies, reflective of one another: the State commanded the obedience of the subjects, the Church supported its demands and provided the moral context within which the State would act. The administrative structures of the Roman State, such as dioceses and vicariates, were exactly duplicated in the Church, and remain even now.

---

[4]The obsequious treatment of Constantine by the bishops of his time shows clearly in *The Ecclesiastical History* by his contemporary and servant, Eusebius, Bishop of Caesarea, of which the most current translation is by C. F. Cruse, New Updated Edition (Peabody, MA: Hendrickson Publishers, 1998).

The *role* of the Church was thus to be the *paradigm to the State*. For more than a thousand years, this *paradigmatic role of the Church*, the Constantinian pattern, remained the norm, and in some odd places we find vestiges of it even today. The Anglican Church, for instance, still has its bishops appointed by royal decree, though actually the choice of the Prime Minister. Acts of State, particularly the ceremonial ones like the coronation of monarchs or royal weddings and funerals, are done under its aegis, even though its actual power in civil matters is as much reduced to figurehead as that of the monarchy itself.

Eventually Constantine himself overstepped, and in his assumption that he was entitled to dictate to the bishops, he became sponsor of the Arian heresy (denial of the divinity of Christ). It was the Church in the West, in regions where the Emperor's influence was weaker, that mounted the principal resistance to this heterodox teaching, to the outrage of Constantine and his successors. Bishops more directly under imperial control tended to conform, but as the Western Church and its papal leadership took up the slack of providing order and stability in the city of Rome and in Italy through the time of barbarian incursions, the rivalries of Emperor and Pope for control over each other—caesaro-papism and papalo-caesarism—became a feature of the normative condition of things. This had eventually, after much tragic conflict, its political advantage for Western culture, as the ability of the community to play off one authority against the other taught us all to keep both authorities accountable to the rest of us.[5]

The conflicts of Church and Empire, Church and State, brought about an incidental change of empires, as papal interventions, independent of the Emperor in Constantinople, established the Carolingian Empire and later the Holy Roman Empire of the German Nation. Emperors made and broke popes in the tenth and eleventh centuries, but the popes demonstrated, in the twelfth and thirteenth centuries, their ability to depose or otherwise control emperors and

---

[5]The Eastern Church, of course, had a different experience. Church and Empire clashed at times, but habitually resolved their quarrels. Church tended eventually to identify with ethnicity, and expected that emperors or their successor authorities in the state would, among other things, have decisive influence on the choice of bishops. This, under the name of Lay Investiture, was the very crux of the conflict between popes and emperors in the West.

kings.[6] And then, with the Holy Roman Empire reduced to a wreck of itself, fortunes were reversed. The kings of France and, to a less extent, of England, were able to bring the Church and the popes to heel. The ability of the Church to exercise powers parallel to and paradigmatic of the State was made more and more a shadow of what had once been until, in the era of Napoleon, it was evident that the paradigmatic role of the Church was at an end.

However much the Constantinian order may have compromised the very faith of the Church throughout its long course, the bishops and other authorities who had grown so used to it saw its demise as a sad event; the deprivation of their accustomed institutional position. They instituted a rear-guard action to preserve as much of the old order as they could. If the Church could no longer parallel all the powers of the State, they would preserve and institutionalize those they could, most especially their control of *marriage*, of *education* and of *the caring services of society* (hospitals, charity, etc.) As a substitute for the no longer feasible paradigmatic role, we can describe this as a PRAGMATIC ROLE OF THE CHURCH.

It was heavily contested by the power of the State, and always exercised with regret for the paradigmatic role that had been lost; both Church and State authorities saw it as second best. We can see it in what Germans call *Kultur-politik*, the administration of these cultural areas of family, school, and welfare, with Church and State competing for control. Especially the nineteenth-century *Kulturkampf* was a concerted effort of the Bismarckian State to wrest control of these functions from the churches, particularly from the Catholic Church.[7] We can see it as well in Nazi campaigns against the churches, in the repressive anti-church activities of the Communist states, and even in a good deal of current American policy of creating obstacles to Church control over schools or hospitals.

---

[6]The best commentary on the growth of papal power and its contests with medieval empire continue to be those of Walter Ullmann (1910–83), among them *The Carolingian Renaissance and the Idea of Kingship* (London: Methuen, 1969); *The Growth of Papal Government in the Middle Ages: A Study in the Ideological Relation of Clerical to Lay Power* (London: Methuen, 1955; 2nd edn, 1962); *Law and Jurisdiction in the Middle Ages* (London: Variorum Reprints, 1988); and *Medieval Papalism: The Political Theories of Medieval Canonists* (London: Methuen, 1945).

[7]For a recent treatment, see Ronald J. Ross, *The Failure of Bismarck's Kulturkampf: Catholicism and State Power in Imperial Germany, 1871-1887* (Washington, DC: Catholic University of America Press, 1998).

What substitute remains to us if these two long-traditional models for the Church's role in society, paradigmatic and pragmatic, have both so failed? If, again, we look to the original experience of Christian community in the early centuries, we will not find it useful or historically true to pretend we live in a time other than our own, when Christians were without a recognized role or responsibility in society. But we can usefully look to the way in which their faith convictions as such, the living out of their faith, rather than institutionalized power, determined the role of Christian community in society.

If our emphasis as Church were consistently on the building up of active faith commitment, that is, basically catechetical, we could expect the presence of a Christian community to influence, in organic and pervasive ways, the free corporate decisions of the society. A useful descriptive term for such a manner of Church activity in society's concern is the mathematical figure of the *parabola*, the plane curve generated by a point moving so that its distance from a fixed point is equal to its distance from a fixed line, the curve widening out between parallel lines without ever touching them. Thus, our *third* model of the Church's activity in society is the PARABOLIC ROLE OF THE CHURCH.[8]

Let us not even pretend that such a procedure is accomplished fact in the Church of our own time, but it was the aspiration of the Second Vatican Council.

That there is a hankering still, for the full Constantinian paradigmatic model can be seen in a couple of extraordinarily instructive episodes of recent history.

Since the publication in the 1960s of Rolf Hochhuth's play, *Der Stellvertreter* ("The Deputy," or "The Vicar [of Christ]"), the complaint has frequently been made that Pope Pius XII, during World War II, failed to act decisively enough against the Nazi Holocaust of the Jews. Much has been said and written for and against this charge. We can properly ask: where were the Catholics of Germany

---

[8]These terms for the roles of Church in society—*paradigmatic* for the Constantinian model, *pragmatic* for the familiar fall-back position, *parabolic* for the more faithful model recommended here—are not my own, but come from a teacher I felt privileged to hear, Argentinian Methodist Professor Jose Miguez-Bonino, when I was in graduate studies at Union Theological Seminary in the late 1960s. Miguez-Bonino uses them extensively in his many works, but I have reflected on them over so many years as to have made my own use of them.

that they needed to be ordered by the Pope to resist the Holocaust? Was their faith not internalized enough to lead them to this without a papal order?

During the Vietnam war, Catholics had a large role in the anti-war movement in the United States, and many of them complained that the Catholic bishops of the United States did not plainly condemn the war as unjust, and prohibit participation in it or payment of taxes that would be spent in prosecuting it. Had the bishops done that, quite probably they might have ended the war. Simultaneously they would have brought down to ruin the democratic structure of the United States with its separation of Church and State. Given the dire consequences of any such action, we can again ask: where were the consciences of US Catholics? Could they not reject an unjust war without the bishops commanding them to do so?[9]

At issue in both these instances, of course, is the question of instrumental use of the structures of Church, in one case by the more "traditionalist," in the other by the more "progressive" elements of the Church. Even where Christian conscience has immediate responsibility to act, as in these cases, we need to question the use of the institution as instrument of power.

We have seen, then, three models of the Church's sense of its role in the world, once again reflecting an enormous range of change in

---

[9]Another fascinating instance of the enduring Constantinian concept of Church-State interdependence is chronicled in David Steele's lucid account of the church role in the 1989–90 transition in East Germany: "At the Front Lines of the Revolution: East Germany's Churches Give Sanctuary and Succor to the Purveyors of Change," in Douglas Johnston and Cynthia Sampson (eds), *Religion, the Missing Dimension of Statecraft* (New York: Oxford University Press, 1994), pp. 199–52. The Evangelische Kirche in Germany had already experienced Nazi efforts to control it as a State Church and established the Confessing Church as an antidote. Faced with Communist determination to make the Church an instrument for its own purposes, the German Protestants crafted a repertory of fine distinctions ranging from the "church *within* socialism" to a "church *for* socialism," to a concept of church as "guardian office" or voice of conscience against abuse of power by the state, to a "church for others" that would focus on support for disenfranchised individuals, and a "critical solidarity" of church with state. This latter was still unacceptable to the state, because it seemed to imply that socialism could somehow be improved. *Op. Cit.*, p. 123, with footnotes 24 and 25, pp. 145f. Fascinating, too, in this regard is Steele's concluding discussion of the relation of Church, as spiritual force and institutional structure, both to the East German state authority and to the largely unchurched public that demanded a revolutionary change of regime, ibid., pp. 139–43.

the Church's self-understanding over the course of its history: (1) the *paradigmatic* role of the long Constantinian era; (2) the *pragmatic* role that sought to supply for the failure of the Constantinian system; (3) the *parabolic* role, based on early Church experience and now simply a hope.

There is another way we can look at the entire course of the Church's history and realize that there have been losses in the course of it. This is in the way the Church, or its leadership, looked on its own members.

We have heard a great deal, since the Council, something that seemed a new idea to us, simply because we had not been hearing of it, that "the Church" is the entire community of faith, with all its members, not merely the clergy or hierarchy but the entire People of God. That, along with the collegial structure of the Church, was one of the most central teachings of the Council.

It is anomalous that this should be a new idea for us, since this is one of the most fundamental teachings of the New Testament, but we continue to need reminding of it. Our press and media have generally not caught on to this yet, except occasionally. When reporters want to know "What has the Church to say about . . ." whatever issue, they still understand it to mean what the bishops have to say on it, or what is in a papal document. It seldom occurs to them yet to ask, in any other form, what is the belief of the Church community on the subject (unless, of course, they are anxious to set up a conflict between official teaching and lay response), or what "the faith" accepted (on principle) by the community has to teach about it.

It is the history of this inclination to think of "the Church" as meaning only or primarily its hierarchical leadership that we will examine in this last excursion through the full two-millenia experience of the Christian community.

The first eight centuries of Christian experiences saw the development of radically new forms, as we saw in discussing the effects of the Constantinian revolution, but in the one respect that will now most interest us, there was a consistency through this whole span of time: the Christian community, centered then on the Mediterranean countries, thought of itself as good people, the focus of God's action in the world, "the saints," happy to be members of the community.

This community, under the pressure of having to resist the doctrinal divisiveness of early heresies, had acquired its hierarchical order: the local church of each city organized under the monarchical government of its bishop. And it had cultivated unity of faith and communion among its bishops and their local churches by emphasizing links of the local communities with "apostolic sees" ("sees" in the sense of seats, or offices of authority), those that could claim foundation by an Apostle: Jerusalem, from which the whole mission of the apostles had gone forth; Antioch, associated with the mission of St Peter; Alexandria, associated (strictly mythically) with St Mark; and Rome, missionized by both St Peter and St Paul. These were the seats of Patriarchs. And when it seemed important to make Constantinople a patriarchal See because of Constantine's establishment of the city as his capital (the "new Rome"), the story was told of the foundation of a Christian community in ancient Byzantium by St Andrew, brother of St Peter and therefore having great seniority among the apostles, making it, too, an apostolic see.

This Mediterranean Church had its shocks: notably the barbarian conquest of the Western part of the Roman Empire, both on the Northern and the Southern shores of the Mediterranean; the poor performance, in terms of witnessing to Christian faith, of the Eastern Empire in its acceptance of unvarnished authoritarianism, and a broad alienation of important segments of its population, which exhibited itself partly in doctrinal divisions and heresies; and finally the loss, mainly because of disillusion with Christian performance, of the Middle Eastern and North African regions of the Christian world and, for many centuries, large parts of Spain, to the new faith of Islam. But by and large, the conviction remained that the Christian community of faith was a world of salvation to which it was good to belong, and in which all had a role.

This sense of the basically holy character of the community ran into a far more fundamental disruption with the conversion of the "barbarian" peoples of Western Europe North of the Alps. I've put an arbitrary date on this of the eighth century. In fact, the process was necessarily more gradual than that.

A radically new thing happened, from the eighth and into the sixteenth centuries, when Christianity crossed the Alps. The Northern "barbarians" were converted to Christianity by a different process than the Mediterranean peoples, not the evangelization from within the community that had characterized the early Church, but instead the conversion of whole peoples from the top down, by decision of their kings.

There had been some of this already, of course, as the Roman imperial system made Christianity its official religion and put anyone who didn't conform at a civil disadvantage in the Empire. But those who had joined the Church earlier and more clearly out of conviction had set the basic tone of Mediterranean Christianity. There had been Christianity North of the Alps earlier too, of course, especially in the Roman Province of Gaul (France and much of Belgium), where the early bishops had been active in opposing the Arian inclinations of the emperors directly after Constantine. Some of the earlier "barbarians" (as we call the horse-borne nomadic invading tribes pouring in from the Eurasian steppes and beyond), like the Lombards and Goths, had become Christian as well, feeling themselves successors to Roman rule, and had brought a wave of Arianism into Italy that was ended only with a short-lived Byzantine reconquest of Italy in the sixth century, when the Eastern Empire was again safely Orthodox. The rapid collapse of that renewed Byzantine hold had left a new instability in the city of Rome and increasingly in more of Italy. And it was because of this that the Popes had taken responsibility for providing order in civil society, and the papal court in Rome had become royal—even imperial—in its trappings.

It was this picture of Christianity that the new "barbarian" powers of Northern Europe encountered when their ambassadors came to Rome, and it was against this background that the Frankish King Chlodwig decided (on his wife Chlotilde's urging) to become Christian himself and mandate the baptism of all his subjects. A similar pattern followed with the conversion of other Germanic and barbarian tribes. The decision was the king's, and a people that had accepted baptism on his *fiat* had to be told afterwards what that was all about.[10]

---

[10]An excellent discussion of this period is given in James C. Russell, *The Germanization of Early Medieval Christianity: A Sociohistorical Approach to Religious Transformation* (Oxford: Oxford University Press, 1994). Russell approaches this from the perspective of Germanic influence on the received Christian faith, emphasizing that the fealty of the tribal warriors to their victorious chieftain, as a measure of their honor, took the place of devotion to a suffering, self-sacrificing Christ. This present paper looks at the same phenomena from the other side: the transformation wrought in the Germanic societies and culture by the Christian missionary effort. Russell, though, in his Preface, makes the observation that the insistence of the LeFebvre disciples on pre-conciliar forms of Church is actually a reversion to that Germanicized culture.

For these kings and their ambassadors, Rome, with its papal court, was the model not only of Christianity but also of culture and civilization. The way to arrange the etiquette of their own courts was in imitation of the papal court. Diplomatic receptions at the court of the Pope took place, of course, in church, and the great public occasions were celebrations of the liturgy of the Mass with all the trappings of a court. Ambassadorial reports contained every detail they could glean of the procedures of these occasions, and our liturgy is marked by it to this day.

Clothing, for instance. Our Mass vestments for the priest are, today, the alb (a long white tunic, the *vestimentum album* which was the staple of late Roman formal dress), a stole (the one element that was from the start an insignia of priestly rank), and a chasuble, the large outer garment in the liturgical color of the day.

This latter was the formal attire (though the liturgical colors are a much later invention) of a gentleman from the fourth century on, the replacement of what had been the *toga* for the ancient Romans. The Roman name for it was *casula*, literally "little house." In its original form, it was a large full-length semicircle of material. It could either be set on the shoulders, hanging open in front (in this form it is the "cope," which we may still occasionally see in church) or be sewn down the front (with an opening for the head), in which case it formed a large cloth cone. To wear it, you had to pull the sides up on your arms so that, like the ancient *toga*, it formed horizontal folds across the body.[11]

The priest, or the Pope, was not the only person so attired. Instead, this was the formal dress of every gentleman present at this Mass which was, effectively, a diplomatic reception at the papal court. We could describe it as a sixth-century tuxedo. But when it was imitated in Northern Europe for Mass at the courts of the Germanic and Frankish kings, it became the priest's vestments, with a supposition that there must be something holy about such garments.

---

[11] This bell-shaped garment, *paenula* in secular usage but called *planeta* in the early liturgical citations, had practically replaced the older *toga* in late imperial times. A good account is in Fr Josef Jungmann, S.J., *The Mass of the Roman Rite: Its Origins and Development*, 2 volumes, trans. Francis A. Brunner, C.S.S.R., 1950, published by Benziger; replica edition published 1986 by Four Courts Press, Dublin; the German original *Missarum Sollemnia*, the revised edition of 1949, published by Herder Verlag, Vienna, vol. I, pp. 276-f.

With the modifications in its shape that have come with time, it remains so.

Imitation of what the ambassadors saw, and heard, at Rome was so much the standard of good usage that other features were all avidly imitated. Incense, for instance, known as symbol of prayer in some texts of the Hebrew Scriptures, was carried before the Pope in procession, as it was before other high-ranking Roman officials, to protect them from the smell of the lower-class multitudes. (The ancient Roman system had been insistent on baths for everyone, with the aqueduct an essential feature of all Roman infrastructure and the public baths the main center of entertainment and social life for the multitudes. But the system had broken down, the aqueducts didn't work anymore, and Roman high society had not gotten used to the smell of poor people.) In the Northern kingdoms, the incense was imitated from Rome, but with the supposition that it was a strictly ritual usage. So the altar, the crucifix, the book of the gospels and all the paraphernalia of the ceremony had to be incensed.

Most important of all, the language of liturgy had to be the language of the Roman court. Latin, in fact, became the international learned language of scholarship and record. In liturgy, it was seen as the right language because it was used for the Mass in Rome, where, of course, it was the vernacular. At an earlier stage, the vernacular language of good society in Rome had been Greek, but had become Latin by about the fifth century. Christian scripture and teaching and liturgy had all gone into the vernacular Greek of the Empire instead of remaining in Aramaic or Hebrew, as it had been at the start. The Eastern (Orthodox) Church has always remained faithful to the tradition that liturgy should be in the language people understand—Greek, Arabic, Russian, whatever. But in the West, Latin became established because the right way was the way it was done in Rome, at the court of the Pope.

What is important about all this is what it reveals of suppositions about the people for whom liturgy was celebrated this way in the Northern countries. It was not regarded as necessary that they understand, merely that they be impressed.

A new faith was taught to them, in many cases even imposed upon them. The suppositions of Mediterranean Christianity, that the community of faith was made up of beloved, redeemed people of God, saints (however weak), were not the suppositions taught North of the Alps. Instead, people were told that they were barbarians, unfit, unworthy to receive the gifts of faith and grace put before them, that they were full of evil inclinations and actions, devil's fodder, deserving of damnation. What was required of them was repentance, contrition, acceptance of their lowly state, recognition of their unworthiness.

Sin and repentance, of course, were familiar themes that had been understood in the happier "communion of saints" from the beginning of Christianity, but this was different. This was a radical supposition of the unworthiness of the congregation: a culture of guilt.

It manifested itself in striking ways. Reception of communion became a fearful thing, incurring danger of condemnation for eating and drinking the Body and Blood of Christ unworthily. Consequently communion became the exceptional thing, something people did only once a year, and that only because they were commanded that they must make their "Easter communion" that once. Confession of sins was a pre-condition for this annual approach to the sacrament. It seemed the practical assumption that it was the normal condition of people to be in mortal sin, and that they could get out of it only briefly, just long enough to receive their Easter communion before falling again.

The prayer formulas of the Mass began to fill up with what the liturgical historians call "apologies." These were confessions of sin, admission of unworthiness, prayer to avoid condemnation for taking part in the sacred ritual. They were particularly elaborate and lengthy around the offertory part of the Mass, but were used by the celebrating priest and all other participants in the ritual at all points of the Mass: before reading from the Scripture or the Gospel, before blessing anything, most especially before communion (which, for the most part, only the priest himself would receive). The penitential rite at the beginning of the present-day Mass is a remnant of these "apologies."[12] They were once so frequent throughout the Mass that the priest would recite them at the same time as someone else would be reading some other text.

For people so radically unworthy, the priority in life was obedience to their betters, to those less unworthy than themselves. Reverence for authority, unquestioning submission became the norm.

---

[12]The multiple "apologies" caught the special attention of Jungmann, *Op. Cit.*, vol. I, pp. 78–80, where he analyzes the series of these formulae.

The qualifications for hierarchical office tied easily into the breeding requirements for ruling-class status. To be made bishop of Fulda, for instance, a candidate had to show 14 "quarterings," that is, the coats of arms to prove patent of nobility for 14 generations. Few others than clergy attained literacy or were trained in such disciplines as the law. Consequently, civil administration was dependent on clerics to carry out essential tasks. This led to constant power struggles between civil and ecclesiastical authority, with all its potential both for aggrandizement and corruption. The authority claims of clergy escalated constantly, building always on the concept of the unworthiness of those they shepherded.

Such an acceptance of ignorance in the general population, with an assumption that the common people need not understand the symbolic importance and intrinsic holiness of words, gestures, clothing, or practices that were used, meant, over an extended period of time, an invitation to superstition and mystification. That anyone should even seek understanding of the actions and rites of the Church came to seem presumptuous, sign of a weakness of faith. A gulf opened between those who were the custodians of the mysteries and those who were to be their passive recipients.

We may speak of all these features of medieval religion as particular to regions North of the Alps. But the example itself was infectious. The same demeaning self-concept of the Christian community slipped back South to the Mediterranean regions and became characteristic for the generality of the Western Church community.

Throughout this period, we can see people striving to overcome the deficiencies of this system through popular religion, which sometimes lived on holdovers of previous pagan beliefs and practices, but often showed extraordinary penetration into a Christian faith whose meaning was so largely withheld from them. If we look at the art of the medieval period, we find images of the saints that witness to the urgency with which these people, with their supposition of their own unworthiness, aspired to the holiness that seemed denied them. In their fear of actual reception of the Eucharist, they invented what amounted to substitute sacraments for themselves: the "spiritual communion" or the cult of (safely) *looking at* the consecrated elements of the sacrament. Their pilgrimages to places associated with the holy, their consciousness of the needs of the poor, the effort to associate themselves and their gifts with the sacramental proceedings that were so remote from them, are all efforts to supersede the limits that this kind of religion placed on them.

We can sum up the principal distorting landmarks of this self-understanding of the medieval Christian under three principal headings:

1 *the guilt culture;*

2 *authoritarianism;* and

3 *mystification.*

There would be a heavy price to be paid for all of them.

We must carry this reading of things the Church had lost or gained further, from the sixteenth century to Pope John's reform, an *aggiornamento* informed by *ressourcement*: recovery, from the original sources, of what had been lost, in the twentieth.

Cataclysm came in the sixteenth century when, after repeated efforts and demands for reform over several centuries, Western Catholic Christianity found its institutions and practices fundamentally challenged by the Protestant Reformation. The Reformers took aim especially at the mystification elements, which they saw as superstition, and at the authority structures that kept the whole fabric so untouchably in place. They had little sense of the damage and distortion of Christian faith brought about by the guilt culture, and so hardly challenged it at all.

With regard to *mystification*, the Protestant Reformers insisted on vernacular language, and removed all sorts of rituals, vestments, gestures, practices that were assumed to be holy without what they considered appropriate understanding. There was much extremism. Music and color were curtailed, for a while, to a grim degree, though they eventually found their way back in many Protestant denominations. In some of the churches, there was a savage period of iconoclasm, with the destruction of images and cult objects on a massive scale. The drawing away from ritual involved an emphasis on word and text. Bible reading and preaching became the principal vehicles of religious expression. Many things were done to such excess that there had to be a corrective action later, in some denominations delayed until the nineteenth or even the twentieth century, but the reaction against mystification and superstition can in general be regarded as the most successful part of the Protestant Reformation.

When it came to battling the *authoritarianism* of the medieval Catholic system, the Reformers were less successful. They struck during an unfortunately authoritarian period, when the pretensions of civil rulers were at an epochal high. The central authority of the papacy was rejected, and in most of the churches that of the bishops also disappeared. Some Reformers took this step very reluctantly, as they appreciated the long tradition of episcopal order in the Church. Yet most of the Reformation, apart from England, found too much abuse and corruption associated with it.

As the old authority structures were uprooted, though, two distinct countervailing tendencies emerged. On the one hand, the civil authority of princes claimed rights over the Church, which they could assert once there were no bishops or Pope to compete with. The position of the Church of England, where the King was recognized as supreme authority over the Church, is a conspicuous example. All over Protestant Europe, though, princes and kings claimed the right to determine the faith of their subjects, prescribing rite and creed in total detail, to such an extent that " *cujus regio, ejus et religio* " (whoever holds the kingship, his is also the religion) became the accepted formula. A century and a half of endemic religious warfare began. On the other hand, the new ecclesiastical authorities tended to build up structures of loyalty tests that amounted, in many cases, to authoritarianisms more rigid than those they overthrew. The net result was, at least in too many cases, the substitution of a new authoritarianism for the old.

In the eyes of the Catholics of the time, of course, what the Reformers had done (in their rejection of what they saw as superstition) was to lose access to the sacraments of the Church. Their dismissal of episcopal order was seen as a break with the apostolic succession which guaranteed legitimacy in the ministry. In their turning from the magisterial authority of bishops and Pope to the Scriptures, they were felt to have lost the essential key to proper understanding of Christian faith. Feeling was so intense over these issues that, down to very recent times, Catholics and Protestants assumed bad faith in one another's positions on all these matters. Not until we had experienced the worst of the twentieth century, the secular tyrannies and the racist and other intolerances that could be resisted only if all Christians and others of basic decency and good will banded together, did we begin to discover one another as resources and to suspect that the others could, in fact, be acting in good faith.

But it was in the matter of the *guilt culture* that the sixteenth-century Reformation fell most short of its opportunities. A terrifying God of wrath underlay much of their teaching. This infected their efforts to impose discipline in an unruly time as the traditional order dissolved. The supposition of radical sinfulness and, in some areas of Reformed teaching, of a predestination to doom, produced, if anything, a deep intensification of the guilt culture.

The Reformation had only very partial success, then, in meeting the crisis that had engendered it, and in part actually exacerbated it. A Catholic effort at Counter-Reformation, crafted in large part at the Council of Trent (1545–63) and developed over succeeding centuries until it reached its high-water mark at Vatican Council I (1869) and in the earlier twentieth century, had similarly mixed results. Like the distortions that had torn at the fabric of Christian faith and communion from the earlier periods, these remaining or even aggravated lesions festered in the Church, but burst into the open after the testing experiences of the World Wars and other violence and infidelity of that century. Vatican Council II was a concerted effort, in which the bishops and most of the People of God accepted the lead of Pope John XXIII to meet head on the crisis they had produced. It has consequently had importance not only for the Catholic world but for all branches of Christianity.

The guilt culture, so poorly met by the Reformation, is at the heart of what is questioned among contemporary Christians. At times this is seen as, and sometimes it actually is, a rejection of the very concepts of sin and repentance, or of accountability for one's acts, and many traditionalists who sense this react vehemently against any such questioning. As the Christian community struggles with this syndrome, recriminations are still the order of the day, within and between denominational traditions. This book speaks of a crisis of confidence within the Catholic Church. If one looks about, it is hard to see any Christian church that does not have a crisis of confidence. It is perhaps especially in this area that those of us who make an effort at faithfulness to the Good News of Christ need to work for responsible reconciliation.

The whole issue is worked out against a renewed background of challenge, often rude challenge, to whatever appears to be authoritarianism in any of the various churches, made more urgent now by the indifferent success in this direction of the sixteenth-century Reformation effort. Here too we run into excess as well as timidity and outright obduracy. We are left the task, before we can expect the Church to regain its stability, of studying the roots of order and accountability in the community of faith.

As had the Reformers of the sixteenth century, the Council addressed the mystification element first. Catholic practice had, in fact, made its effort to crop out superstitions during the Counter-Reformation. Now, however, the liturgical reform initiated by Vatican II gave new access to the basic sacramental expressions of the Church's life of faith and the chance of a deepened understanding of them. Liturgy was made comprehensible with the shift to vernacular languages, the readings made far more representative of the breadth of the Scripture. The Constitution on Revelation, with its renewed understanding of the revelation of God and its relation to Scripture and the tradition of the Church's teaching, complemented that greatly increased exposure of Catholic people to the scriptural tradition. A real effort to improve the quality of preaching, if successful, would open up a renewed understanding of the basics of faith. Word and sacrament, so long separated into the realms of Protestantism and Catholicism, could both take their place now in people's habits and expectations of worship.

The separation of sacramentality from rest of life, a debasement of liturgy as old as the importation of Roman ceremonial and Latin language into the Carolingian Frankish kingdom, could now be addressed. Restoration here would be a slow and gradual work. The shame culture that had characterized the Church as its message was preached North of the Alps had already been partly addressed by Pius X's call for more frequent communion at the beginning of the century, but now a restored liturgy would constitute its own invitation. This, along with the recognition of religious freedom and the primacy of conscience, could now peel back the age-old reduction of Christian religion to its usefulness to the state, the great obstruction that had existed since the time of Constantine to any understanding of the whole of the person's life and that of the community as witness to Christ.

The fresh view of the Church as constituted by the People of God addressed the deep wounds of clericalism, which had afflicted the Church throughout the time when power and submission had been its characteristics. A restoration of collegial governance in the Church would also work in that direction, making the core leadership of the Church aware of what was going on in its many parts and breaking the concentration of power in the hands of an insular Curia. Resistance had already been seen here, even as the Council proceeded, since the rules for synodal meetings had by now been drawn in terms that would make them subordinate to the Curia in every way.

In addressing the great crimes of Christian history, the Council had done monumental work. His experience of Jewish suffering during World War II had been a principal motivator for John XXIII in calling the Council. The same Cardinal Bea who would be his principal assistant in doing that work in the Council would promote the healing of relations with all those other Christians, the Orthodox and Protestants whom Catholics had treated as discarded members for centuries but who were their fellows in faith.

That is to give only a sampler of accomplishments the Council brought to a Church which the centuries had disfigured in so many ways. Released from constraints on their life as a communion in Christ, the entire Church had sought its restoration in profound return to the ways of Jesus. Subsequent years would show how well it had succeeded.

9

The crisis begins to set in

We've seen a great deal of distortion of purpose and mission in our look through the history of the Church, leading to two great previous crises in the eleventh and sixteenth centuries, and rather a terrible state of paralysis in the Church of the nineteenth century after the French Revolution. For all this, Catholic practice and the recruitment of clergy persisted strongly, and the grand accomplishments of the Second Vatican Council, though far from perfect, had managed to address to a remarkable extent the worst of the major self-inflicted wounds of the Church. The sense of crisis we experience now is consequently something that has developed since the Council, and has much to do with its implementation.

Reception of the Council in most of the Catholic world took an exuberantly positive form. The exuberance itself, however, would create certain problems. People who were anti-change, and there were many of those even beyond the hard-bitten but minuscule opposition within the Council, found plenty of examples of excess.

Liturgy made for the first concrete experiences Catholics had of what had changed with the Council. Though Pope Paul had begun saying Mass in Italian in Roman parishes as early as March, 1965, even before the final period of the Council's sessions,[1] it took some years before approved translations were ready in the various vernacular languages.

I can recall my own experience in Germany, after my 1963 ordination, when certain of the direct addresses to the congregation, as well as the readings, began to be spoken in German. It loved to intone: "*Sieht das Lamb Gottes. Sieht der hinweg nimmt die Sünden der Welt.*" The

---

[1] Cf. *supra*, Chapter 7, 2.

French as well as the Germans authorized the readings in vernacular, but the English and Americans did not. As I made my way back to the United States on the liner Queen Elizabeth in the summer of 1964, the ship having stops both in Southampton and in Le Havre, I would do the readings for the morning congregations first in French, followed by English translation. Yet when, in Spring of 1965, the American bishops authorized the readings in English, I went out one Sunday from my Jesuit Tertianship in Connecticut to say Sunday Mass in a parish I had not visited before. The Pastor told me before Mass that there was something of great importance to be announced at the Mass, so I was to go to the chair after the Gospel and let him do the speaking. He rose to announce to his congregation: "Next week, everything is going to be confused. I'm going to be confused. You're going to be confused. I won't like it. You won't like it. But they tell us we must do the readings of the Mass in English, and we'll just have to put up with it."

During the time I returned to teaching in Jamaica, 1965–67, first permission for the use of English vernacular for the entire Mass was granted, as an experiment, to two areas, the Antilles conference of bishops and the Philippines, before it would be extended to other English-speaking countries. I was invited by Monsignor Frederick McManus, major figure in the composition of the Council's Constitution on the Liturgy and, since 1963, founding member of the International Committee on English in the Liturgy, to take part, with a few others, in preparing the translations of the Ordinary of the Mass, particularly the Roman Canon. We were quite clear that its language should be the English that we actually speak, neither archaic nor artificial. We had it ready before 1967 was out and three other, novel, eucharistic prayers came out from Rome and were duly translated.

Not until 1973 were these translations authorized for use in the United States, with Roman approval. But meanwhile some enthusiasts were composing Eucharistic prayers of their own, with little knowledge of the structure. Various others extravagances saw the light: clown performances in the liturgy, and the more conservative were becoming alienated. Many hymns composed for the vernacular liturgy sounded trivial by comparison with the great Latin musical heritage, and here too some performances in church ran to the bizarre. Some disliked having a liturgy that demanded their actual engagement, as in the case of a British Member of Parliament, Catholic and Unionist, who complained to me that he could now no longer get away from the personality of the priest. I well remember a liturgy in Paris, prepared obviously with some care, at which I felt quite estranged. There were three enthusiastic super-stars: celebrant, homilist and leader of song. They seemed to be in competition.

Of course, there was much more than these early impressions of liturgy, the most obvious way that Catholic experience had changed.[2] Some stirrings of discontent began to show, but they were still isolated against a general background sense of liberation and new understanding among Catholics.

Settled opposition, though, was in these early days mostly within the groups of bishops, many of them in curial positions in Rome, who had made up the *Coetus Internationalis Patrum* during the Council. For those who saw the whole 4 years as an aberration, it was a relief to see the foreign bishops, "*questa gente da fuori*," depart. Restoration was now their program, as Cardinal Ottaviani, who still remained in charge of the Doctrinal Congregation, remarked: "You go home, but we remain."[3]

Pope Paul VI himself appeared troubled by this Council he had inherited from his predecessor, Pope John XXIII. Always the faithful admirer of Pius XII, for whom prudence and caution were primary virtues, Paul VI was a humble, even a holy man. When he and the later Cardinal Domenico Tardini served Pius XII for years as his closest consultants, seeing and advising him every day, they both turned down the prospects of being made Cardinal. Carlo Montini became one only under John XXIII, after he had already spent some years as Archbishop of Milan, a post which almost automatically called for a Cardinal. He had responded with the well-known skepticism when John announced the coming Council, doubting whether the "old boy" knew "what a hornet's-nest he has stirred up."[4]

It must be a strange thing for any man to live as Pope, surrounded on all sides by incessant adulation, especially so for this man. John XXIII had managed somehow to live in this atmosphere without losing the sense of his mere humanity, but he had discerned a task that would engross him, to which he dedicated himself. The office was his instrument for meeting the challenges of the Church. Paul VI

---

[2]This is carefully laid out in Mark S. Massa, S.J., *The American Catholic Revolution: How the '60s Changed the Church Forever* (New York: Oxford University Press, 2010), Preface, xi–xvi, and Chapter 1, 1–6.

[3]Quoted by Peter Hebblethwaite, *Paul VI: The First Modern Pope* (New York/Marwah: Paulist Press, 1993), 455.

[4]Cf. *supra*, Chapter 3, 20. Quoted by George Weigel, "Thinking Through Vatican II," *First Things*, June/July 2001.

brought to the office all the devotion he had given to Pius XII and to this new Pope Roncalli and saw it as a sacred trust to bring his Council to a good conclusion, yet his central anxiety was for his office as Pope, its dignity and its prerogatives, complete unavoidably with all that adulation. He had waited to the last moment in the opening year of the Council before making his first intervention, endorsing the early concept of what would become the Pastoral Constitution On the Church in the Modern World.[5]

He agonized over every step of the Council, often crying out with his hesitations as he intervened at critical moments, and he had experienced that foreboding close of the third year of the Council when he was carried grimly out of the basilica on his *sedia gestatoria* to thin applause and the manifest doubts of the Council Fathers.[6] The characteristic tone of the Pope's exhortations in the succeeding years was that of his address to the Council at the Public Session of 18 November 1965, its last year, when he warned against any exaggerated reading of its documents, invoking the term "relativism,"[7] which would be the standard language of doubters in the years to come.

Priests who could not stomach the reforms of the Council, particularly the changes in liturgy, were to be found early. I came to think of them as the nonsurvivors of the Council, and they included one favorite counselor of my own who became terribly bitter and estranged, unable to function any more. A powerful opposition to the Council was soon forming on the Right around the figure of Archbishop Marcel Lefebvre.[8]

---

[5] Cf. *Supra*, Chapter 5, 16.
[6] Cf. *Supra*, Chapter 6, 20.
[7] Cf. *Supra*, Chapter 7, 15.
[8] A considerable literature exists on Archbishop Lefebvre, especially from writers in the Society of Pope Pius X, particularly Ramón Anglés (March 1991). *His Grace Archbishop Marcel Lefebvre (1905-1991) – A short biography by one of his priests* (Society of Saint Pius X March 1991). Archived from the original on 24 August 2011. Also partially available from the official website of the Society of Saint Pius X; also Michael Davies, *Apologia pro Marcel Lefebvre, Volume 1: 1905-1976* (Devon: Augustine Publishing Company, 1980); *Volume 2: 1977-1979* (Devon: Augustine Publishing Company, 1980, 1999); *Volume 3: The Historical Defense of Archbishop Marcel Lefebvre and the Society of Saint Pius X* (Kansas City, MO: Angelus Press, 1999); Bishop Bernard Tissier de Mallerais, *Marcel Lefebvre: The Biography* (Kansas City, MO: Angelus Press, 2004). Other than these biographies by his disciples, there is William D. Dinges, "Marcel Lefebvre," in Catholic University of America. *New Catholic Encyclopedia*, vol. 8 (Jud–Lyo), 2nd edn (Washington, DC: Gale, 2003), 446–9; and Yves Congar, *Challenge to the Church: the case of Archbishop Lefèbvre* (London: Collins, 1977).

Long a missionary of the Holy Ghost Fathers in Africa, where he had been, as bishop, Apostolic Vicar in Dakar, he became, from 1948, Apostolic Delegate to all of French Africa, responsible for choosing bishops for many newly formed dioceses. Close to Pope Pius XII, he had advised him closely during the writing of his Encyclical *Fidei Donum*[9] in 1957.

He was given the choice by the new Pope John XXIII, in 1959, between remaining Apostolic Delegate or becoming Archbishop of Dakar. Choosing the latter, he served as Archbishop until 1962, when, on 26 July, he was elected Superior General of the Holy Ghost Fathers by their Chapter General. His authoritarian administrative style soon alienated the more progressive elements in the order but he remained in that position until September 1968, when a new Chapter General, convened to adapt the order to Vatican II, elected several Moderators for their sessions without including him. He then resigned, saying it had become impossible for him to remain superior of an institute that no long wanted or listened to him.[10]

John XXIII had appointed Lefebve, in 1960, to the Central Preparatory Commission that prepared the preliminary draft documents which were so decisively rejected by the Council. Alarmed at this development, he became a key figure in the *Coetus Internationalis Patrum*, the central group in opposition. Especially offensive to him was the draft On Religious Liberty. It was entirely foreign to this scion of the old monarchist Right that had flourished in France since the French Revolution, polarizing French politics between a Catholicism identified with the Right and an anti-clerical Left. Along with Cardinal Ottaviani, Lefebvre favored an alternative document called "Relations Between Church and State and Religious Tolerance." Once it became evident that Paul VI did not approve that measure but had handed over the drafting of a draft "On Religious Liberty" to the Secretariat for Promoting Christian Unity,[11] the *Coetus* concentrated its efforts on delaying consideration

---

[9]Vatican website, Fidei Domum, On the Present Condition of the Catholic Missions, Especially in Africa, 21 April 1957, vatican.va/holy_father/pius_xii/encyclicals/documents/hf_p-xii_enc_21041957_fidei-donum_en.html. Consulted 30 November 2012.

[10]Tissier de Mallerais, 390.

[11]The well-informed Robert Kaiser reported, for the 23 October 1964 issue of *Time Magazine*, "In interviews with Bea and Frings, Paul VI agreed that the Christian Unity office would bear the major responsibility for revising the two declarations."

of the document by the Council. Yet when on 7 December 1965, in the last moments of the Fourth Period, the Council finally approved and the Pope promulgated the Declaration *Dignitatis Humanae*, Lefebvre, while he was among the small number (70, or 3 percent) who voted against it, signed the document after the signature of the Pope, though some other opponents had refused to sign.[12]

As soon as he resigned as Superior General of the Holy Ghost Fathers, Lefebvre was approached by traditionalist seminarians from the French Seminary in Rome who had been refused the tonsure, traditional *entreé* (until it was abolished in 1973) into the clerical state.[13] They requested that he direct them to a conservative seminary, and after first sending them to the University of Fribourg he decided he would teach these seminarians personally. In 1969, he received the permission of Bishop François Charriere of Fribourg to found a seminary there, which opened with nine students, later moving it in 1971 to Écône, Switzerland. In November, 1970, Bishop Charriere established, on a provisional basis (*ad experimentum*) for 6 years, the International Priestly Society of Saint Pius X (SSPX) as "a pious union."

There was more than this. Lefebvre soon made it clear that, of the Council's teachings, he rejected altogether the concept of ecumenism, choosing rather to favor an exclusive claim to truth for the Catholic Church. Much later he would say, in an address to the United States district of the Society of Saint Pius X: "This spirit of adultery is made clear in the ecumenism instituted by The Secretariat for the Unity of Christians."[14] It was in connection with

---

[12]Lefebvre later tried to challenge that signature of his, saying the document he signed merely indicated his presence at the vote and was not a vote for or against. Yet the paper he signed was not "the relatively unimportant attendance sheet which Lefebvre recalled in his interview," but bore "the title *Declaratio de Libertate Religiosa* (along with the titles of three other documents) at the top," and "(t)he fathers were informed that if they wished to sign one or more documents, but not all of them, they could make a marginal annotation beside their name, specifying which documents they did or did not wish to sign. No such annotation is found beside the names of either Lefebvre or de Castro Mayer, which proves that they were prepared to share in the official promulgation of that Declaration on Religious Liberty which they later publicly rejected." (Brian W. Harrison, "Marcel Lefebve, Signatory to *Dignitatis Humanae*," *Fidelity Magazine*, a Journal of the Wanderer Forum Foundation, 1994).
[13]Luc Gagnon, "The Wanderer Interviews Fr. Aufagnier, SSPX," *The Wanderer*, 18 September 2003.
[14]Address of 19 October 1983.

this that he rejected the principle of religious liberty. "Hence, to accept Religious Liberty was in principle to accept the 'rights of man' within the Church. Now, the Church has always condemned these declarations on the 'rights of man,' which have been made against the authority of God."[15]

He objected on principle to collegiality within the Church, seeing it as a contradiction to papal supremacy. And he wholly rejected replacement of the Tridentine Mass (i.e., the Missal of Pope Pius V) by the Mass of Pope Paul VI.[16] As early as 1974, he denounced the modernist and liberal trends he saw in the reforms being undertaken in the Church.

In 1975, when the 6-year license of the Society of Saint Pius X as a "pious union" expired, a new Bishop of Fribourg stated his intention to withdraw the status. He put this into effect on 6 May 1975, thereby officially dissolving the Society.[17] Pope Paul VI then confirmed this action, writing personally to Lefebvre in June, 1976, but to no avail, though Pope had criticized Lefebvre by name in the Consistory of 24 May 1976, appealing to him and his followers to change their minds.[18] Lefebvre continued regardless.[19]

---

[15]Conference of His Excellency Archbishop Marcel Lefebvre, held on Long Island, New York, 5 November 1983, hosted by SSPXasia.com. These last two citations were long maintained on the website of the Society of Pope Pius V, but are no longer to be found there.

[16]Thomas J. Reese, "Archbishop Lefebvre: Moving Toward Schism?" *America*, 4 June 1988, 573f. "Archbishop Lefebvre is known most widely for his support of the Tridentine liturgy and his attacks on the liturgical changes initiated by Vatican II. But his complaints against Vatican II go far beyond liturgical reforms. He also rejects conciliar developments in collegiality, religious liberty and ecumenism. These are seen by him as corresponding to the Revolution's égalité, liberté, and fraternité." Pete Vere, "My Journey Out of the Lefebvre Schism," *Envoy Magazine*, 4 March 2001, "However, Lefebvre's continued use of the Tridentine Mass eventually became an issue with the Vatican."

[17]Davies, vol. I (1980), ch. 4, expounds on this whole period in the history of the Society.

[18]Vatican website, vatican.va/holy_father/paul_vi/speeches/1976/documents/hf_p-vi_spe_19760524_concistoro_lt.html, Consistorio Segreta del Santo Padre Paulo VI Per la Nomina di Venti Cardinali, 24 maggio, 1976: "Saepius per Nosmet ipsos, per Nostros adiutores aliosque amicos Reverendissimum Lefebvre monuimus de gravitate ipsius agendi modorum; de illegitimitate praecipuorum eius inceptorum in praesens exstantium; de inanitate ac saepe de falsitate principiorum doctrinalium, quibusille tum suum agendi modum tum sua incepta suffulcire studet; denique de damnis quae exinde Ecclesiae universale oriuntur." Consulted 30 November 2012.

[19]Davies I (1980), ch. 11.

Lefebvre held his first ordination of priests of his Society on 29 June 1976, without the approval of the local Bishop and despite receiving letters from Rome forbidding it. He was then suspended "*a collatione ordinum*," that is, prohibited from ordaining priests. The Prefect of the Congregation for Bishops, Cardinal Sebastiano Baggio, then informed him that, to regularize his position, he required pardon from the Pope. In response, Lefebvre, now in full cry against the Council itself, wrote to the Pope, saying the modernization of the Church was "compromise with the ideas of modern man," originating in a secret agreement between high dignitaries in the Church and senior Freemasons prior to the Council.[20] He received notification, then, that since he had not apologized to the Pope, he was suspended "*a divinis*," that is, could no longer administer any sacrament. Undeterred, Lefebvre continued to say mass regularly and to ordain the students of his seminary.

High officials of the Church appear to have great trouble in exercising discipline over dissidents from the Right, much more than if they are from the liberal left. Pope Paul VI received Lefebvre in audience on 11 September 1976.[21] A month later he wrote again personally to him, repeating the appeal he had made to him in that audience, asking him to accept the documents of the Second Vatican Council in their obvious meaning, the legitimacy of the revised liturgy, the obligatory character of the norms of canon law then in force, and the authority of the diocesan bishops over preaching and administration of the sacraments in their dioceses.[22] That producing no result, the new Pope John Paul II again received Lefebvre in audience 60 days after his own election as Pope in 1978, still without effect.

The situation continued unchanged until 1987, when Archbishop Lefebvre, now 81, announced his intention to consecrate a bishop to carry on his work after his death. This was a new offense, as the consecration of a bishop requires the consent of the Pope, but Vatican efforts to bring about a reconciliation continued unchecked. On 5 May 1988, Cardinal Joseph Ratzinger, then Prefect of the

---

[20]Letter of Mgr. Lefebvre to Pope Paul VI, 17 July 1976, quoted in: Davies I (1980), ch. 12.
[21]Davies I (1980), ch. 14.
[22]Text on the Vatican website, vatican.va/holy_father/paul_vi/letters/1976/documents/hf_p-vi_let_19761011_arc-lefebvre_lt.html, "Pauluis PP. VI, Epistola Marcello Lefebvre, Archiepiscopo-Episcopo Olim Tutelensi." Consulted 3 December 2012.

Congregation for the Doctrine of the Faith and now Pope Benedict XVI, signed an agreement with Lefebvre which permitted him, as sign of regularizing the Society of Saint Pius X, to consecrate one bishop for the Society. Lefebvre, however, reneged on the agreement, declaring that he now felt obliged both to reject it and to consecrate a bishop without the approval of the Pope. Pope John Paul II sent a personal letter, dated 9 June, reminding Lefebvre of the agreement of 5 May, and appealed to him not to proceed with what "would be seen as nothing other than a schismatic act, the theological and canonical consequences of which are known to you."

On 30 June, Lefebvre consecrated not one but four new bishops for his Society, Bernard Tissier de Mallerais, Richard Williamson, Alfonso de Galarreta, and Bernard Fellay, his old comrade in the *Coetus Internationalis Patrum* of the Council, Antônio de Castro Mayer, now Bishop Emeritus of Campos, Brazil as his co-consecrator. Lefebvre's sermon for the consecration was defiant:

> That is why, taking into account the strong will of the present Roman authorities to reduce Tradition to naught, to gather the world to the spirit of Vatican II and the spirit of Assisi [Pope John Paul's interreligious prayer celebration at Assisi in October, 1987], we have preferred to withdraw ourselves and to say that we could not continue. It was not possible. We would have evidently been under the authority of Cardinal Ratzinger, President of the Roman Commission, which would have directed us; we were putting ourselves into his hands, and consequently putting ourselves into the hands of those who wish to draw us into the spirit of the Council and the spirit of Assisi. This was simply not possible.

Excommunication followed on the next day, 1 July 1988, by decree of the Congregation of Bishops, which declared that this was a schismatic act and that all six persons involved, Lefebvre, de Castro Major, and the four new bishops, incurred automatic excommunication. The Pope himself issued an Apostolic Letter, *Ecclesia Dei*, which stated that this was a schismatic act and that all six people directly involved had thereby incurred the automatic excommunication.[23]

---

[23]Vatican website, vatican.va/holy_father/john_paul_ii/motu_proprio/documents/hf_jp-ii_motu-proprio_02071988_ecclesia-dei_en.html, Apostolic Letter, "Ecclesia Dei" of the Supreme Pontiff John Paul II, Given Motu Proprio. Consulted 3 December 2012.

Offers of reconciliation still did not cease. In 2009, long after the death of Archbishop Lefebvre at the age of 85 in 1991, Pope Benedict XVI lifted the excommunications on the four surviving bishops, at their request. Nothing had changed in their position but the Pope declared:

> With this decision I intended to remove an impediment that might have jeopardized the opening of a door to dialogue and thereby to invite the Bishops and the "Society of St Pius X" to rediscover the path to full communion with the Church.[24]

The lifting of the excommunication produced a firestorm of objections for an extrinsic reason. Bishop Richard Williamson, an English "traditionalist," had distinguished himself by his flagrant anti-Semitism and Holocaust denial, describing Jews as "enemies of Christ" and blaming them and Freemasons for contributing to the "changes and corruption" in the Catholic Church.[25] Of all this, the Vatican had apparently taken no notice. Jewish sources took this indulgence toward Williamson as a deliberate insult on the part of the Vatican itself. Frantic apologies and disclaimers followed but the hurt feelings could not be assuaged. In 2010, he was convicted of incitement in a German court in relation to those views, a conviction that was later voided due to formal weaknesses in the original indictment.[26]

Bishop Williamson, however, was not to be restrained, even by the SSPX. For him even he Society was not far enough to the Right. In June of 2012, he demanded, at a conference of the SSPX, that Bishop Bernard Fellay, who since the death of Archbishop Lefebvre in 1991 had led the Society, should be deposed as Superior General. In August, acting independently of the Society, he confirmed some 100 lay people at the Benedictine Monastery of the Holy Cross at Novo Friburgo in Brazil, his visit to Brazil itself unauthorized by the Society.

---

[24]Vatican website, vatican.va/roman_curia/congregations/cbishops/documents/rc_con_cbishops_doc_20090121_remissione-scomunica_en.html, Congregation for Bishops, Decree remitting the Excommunication "Latae Sententiae" of the Bishops of the Society of St Pius V. Consulted 3 December 2012.

[25]*National Catholic Reporter*, 30 March 2001, quoting a letter from Williamson of 3 October 2000.

[26]*Hamburger Abendblatt*, 22 February 2012.

History was repeating itself in imitation of Archbishop Lefebvre's expulsion from the Catholic Church. The South American district superior of the SSPX, Very Reverend Christian Bouchacourt, posted an official letter of complaint on the Society's website and a German website, kreuz.net, saying that because of Williamson's divisive acts, including his refusal to stop publishing his weekly blog, Fellay, as the society's superior, should expel him.

Fellay gave Williamson an ultimatum to take effect on 23 October 2012. On 24 October 2012, a communiqué of the General House of the Society of Saint Pius X confirmed his expulsion, stating that Williamson "was declared excluded from the SSPX by decision of the Superior General and its Council."

Even through 2012, strenuous Vatican efforts to bring about rehabilitation of SSPX continued. In June, Bishop Fellay was offered, in a personal meeting with Cardinal William Levada, Prefect of the Congregation for the Doctrine of the Faith, a Personal Prelature for the Society, similar to that granted to Opus Dei: its own jurisdiction over its members rather than submission to any other leader except the Pope.[27] This was on the provision that they agree to some new "explanations and clarifications" in the "doctrinal difficulties" they had with the Second Vatican Council and the liturgical reforms. Their answer was to delay their response until after a meeting of their General Chapter at Écône in mid-July.[28] By then there was a new Prefect of the CDF, Archbishop Gerhard Müller.[29] In early October, Archbishop Müller still talked hopefully, though the talks had hit an impasse,[30] but by 16 October, Fr Niklaus Pflüger, 1st Assistant General of SSPX, announced that the whole effort had failed.[31]

All efforts were not in vain, but an agreement in the near future is improbable. In both our estimation and that of the Curia, any agreement would be pointless unless we are on the same page about what the Faith really means.

---

[27]*Catholic News Service*, 14 June 2012, "SSPX says doctrinal difficulties could prolong talks with Vatican."

[28]*Whispers in the Loggia*, 14 June 2012, "From SSPX: A Response 'In Reasonable Time.'"

[29]*Catholic News Service*, 25 July 2012, "New Vatican doctrinal chief talks of SSPX, LCWR discussions."

[30]*Catholic News Agency*, 5 October 2012, "Archbishop Muller stresses hope as SSPX talks hit impasse."

[31]*Kirchliche Umschau*, 16 October 2012, "We're back to square one."

Ought we judge, then, that the Lebevrists are altogether removed from reality? Pfügler continues:

> The facts are what they are. The Church everywhere in the world, with some rare exceptions, is undergoing a process of self-destruction, and not just in Europe. In Latin America, for example, things don't seem to be any better. Where the economy is relatively strong, as in Germany, Switzerland, and the United States, the external structures remain. But the loss of the Faith can be seen everywhere. Now, without the Faith, there is no Church. In Germany, the bishops recently sent a clear message: the right to collect taxes from Church members is more important than 120,000 Catholics leaving the Church every year. We are witnessing a march to destruction unseen in history, a rising tide which not even the bishops can stem, using, as they do, tactics devoid of the spirit of Faith. Joseph Ratzinger, as a Council father 50 years ago, spoke of a Church, "*imbued with the spirit of paganism*," which the Council did its part to usher in. I am convinced that this turn of events, on the one hand, will bring the bishops to a more sober frame of mind, and, on the other hand, will leave only the conservatives holding fast, meaning those who quite simply wish to believe as the Church has always believed, and to persevere in their Catholic Faith. With those holding fast, we will no longer need to argue. Agreement in the Faith will soon follow.

He is looking, then, at the same crisis of confidence in the Church by its members that is the subject of this book. Reminded, by his interviewer, that the Church's liberals would see things differently, seeking more reform to ensure the survival of a living Church, he replies:

> I am inventing nothing. I see events and where they lead. Which religious order or diocese has younger members to ensure its future growth, and which ones are dying out? We can observe that decline and dissolution are most apparent in those places where the so-called conciliar reforms are most eagerly followed. I don't deny that, in the arena of public opinion – and on the parish level – the liberal approach is more acceptable. But the Church does not live by social acceptance or by human applause. She derives

her energy from men and women who believe and practice their Faith, who are prepared to renounce worldly pleasures to become priests, monks, or nuns. These latter are conspicuously absent among the liberals, and that is why they now want to receive priestly ordination, but of course without celibacy, without any self-denial. And they naively expect to increase their vocations by lowering the standards!

And so it comes down at last, for him, to celibacy, a valuable gift of service within the Church, but one that, if seen as the very essence of Christian life, becomes a dangerous fixation, at times an exercise in hypocrisy. Fr Puglisi, on behalf of the SSPX, is looking at the same crisis the rest of us see. He has a different formula to meet it, one that is incumbent basically on bishops, and not much related to the "People of God."

This challenge from SSPX represents the extreme of dissidence from the Right. It is not alone. Demand for the Latin Mass, taken as sign of the true faith by many Catholics, has been growing ever since the Council, and definition of doctrine in rigidly formalistic terms has become a common expectation of those Catholics closest to the Protestant Religious Right. Yet from the earliest days after the Council, this kind of dissidence has been met with an indulgence from Church authorities and Roman curial officials that is not shown to more liberal challenges.

The range of such reaction reaches from (1) simple anxiety for the Church such as Pope Paul VI himself always showed, despite his determination to be the Pope of the Council, to (2) suspicion of any change in the accustomed routine of things, which had been the reaction of Pope Pius XII and his curia during the years after World War II, to (3) an understanding of the Church's basic task as rooting out all questioning of authority, the understanding of the *Coetus* during the Council years and their followers since, to (4) this outright rejection of the Council itself and all its works. Up to that last stage, represented by SSPX, the doubters have wanted to profess their acceptance of the Council but argue that it is misinterpreted. Each of these attitudes leads, in varying degrees, to a "Restorationist" view of the Church, a drawing back from the reforming work of the Council.

Meanwhile, a Catholic public that had found itself liberated through the Council began to find unexpected hesitancy on the part of the hierarchy to implement what had been decided, always accompanied by warnings from Pope and Vatican authorities against going too far. Greater expectations had been raised.

In our own time, as we begin the 50-year celebrations of the Council, Pope Benedict XVI has spoken eloquently of the daunting tasks set before it:

> It was a moment of extraordinary expectation. . . . Christianity, which had built and formed the Western world, seemed more and more to be losing its power to shape society. It appeared weary and it looked as if the future would be determined by other spiritual forces. The sense of this loss of the present on the part of Christianity, and of the task following on from that, was well summed up in the word *"aggiornamento"* (updating). Christianity must be in the present if it is to be able to form the future. So that it might once again be a force to shape the future, John XXIII had convoked the Council without indicating to it any specific problems or programmes. This was the greatness and at the same time the difficulty of the task that was set before the ecclesial assembly. . . . The Church, which during the Baroque era was still, in a broad sense, shaping the world, had from the nineteenth century onwards visibly entered into a negative relationship with the modern era, which had only then properly begun. Did it have to remain so? Could the Church not take a positive step into the new era? Behind the vague expression "today's world" lies the question of the relationship with the modern era. . . .

Assessing the success of the Council in meeting this challenge, the Pope acknowledged the great importance of the liturgical reform and the great lessons of ecumenism which had come, for both Protestants and Catholics, from their experience of shared persecution during the Nazi era, and were now "to happen at the level of the whole Church, and to be developed further." Those, I would believe myself, have been major and enduring accomplishments. The reformed liturgy has made it possible for the ordinary Catholic, perhaps for the first time in many centuries, to live his Christian life in a truly sacramental landscape. To be told, before the reforms, that the Eucharist should be front and center in our entire experience of life stretched credibility.

What we were seeing in our experience of the Mass seemed something quite other than living. But that assertion has made sense since. An intelligible Eucharist, shared in a communion of faith, links into the ordinary things of people's live and makes sense of that assertion. Yet this very comprehensibility of the Eucharist has enraged people who lived on the distant majesty of a transcendently incomprehensible mystery. Ecumenical cordiality has waned much in the years since the Council, largely as the result of the Church's preoccupation with the "social issues," but we no longer start from an assumption that the others are not really Christians.

The major steps toward relating to the Church to the modern world, the Pope felt, had not been the Pastoral Constitution on the Church in the Modern World, "but instead in two minor documents, whose importance has only gradually come to light in the context of the reception of the Council. First, there is the *Declaration on Religious Liberty*, which was urgently requested, and also drafted, by the American Bishops in particular."

With developments in philosophical thought and in ways of understanding the modern State, the doctrine of tolerance, as worked out in detail by Pius XII, no longer seemed sufficient. At stake was the freedom to choose and practice religion and the freedom to change it, as fundamental human rights and freedoms. Given its inner foundation, such a concept could not be foreign to the Christian faith, which had come into being claiming that the State could neither decide on the truth nor prescribe any kind of worship. The Christian faith demanded freedom of religious belief and freedom of religious practice in worship, without thereby violating the law of the State in its internal ordering; Christians prayed for the emperor, but did not worship him. To this extent, it can be said that Christianity, at its birth, brought the principle of religious freedom into the world.

The second document that was to prove important for the Church's encounter with the modern age came into being almost by chance and it developed in various phases. I am referring to the *Declaration "Nostra Aetate" on the Relation of the Church to Non-Christian Religions*. At the outset the intention was to draft a declaration on relations between the Church and Judaism, a text that had become intrinsically necessary after the horrors of the

Shoah. Then, following naturally, came a brief indication regarding dialogue and collaboration with the religions, whose spiritual, moral, and socio-cultural values were to be respected, protected and encouraged (ibid., 2). Thus, in a precise and extraordinarily dense document, a theme is opened up whose importance could not be foreseen at the time.[32]

Pope Benedict's insights into the lasting values of the Council, coming all these years later from the able theological adviser to the great Cardinal Frings and colleague of Karl Rahner, portray accurately the lasting legacy of those years, even as he recognizes that these were peripheral issues at the Council itself. What has not happened, though, is an implementation of what we all understood at the time to be the core teachings of the Council: collegial governance in the Church and the understanding of the Church as People of God.

Those basics had been heavily eroded since the time of the Council's conclusion. The regular meetings of a Synod of Bishops had, even from the day Pope Paul VI had proclaimed its ground rule to the Council, 15 September 1965, been fundamentally neutered.[33] The voice of the people was encouraged by the Council's teaching and began to be heard clearly. Yet, as we would see when an organization sprang up under that name and spread widely across the United States and some other countries after the sexual abuse crisis of 2002, it was seen as basically something to be contained and controlled. It was welcome only when leading cheers for the pastors and bishops.

A tremendous shock came to both of those concepts with the publication of the birth control Encyclical, *Humanae Vitae*, Of Human Life, on 25 July 1968. Pope Paul VI had agonized over

---

[32]*L'Osservatore Romano*, publishing, on 19 November 2012, the preface Pope Benedict had written 2 August 2012, for the 16-volume collection of his own writings, Joseph Ratzinger, Gesammelte Schriften, edited by then Bishop of Regensburg Gerhard Ludwig Müller (now prefect of the Congregation for the Doctrine of the Faith), published by the Pope Benedict XVI Institute of Regensburg on 11 October 2012, fiftieth anniversary of the opening of the Second Vatican Council. To be issued also in English.

[33]*Supra*, Chapter VII, 2–3. Vatican website, vatican.va/holy_father/paul_vi/motu_proprio/documents/hf_p-vi_motu-proprio_19650915_apostolica-sollicitudo_en.html; and *Acta Apostolicae Sedis* 57 (1965), 776. Consulted 3 December 2012.

this Encyclical ever since the topic first came up during the Council itself. Whatever one may think of his conclusions, contained in this Encyclical, it was a tragedy for him. The scale of rejection it met in Catholic circles was something not seen before in centuries. He was himself so shaken by it that he never wrote another encyclical on any subject.

The topic was framed in massive concerns about a population explosion. Scientific thinkers and responsible policy planners agreed that the planet's capacity to harbor and feed a population growing in exponential terms could be exceeded, with threats to habitat not only for humanity itself but to all the plant and animal sources that sustained it. We weren't yet thinking of global warming or even of the depletion of the earth's ozone layer, but the perils were already enough to alarm the world. It seemed the traditional concerns about natural law and direct or indirect means of birth control were simply frivolous by comparison. If the Church were to respond to the realities of life, it had to rethink these questions. The old answers were no longer givens.

That concern remains powerfully alive to this day, but 50 years later the terms of debate have changed, as we have seen many developed countries fail to maintain their populations, the rise of an aged population, and in such a country as China, where mandatory abortions were so long maintained to limit births to one per couple, a drastic imbalance in the numbers of males to females.

In the context of his time, Pope John XXIII had set up a commission of six European non-theologians in 1963 to study questions of birth control and population.[34] Oral contraceptives had made their first appearance in 1960, and this commission was to advice the Church on acceptable methods of birth control. It met once in 1963 and twice in 1964, but as the Council was concluding, in 1965, Pope Paul enlarged it to 58 members, among them lay women, married couples, theologians, and bishops, reserving, however, the ultimate decision to himself.[35] A long history of rejection of any kind of

---

[34]William Henry Shannon, "The Papal Commission on Birth Control," in *The lively debate: Response to Humanae vitae* (New York: Sheed & Ward, 1970), 76–104. Robert McClory, *Turning point: The inside story of the Papal Birth Control Commission, and how Humanae Vitae changed the life of Patty Crowley and the future of the church* (New York: Crossroad, 1995).

[35]Cf. *supra*, Chapter 6, 16.

birth control lay behind the study, which Paul VI himself often cited during his first year in office, when many of the Council Fathers expressed readiness to see some change.

Some ambiguity had crept into the discussion with the Encyclical *Casti Connubii* of Pope Pius XI,[36] issued in 1930 in response to the action of the Lambeth Conference that year, which had approved some limited use of birth control for the Anglican community. The Encyclical, while condemning artificial birth control, had given its approval to the rhythm method of avoiding conception. What exactly was disapproved? Was it the limitation of births itself, a refusal to welcome new life, or particular physical apparatus used for that purpose? Were the sexual relations of married couples permissible only for the purpose of having children, or for what other purposes?

Cardinal Suenens, in particular, had questioned "whether moral theology took sufficient account of scientific progress, which can help determine, what is according to nature. I beg you my brothers let us avoid another Galileo affair. One is enough for the Church."[37] Bishops supporting the position included Cardinals Léger and Alfrink, Bishop Josef Reuss (Auxiliary of Mainz), speaking for 145 bishops "from various countries and parts of the world," and Bishop Rudolf Staverman of Sukarnopura, Indonesia.[38]

The pastoral Constitution *Gaudium et Spes*, on the Church in the Modern World, included a section on "Fostering the Nobility of Marriage,"[39] which made reference to a "duty of responsible parenthood," but did not make the determination, still reserved to the Pope of licit or illicit means. The Pope called a fifth and final meeting of the Commission after the close of the Council, enlarged this time to include an executive committee of 16 bishops. This commission issued a majority report, consultative only, proposing that the Pope might use his authority to life the general ban on all forms of contraception for married couples, but a minority number of members opposed this report and issued a parallel report to

---

[36]Vatican website, vatican.va/holy_father/pius_xi/encyclicals/documents/hf_p-xi_enc_31121930_casti-connubii_en.html, Casti Connubii, Encyclical of Pope Pius XI on Christian Marriage, 31 December 1930. Consulted 20 December 2012.

[37]Quoted in Peter Hebblethwaite, *Paul VI* (New York: Paulist Press, 1993), 394.

[38]Cf. *supra*, Chapter 6, 17.

[39]Gaudium et Spes, ##47–52.

the Pope. Two more years would elapse before the Pope issued his encyclical,[40] with a few paragraphs explaining why he did not accept the opinion of the majority report.[41]

What had happened?

It was, in fact, a small faction who opposed the majority recommendation. American Jesuit John Ford was a member of the commission, and had brought with him as assistant Fr Germain Grisez, who at Ford's direction had drafted the minority report, saying the Church should not and could not change the traditional position. Only two other commission members signed it with them, but it said substantially what the Pope had wanted all along. That made them a minority of four in a seventy-six-person commission.

---

[40]Vatican website, vatican.va/holy_father/paul_vi/encyclicals/documents/hf_p-vi_enc_ 25071968_humanae-vitae_en.html, Encyclical Letter Humanae Vitae of the Supreme Pontiff Paul VI On the Regulation of Birth, 25 July 1968. Consulted 20 December 2012.

[41]*Humanae Vitae*, ##5 and 6. To quote them in full: "*Special Studies, 5.* The consciousness of the same responsibility induced Us to confirm and expand the commission set up by Our predecessor Pope John XXIII, of happy memory, in March, 1963. This commission included married couples as well as many experts in the various fields pertinent to these questions. Its task was to examine views and opinions concerning married life, and especially on the correct regulation of births; and it was also to provide the teaching authority of the Church with such evidence as would enable it to give an apt reply in this matter, which not only the faithful but also the rest of the world were waiting for. When the evidence of the experts had been received, as well as the opinions and advice of a considerable number of Our brethren in the episcopate—some of whom sent their views spontaneously, while others were requested by Us to do so—We were in a position to weigh with more precision all the aspects of this complex subject. Hence We are deeply grateful to all those concerned. *The Magisterium's Reply,* 6. However, the conclusions arrived at by the commission could not be considered by Us as definitive and absolutely certain, dispensing Us from the duty of examining personally this serious question. This was all the more necessary because, within the commission itself, there was not complete agreement concerning the moral norms to be proposed, and especially because certain approaches and criteria for a solution to this question had emerged which were at variance with the moral doctrine on marriage constantly taught by the magisterium of the Church. Consequently, now that We have sifted carefully the evidence sent to Us and intently studied the whole matter, as well as prayed constantly to God, We, by virtue of the mandate entrusted to Us by Christ, intend to give Our reply to this series of grave questions."

Much more recently Fr Gerald Slevin has published an analysis[42] of the background papers released by Grisez, including an extensive online biography of Ford[43] that covered his activities and correspondence on the issue. Grisez and Ford were of the opinion that Dominican Fr Henri de Riedmatten of the Vatican's office of Secretariat of State had placed undue pressure on the members of the commission to approve birth control. Their papers, however, revealed the powerful hand of Cardinal Ottaviani controlling the work of Ford and Grisez, and the strong encouragement of Cardinal O'Boyle of Washington. Pope Paul clearly approved in this case the influence of Cardinal Ottaviani.

One other contribution carried considerable weight, a member appointed to the commission who had been unable to come to Rome because he was refused a passport by the Polish government: Archbishop Karol Wojtyla of Kraków,[44] as revealed by George Weigel in his monumental biography Pope John Paul II. The future Pope, generally very positive in his view of marital sexual intercourse as symbol of God who is love, had published a book called *Love and Responsibility* in 1960,[45] and had convened his own diocesan commission to study the same issues as the Papal Commission in 1966. His written advice had strong influence on the eventual encyclical, though Weigel believes his argumentation was not sufficiently used and would have won the Encyclical a more positive reception had it been. This is important inasmuch as Wojtyla, as Pope, would be even more absolute on this teaching than Paul VI himself, even making assent to the Encyclical a litmus test for the appointment of bishops in his time.

The die was cast. In his Encyclical, Pope Paul expressed his own conviction that "an act of mutual love which impairs the capacity to transmit life which God the Creator, through specific laws, has built into it, frustrates His design which constitutes the norm of

---

[42]*National Catholic Reporter*, 23 March 2011, "New birth control commission papers reveal Vatican's hand."

[43]twotlj.org/Ford.html. Consulted 24 December 2012.

[44]This episode is narrated extensively by George Weigel in his *Witness to Hope: The Biography of Pope John Paul II* (New York: HarperCollins Publishers, Inc., 1999), 206–10.

[45]1960 Original in Polish; English translation, Karol Wojtyla, *Love and Responsibility* (London: William Collins Sons & Co., Ltd., 1981).

marriage, and contradicts the will of the Author of life. Hence to use this divine gift while depriving it, even if only partially, of its meaning and purpose, is equally repugnant to the nature of man and of woman, and is consequently in opposition to the plan of God and His holy will."[46]

Dissent, of an unprecedented sort, sounded immediately. Some sort of contraceptive practice was so widespread among faithful Catholics in the United States that all of us who dealt with people pastorally understood that people would need immediate help with their reaction. I was at that time studying in New York and going out to a Long Island parish regularly every weekend. The Encyclical was released on a Tuesday and every priest who would be preaching on Sunday knew that this was an emergency. On the Thursday evening, many of us attended a hastily convened lecture at Fordham by outstanding canon lawyer and theologian Ladislas Orsy, a Hungarian Jesuit, who helped us to understand how we could reassure people who were acting in the matter in good conscience.

That was exactly the tack taken by the Canadian Conference of Catholic Bishops in their *Winnipeg Statement*, issued 2 months later on 27 September 1968. These bishops had been among those expressing themselves as in favor of change in the teaching during the Council. On the advice of their *peritus* Gregory Baum, Cardinal Léger of Montreal had defended the position that the duty of bearing children should be seen as pertaining to the state of matrimony as a whole rather than to an individual act, and had told the Third Session of the Council that "Confessors are assailed by doubts. They no longer know what to answer."[47] The statement said that many Catholics, though bound by the Encyclical, would find it "either extremely difficult or even impossible to make their own all elements of this doctrine." They "should not be considered, or consider themselves, shut off from the body of the faithful. But they should remember that their good faith will be dependent on a sincere self-examination to determine the true motives and grounds for such suspension of assent and on continued effort to understand and deepen their knowledge of the teaching of the Church." In that case, "the confessor or counsellor must show sympathetic

---

[46]*Humanae Vitae*, #13.
[47]Quoted by Msgr Vincent Foy in his article "Tragedy at Winnipeg," first published by *Challenge Magazine* in 1988.

understanding and reverence for the sincere good faith of those who fail in their effort to accept some point of the encyclical."[48]

The Canadians were not the only bishops who spoke, individually or as conferences, on these lines, but their statement attracted particularly much attention. There was fierce opposition to them over the succeeding years and demands for retraction, and in 1969 they had to issue a confirmation of their statement:

Nothing could be gained and much lost by an attempt to rephrase what we have said in Winnipeg. We stand squarely behind our position but we feel it is our duty to insist on a proper interpretation of that position.

We wish to reiterate our positive conviction that a Catholic Christian is not free to form his conscience without consideration of the teaching of the *magisterium*, in the particular instance exercised by the Holy Father in an Encyclical letter. It is false and dangerous to maintain that because this Encyclical has not demanded "the absolute assent of faith", any Catholic may put it aside as if it had never appeared. On the contrary, such teaching in some ways imposes a great burden of responsibility on the individual conscience.

The Catholic knows that he or she may not dissent from teaching proposed as infallible. With regard to such teaching one may seek only to understand, to appreciate, to deepen one's insights.

In the presence of other authoritative teaching, exercised either by the Holy Father or by the collectivity of the bishops one must listen with respect, with openness and with the firm conviction that a personal opinion, or even the opinion of a number of theologians, ranks very much below the level of such teaching. The attitude must be one of desire to assent, a respectful acceptance of truth which bears the seal of God's Church.[49]

As late as 1998, the bishops of Canada voted by secret ballot on a resolution to retract the Winnipeg Statement, but it did not pass.

---

[48]Canadian Conference of Catholic Bishops, 27 September 1968. *Canadian Bishops' Statement on the Encyclical Humanae Vitae,*" ##17, 25.
[49]Canadian Conference of Catholic Bishops Plenary Assembly, 18 April 1969, *Statement on Family Life and Related Matters.*

Neil MacDonald, in an article, "Freedom and Responsibility," posted without date on the internet, testifies that a month after the Canadians' *Winnipeg Statement* Pope Paul VI told his Secretary of State, privately, that he had taken cognizance of it "with satisfaction."[50] That was fiercely denied by Joseph Pope in an article of September 1998.[51]

In an interview published on 15 May 1969, in *Informations Catholiques Internationales*, Cardinal Suenens criticized the Pope's decision again as frustrating the collegiality defined by the Council, calling it a noncollegial or even an anti-collegial act.[52] His position was endorsed by theologians Karl Rahner and Hans Küng and Dom Christopher Butler, OSB, longtime Abbot of Downside Abbey and, from 1966, auxiliary bishop to Cardinal Heenan of Westminster, who called it one of the most important contributions to contemporary discussion in the Church.[53] Within a couple of days of the encyclicals' release, a group of some 600 dissident theologians, led by Rev Charles Curran, then of The Catholic University of America, issued a statement claiming that Catholics' individual consciences should prevail in such a personal and private issue. Ten prominent signers in Washington, where Cardinal O'Boyle, one of the leading supporters of the Pope's position, was Archbishop, were immediately suspended from the exercise of their priestly office.[54]

It was clear, then, that the Encyclical had not won universal assent from the Catholic bishops or faithful. That raises questions about the canonical doctrine of Reception, as a necessary element in the authority of Catholic teaching. This is an ancient doctrine of deeper complexity than this present discussion will bear, but with roots in the twelfth-century teaching of John Gratian, who drew on Isidore of Seville in the seventh century and Augustine in the fifth. An extensive study of it in the light of contemporary Canon Law by James E. Coriden can be found on the website of the Association for

---

[50]Mission of the Holy Spirit, "A lay Catholic Perspective," peace.mb.ca/07.Mission_of_HS/xneil07.html. Consulted 26 December 2012.

[51]Joseph Pope, "That Winnipeg Statement Again", *Catholic Insight*, September 1998.

[52]Quoted by Hebblethwaite, *Paul VI*, 528.

[53]Hebblethwaite, *Paul VI*, 533.

[54]I know of this from Jesuit Fr Horace McKenna, blind old man when I knew him in the early 1980s, who had been confessor to Cardinal O'Boyle. At regular intervals, the Cardinal would summon him, scold him a bit, then lift the suspension long enough for Horace to hear his confession, suspending him again at the end.

the Rights of Catholics in the Church.[55] I myself did a study of the teaching on bishops in the letters of St Ignatius of Antioch, in which I saw this as the view of this early Christian Father.[56]

Catholic belief and practice on the topic, according to a Gallup Poll taken 3–6 May 2012, show 82 percent of American Catholics and 89 percent of all Americans regard birth control as morally acceptable. A *Wall Street Journal* article of 16 March 2012 says that "Americans overwhelmingly agree that employers should be required to offer birth control, but a slight majority opposes the rule mandating Roman Catholic and other religious institutions from having to provide the service," a measure that the American bishops are vigorously opposed during the 2012 Presidential election campaign. That the American bishops should be making that a most serious issue for the candidates is surprising, given the enormous extent of Catholic dissent, and may even indicate that the bishops' displeasure is really about something else.

Yet, since the Encyclical, Catholic traditionalists have treated it as a primary concern of the Church to hold adherence to the encyclical as of the essence of Catholicism. Since the 1958 advent of Pope John Paul II, it has even been quite an absolute litmus test for the suitability of priests to be named bishops, thereby producing a generation of bishops whose commitment to this teaching is total. If any have doubts they know how to keep their counsel.

What is most important about this, though, is its effect on the Church. A measure of confidence has to be a principal concern of this book, and it would be presumptuous to argue that any one cause was responsible for the devastation we've seen, yet the first stages of the hemorrhage of priests leaving the priesthood and the decline both of priestly vocations and of Sunday attendance, a growing phenomenon ever since, do date from this period, which was one of disillusionment with the Church. There are, of course, rival explanations: either that the decline was caused by the Council or that it resulted from the neglect and deliberate bypassing of the Council.

---

[55]arcc-catholic-rights.net/doctrine_of_reception.htm, "The Canonical Doctrine of Reception," prepared for the Association for the Rights of Catholics in the Church, n.d. Consulted 26 December 2012.

[56]Unpublished lecture originally given at St Andrew's Theological College, Moscow, 31 May 2002.

Accurate statistics on Catholic practice are hard to come by, despite polling by a variety of groups. Gallup polls tend to give much higher figures than others. Pew Foundation and CARA studies differ somewhat too, and the taking of these statistics seemed less urgent in the earlier stages of what we recognize as steady decline in Mass attendance, in numbers and vocations of priests, and of men and women religious. Mass attendance in the years of the Council tends to be reported very high, typically around 75 percent of Catholics at Sunday Mass each week, but this was still under the circumstances, much diminished since, of strong ethnic identities—Irish, Italian, German, Polish—which saw Catholic practice as of the essence of their ethnicity, and a carefully cultivated mind-set among Catholics that the penalty for missing Mass on any Sunday was eternal damnation, unless the fault were mended by a good confession. People, even the most faithful Catholics, no longer think that way. Yet statistics from the same variety of sources generally find that Sunday attendance had dropped to the neighborhood of 25 percent by 2000, which was still before the further shattering blow of the sex-abuse crisis, and by 2012 it was down to a normal 15 percent if that.

Numbers of priests have been more carefully measured. According to Kenneth Jones' *Index of Leading Catholic Indicators* the number of priests in the United States had jumped from about 27,000 in 1930 to 58,000 in 1965. The number dropped to 45,000 in 2002. By 2020, it was predicted that there would be only about 31,000 priests, and only 15,000 of those under the age of 70. As of the last update of these statistics, 12 April 2012, there were more priests aged 80–84 than were aged 30–34.

Of ordinations or priests, there were 1,575 in 1965, only 450 in 2002, for a decline of 350 percent. The number of seminarians, 49,000 in 1965, had dropped to 4,700 in 2002, a loss of 90 percent. With that decline, seminaries across the country were being closed and sold, the number dropping from 596 in 1965 to 200 in 2002.

The number of professed brothers decreased from about 12,000 in 1965 to 5,700 in 2002, with a further drop to 3,100 projected for 2020.

Sisters had been the backbone of the Catholic school and hospital system through more than the previous century, and the mainstay of Catholic upbringing along with the family. With 180,000 sisters in 1965, there were in 2002 only 75,000, with an average age of 68.

By 2020, the number of sisters was predicted to drop to 40,000, and of those, only 21,000 aged 70 or under. In 1965, 104,000 sisters were teaching, while in 2002 there were only 8,200 teachers.

There were 10,503 parochial grade schools in 1965 and 6,623 in 2002. The number of students went from 4.5 million to 1.9 million.

Religious orders had suffered proportionally. In 1965 there were 5,277 Jesuit priests and 3,559 seminarians; in 2000 there were 3,172 priests and 38 seminarians. There were 2,534 OFM Franciscan priests and 2,251 seminarians in 1965; in 2000 there were 1,492 priests and 60 seminarians. There were 2,434 Christian Brothers in 1965 and 912 seminarians; in 2000 there were 959 Brothers and 7 seminarians. There were 1,148 Redemptorist priests in 1965 and 1,128 seminarians; in 2000 there were 349 priests and 24 seminarians. Every major religious order in the United States mirrors these statistics.[57]

The year 2002, so often cited in these statistics, was another key year in the decline, with the onset of a shocked public awareness of the sex-abuse crisis, which, of course, was by then a long-established fact, only then widely perceived. We will have to return to reading such statistics later, as the decline became all the more precipitous then. The attrition up to that time is clear evidence that the actual crisis of confidence was of much longer standing.

The reasons for these dismal statistics can't be put down simply to any one cause. Putting less value on the celibacy tradition was one factor. There were individual instances of priests leaving to get married, not widespread but enough initially to astonish people, for a year or so before the appearance of the birth-control Encyclical. The disillusion that followed the appearance of *Humanae Vitae*, however, was an enormous factor. Priests everywhere were left the impression that they were being required to hold people to an impossible standard. Introduction of the most substantive of the Council decisions, those on collegiality and the People of God, was glacially slow and already constantly impeded. The criteria to know what is happening for either of those are, of course, hard to define, but the sense was spreading that, for the governing bodies of the

---

[57]The surveys that place such statistics on the internet come largely from alarmed people anxious to find whom to blame. This survey, seen 27 December 2012 at tldm. org/news6/statistics.htm, draws on Kenneth C. Jones, *Index of Leading Catholic Indicators: The Church since Vatican II* (London: Orion Publishing Co, 2003).

Church in Rome, outright opponents even during the Council, these were not at all welcome concepts. Papal statements from Paul VI spoke more and more of anxiety, and the enforcement mechanisms exercised over the likes of Charles Curran left doubts over how seriously the freedom of conscience was being taken. It began to feel more and more like the period after 1950 when Pius XII and his counselors had taken panic at the flow of new ideas.

A sense of malaise spread gradually through the Church. Manifestations of clericalism, which people had complained of in the past but taken for granted, were now more resented. As the reign of the sad Pope Paul VI drew to its bleak close, there was a yearning felt throughout the Church for "a smiling Pope." We got one, ever so briefly, in the person of Pope John Paul I, who, after the death Paul VI on 6 August 1978, died unexpectedly after a reign of only 33 days, 26 August–28 September 1978. What would happen in the future would be under the aegis of the new Polish Pope John Paul II.

10

Pope John Paul II

For close to 27 years, the Pope was John Paul II, Karol Wojtyla, tested Polish veteran of the great conflicts of the twentieth century, tremendously popular world celebrity, traveling as no Pope had ever done before to all parts of the world, 129 countries in all, charismatic figure of tremendous energy and zeal for bringing the Good News of Jesus Christ to the world. No one other than an Italian had been elected Pope in 455 years. When, on 16 October 1978, the Dean of the College of Cardinals, Cardinal Jean Villot, stood on the balcony of St Peter's Basilica and announced to the world: "*Annuntio vobis gaudium magnum. Habemus Papam,*" and then proceeded to name him: "Carolus Wojtyla," Archbishop Bavone, Secretary of the Congregation for the Doctrine of the Faith, watching from the Palace of the Inquisition next door to St Peter's Square, was heard to exclaim "*Povera Italia!*"

A vigorous 58 when elected, the youngest Pope since Pius IX was elected in 1846 at the age of 54, he went on skiing holidays and had a swimming pool installed at the Castel Gandolfo villa.[1] By the time of his death, 2 April 2005, a sick old man bravely carrying his final afflictions, a whole new generation of priests, far fewer than before and basically very conservative, regarded themselves as "John Paul II priests," and referred to their hero as "John Paul the Great," the first Pope to be given that soubriquet since Gregory I in the seventh

---

[1]When the usual snipers complained about the cost of the swimming pool, the Pope, successor to a man who had succumbed to a heart attack 33 days after his election, replied that he needed the exercise, and that the pool was less expensive than holding another conclave. George Weigel, *Witness to Hope: The Biography of Pope John Paul II* (New York: Harpers Collins Publishers, 1999), 332, citing *Our Sunday Visitor*, 3 June 1979.

century. He was by then the only imaginable face of the papacy. At his funeral, the cry resounded: "Santo subito," a call for instant canonization. That did not happen, but the new Pope, Benedict XVI, who had heard that call while saying the funeral Mass, waived the normal requirement of waiting 5 years before beginning a beatification process. The beatification followed on 1 May 2011.

Wojtyla was a compromise candidate when elected. Details of the conclave, always expected to be super-secret, slipped out immediately and were widely reported in the international press. Two strong candidates were brought forward, the ultra-conservative Cardinal Giuseppe Siri of Genoa and the moderate-to-liberal Archbishop of Florence, Cardinal Giovanni Benelli. Benelli had only recently been made Archbishop of Florence and a Cardinal, in 1977. Before that, since 1967, he had been *sostituto*, or Deputy, to the Secretary of State, the aging Cardinal Amleto Cicognani. Since, however, Cicognani was no longer able to perform most of his duties, Benelli became the powerful Number Two to Pope Paul VI, so tightly controlling Vatican business that other curial cardinals channeled their business through him. Nicknamed "the Vatican Kissinger"[2] and "the Berlin Wall,"[3] his reputation was such that one heard it said commonly at the time: "all roads lead to Rome, and they are all named Benelli."[4]

In the conclave, though, it quickly became clear, in the first few ballots, though Benelli came within nine votes of election, that neither could overcome the opposition. Cardinal Franz König of Vienna then suggested the Polish Cardinal Wojtyla of Kraków as compromise, and on the eighth ballot he won 99 of the 111 votes cast.[5]

As he appeared on the balcony before the crowds in St Peter's Square, the Polish Pope broke precedent by addressing his largely Italian hearers: "I am speaking to you in your – no, our Italian language. If I make a mistake, please correct me. . . ."[6]

---

[2]*Time Magazine*, 8 November 1982, "Recent Events."

[3]*Time Magazine*, 14 March 1969, "The Pope's Powerful No. 2."

[4]Personal memory.

[5]*Time* Magazine, 30 October 1978, "A 'Foreign' Pope." This chatty column drew liberally on common reporting throughout the Italian press.

[6]Edward Stourton, *John Paul II: Man of History* (London: Hodder & Stoughton, 2006), 171. Weigel, 256. There are numerous biographies of John Paul II, most of them worshipful. Weigel's enormous work, xiv–992 pages, nearly hagiographic apart from instances where John Paul's judgment, in his assessment, slips, as when he criticizes America's wars or is insufficiently appreciative of the virtues of capitalism, is the gold standard, meticulously researched and comprehensive.

Already, from the moment of his election, he had been breaking precedents. As he returned from the robbing room to the Sistine Chapel in his white garments and was told to seat himself on a throne before the altar to receive the homage of the cardinals, he had replied: "I receive my brothers standing."[7]

Wojtyla had been made Archbishop of Kraków and Cardinal at the beginning of Pope Paul's *appertura a sinistra*, of which the main instrument became Cardinal Casaroli. This represented a judgment on the part of the Pope that the Communist regimes, in Poland and elsewhere, had to be treated as really in charge of their respective countries and dealt with by means of diplomacy rather than simply loaded with condemnations. The Church in Poland was under the general charge of Cardinal Stefan Wyszyński, Archbishop of Warsaw and Gniezno and Primate of Poland, an implacable foe of the Communist regime, always outspoken in opposition. Wojtyla was expected to represent the *appertura a sinistra* dear to Pope Paul and Casaroli, not any kind of cordiality but an openness to diplomatic negotiation with the Communist authorities, and to do so without detracting from the role of the senior Cardinal Wyszyński. He did this so well that he became a trusted figure to the Pope.

His immediate predecessor as Pope, "*Il Papa del Sorriso*," the Smiling Pope, Albino Luciani, who lived only 33 days after his election, had taken the name John Paul, in honor of his two predecessors, John XXIII and Paul VI. Wojtyla did likewise, choosing to be known as John Paul II, and like John Paul I he refused to be crowned with a triple tiara, in a move to "humanize" the papacy, or to ride the *sedia gestatoria*, and began to refer to himself as "I" rather than "We." John Paul II did likewise and had, on 22 October 1978, a simple inauguration in place of the traditional papal coronation. Those trappings of royalty, one may hope, are gone forever. When, during the inauguration, the cardinals knelt, one by one, to promise their fealty and kiss his ring, he rose to prevent Wyszyński from kneeling and embraced him, rather than let him kiss the ring.[8]

---

[7]Weigel, 254.
[8]Website of the Holy See Press Office, updated 30 June 2005, Events in the Pontificate of John Paul II, for 23 October 1978, John Paul II's Historic Embrace of Cardinal Wyszyński. Vatican website, vatican.va/news_services/press/documentazione/documents/santopadre_biografie/giovanni_paolo_ii_biografia_pontificato_en.html#1978. Consulted 29 December 2012.

Quickly there followed a whirlwind tour of countries all over the world. Pope Paul VI had broken the old convention that the Pope would always be seen only in Rome with his lightning trips to the Holy Land and to the United Nations even as the Council still proceeded. He went to Eucharistic Congresses in Bombay, India, in 1964 and in Bogotá, Columbia, in 1968. On the latter occasion, he endorsed the concept of the "preferential option for the poor" that had been introduced at the Medellin Conference of Latin American Bishops (CELAM). With his own strong social activism, he, with the CELAM bishops, would long be invoked as inspiration for the Liberation Theology movement, even when it fell under the suspicions of his successors.[9] He went to the fiftieth anniversary of the apparitions at Fátima in 1967 and made a pastoral visit to Africa in 1969. In November of 1970, he was target of an assassination attempt at the Manila International Airport in the Philippines.[10] Yet these were brief interludes in his papacy. The new Pope John Paul would be constantly on the road, visiting countries that had never seen a Pope before, an enormously popular figure sometimes referred to as the "rock-star" Pope.

First in line were the Dominican Republic and Mexico in January, 1979. He would be back to the Dominican Republic twice more, in 1984 and in 1992, when the occasion was the 500th anniversary of Columbus's discovery, but in 1979 it was a visit to the first country in the New World to receive missionaries of the Christian Gospel. Mexico was a more difficult visit. In this profoundly anti-clerical country where clergy were banned from wearing clerical dress, the Pope emerged from his plane on 26 January in his white cassock. Clergy and bishops of the country followed suit. President Lopez-Portillo, the women of whose family were devout Catholics, came to the airport to give an "unofficial" welcome. A million Mexicans witnessed the motorcade that took the Pope into the city, covering just five miles in an hour, to be met by 300,000 waiting in Constitution Square.

---

[9]Good information on Pope Paul's relation to the preferential option for the poor can be found in Manfred K. Bahmann, *A Preference For The Poor: Latin American Liberation Theology from a Protestant Perspective* (Lanham, MD: University Press of America, 2005). (Google eBook).

[10]"Apostle Endangered," *Time Magazine*, 7 December 1970.

The main business of the Pope's visit was to attend the Third General Assembly of CELAM, the Latin American bishops' conference, beginning 28 January in Puebla. John Paul had brought with him from Poland an insistent resistance to anything smelling of Marxism, and he suspected the Liberation Theologians of sympathy with it, a divisive topic among the clergy of Mexico. He was therefore at pains to discourage it, while at the same time concerned for the plight of the vast indigenous population of Mexico, largest in the Americas, who were drifting away from Catholicism because of their deprived situation, their oppression often ignored by an ambivalent Catholic hierarchy. The Pope wanted to emphasize human rights concerns, the importance of the Catholic Church's witness in Mexico and an affirmation of the indigenous peoples. It was his conviction that the defense of human rights was the best sort of evangelization. The Pope's speeches on the subject, straddling issues of human rights, and his opposition to Liberation Theology, often left an ambiguous impression. He would be back to Mexico three more times, in 1990, 1993, and 1999, always with these same concerns.[11]

Yet the *piece de résistance* of the early papal travels was his first visit to Poland in June, 1979. The Communist authorities in the Kremlin had been terrified from the time of the Polish Pope's election.[12] Soviet Foreign Minister, Andrei Gromyko had traveled to the Vatican on 24 January, two days before the Pope's arrival in Mexico, to scout the landscape. The Pope had made several moves before his Polish trip that raised alarms. On 2 March he sent a letter to strengthen Czechoslovakian Catholicism through better resistance to tyranny. On 19 March, he sent a papal letter to Cardinal Slipyi of the Ukraine, anticipating the 1988 millennium of Christianity in the Kievan Rus, which pointedly defended the principle of religious freedom for all. On 20 April, he named Cardinal Agostino Casaroli, representative of the *appertura a sinistra*, which so worried the Kremlin, his new Secretary of State.[13]

---

[11]For the Mexican visits, Weigel, 282–7; Maria M. Weir, 2000–01 Undergraduate Research Fellow at the Regional Research Institute of the West Virginia University, mentored by Joe Super, Ph.D., Professor of History, West Virginia University, "Pope John Paul II: Treatment of Mexico's Indigenous Peoples," June 2001.
[12]Weigel, 279–81, chronicles their reaction.
[13]Ibid., 291, lists these moves.

The sojourn in Poland would last from 2 to 10 June. In what could have been a very volatile situation, the Pope showed the wisdom to avoid any openly confrontational talk. The Communist authorities were hoping he would give a show of complacent acceptance of their regime, discouraging popular resistance. If his appearances caused a riot, they were prepared to put it down bloodily and impose full responsibility for it on him. The pope, instead, representing the one institution most radically opposite to them, hardly mentioned or took cognizance of them, but exhorted the Polish people to believe their one refuge was in God and to put their hope and their trust in him alone.

The reception of the Pope was ecstatic, all jubilation, no disorder. Hundreds of thousands of people lined his route from the airport to the city of Warsaw, kneeling for his blessing, hurling bouquets, cheering, and in uncontrollable tears. For his Mass in Victory Square, 230,000 tickets had been distributed but 300,000 crowded into the square, with another three-quarter of a million swarming the surrounding streets. In his sermon, which Weigel regards as the greatest of his life, he presented himself as pilgrim to this "land of a particularly responsible witness" to the faith. The cry of the crowd through the Mass was "We want God, we want God . . .!" It was the centennial of the martyrdom of St Stanislaw in 1079, the great resistor to the power of an autocratic state, and the Vigil of Pentecost. His hearers were to return in their imagination to the Upper Room, where Mary and the apostles awaited the coming of the Holy Spirit, who would make them witnesses of Christ's resurrection to the ends of the earth.[14]

The Pope had trumped the Communist tyranny. He had transcended politics simply by appealing to the deepest loyalties of Catholic Poland. He regarded the regime as not only oppressive, but tired. *Quo usque tandem, Catalina, abuteris patientia nostra?* Cicero had shouted across the Roman Senate to the repeatedly failing conspirator against the Republic, "How far, at last, Cataline, will you abuse our patience?" So did John Paul dismiss the claims of the exhausted Communist system. More would happen over the

---

[14]Besides Weigel's account of the events, 291–5, a superb political-religious analysis of the visit is given in Angelo M. Codevilla, "Political Warfare: A Set of Means for Achieving Political Ends," in J. Michael Waller (ed.), *Strategic Influence: Public Diplomacy, Counterpropaganda and Political Warfare* (Philadelphia, PA: Institute of World Politics Press, 2008).

remaining decade before the dissolution of its despotism in 1989–90: the formation of the Solidarity movement, encouraged by the Pope on each of his subsequent visits to Poland, even a Communist effort to assassinate him, but he had struck a mortal blow to the Polish regime, to the Soviet Empire, to Communism itself. The outbreak of democratic life to Poland in 1989–90 would spread to all of Eastern Europe between 1990 and 1992. The Marxist ideological empire had collapsed.

More papal travels would follow. The Pope was in Ireland on 29 September to 1 October 1979, appealing against the violence of Christian upon Christian. From 1 to 7 October, he undertook a comprehensive visit to the United States, beginning in Boston. On 2 October, he flew to New York, where his address to the United Nations centered on a bold defense of human rights and religious freedom against all totalitarianism. His new Secretary of State and custodian of his *Ost Politik*, Cardinal Casaroli, had thought these passages too confrontational and bracketed them out from the speaking version, reserving them for the longer text that would be published, but a junior official of the Secretariat of State, Fr Jan Schotte, appealing over the head of his boss, convinced the Pope during the short flight from Boston that he should restore them to the spoken text.[15] Their result was to make John Paul a principle spokesman for human rights for the duration of his papacy.

As the Pope turned up to kiss the ground on more tarmacs all over the world, a major feature of his travels became the World Days of Youth. These were set for every 2 years in different cities of the world. They always attracted young people in their many thousands, organized, with their priests, teachers, and parents from dioceses and parishes everywhere, always put up in fairly primitive surroundings and responding with tremendous enthusiasm to the energetic super-star Pope. His address would usually begin, in his slow, sonorous voice, intoning: "The reason for my journey is to preach Christ." He did exactly that, and created such a following among the youth of the world as had seldom been seen before.

The Francis of Assisi style of these pilgrimages was matched, in October 1986, by a World Day of Peace, inviting other Christians and representatives of the world's religions to Assisi to pray for peace.

---

[15] Weigel, 332-f.

Announced on 25 January 1986, the guardians of Catholic super-orthodoxy denounced it instantly for implying that other religions could be assigned some validity and their prayers respected. The Pope was undeterred. He had discussed with African Cardinal Francis Arinze of the Secretariat for Non-Christians and with Cardinal Roger Etchegaray of the Pontifical Justice and Peace Commission the deep resources in the world's religious traditions for addressing international world conflict.[16]

On 31 January as the curia muttered, John Paul took off for an extended tour of India, to be sure the invitation was properly communicated. He was in Delhi, in Calcutta, where he met with Mother Teresa, in Madras, in Goa, in Mangalore, Trichur, Cochin, Ernakulam, Verapoly, Kottayam, Trivandrum, Vasai, Puna, Goregoan, and Bombay. At the site of the cremation of Mohandas Ghandi, he preached on the Beatitudes. He visited the tomb of St Thomas in Madras and got to the far northeast state of Assam, normally closed to foreigners, and said Mass for the local peasants in a field. Everywhere his theme was service to the poor and the abandoned.[17]

Preparations went on in Assisi as summer turned into autumn, under the care of the Catholic renewal groups, Community of Sant' Egidio and Focolare, who would be responsible for hospitality. Bishop Jorge Mejía, the Pope's classmate from the Angelicum University and then Cardinal Etchegaray's Deputy at the Commission on Justice and Peace, was asked to publish an article in *L'Osservatore Romano* explaining that while "it is difficult to see how we, as Christians, can insert ourselves into the prayer of others" who did not share our faith in the God of Abraham, it remained true that "being present when another prays, or when many come together to pray, cannot but enrich our own proper experience of prayer." He reminded the doubters in the curia that: "In a world where there is too little prayer, the unheard of fact that believers of the different religions find themselves together to pray acquires an exceptional value. . . . What better response can we make to widespread secularism, if not this journey, this mutual encounter, for no other reason than to speak to God, each in his or her own way?"[18]

---

[16]Ibid., 511-f.
[17]Ibid., 512-f.
[18]Jorge M. Mejía, "To Be Together to Pray," *L'Osservatore Romano*, English World Edition, 13 October 1986. Weigel, 513f.

The participants of the different faiths would not attempt to pray together in chorus. Instead all the religious leaders first met the Pope at the Portiuncula, the small chapel in the plain below Assisi that Francis had so assiduously restored from ruin. Then all went to separate sites in the town where they prayed with their followers for ninety minutes. After this, everyone took the long walk up the hill to meet in the grand plaza before the Basilica of St Francis, where each led a prayer according to his own tradition. After a closing speech by the Pope, all broke their fast together in a common meal.[19]

That openness to other religions and to all Christian churches was consistent with Pope John Paul's constant priorities of ecumenism— Christians of other traditions were to him fellow Christians—and inter-religious activism.

The Pope's ecumenical activity started quickly after his October election in 1978.[20] It had been customary since Vatican II that on 29 June, Feast of Sts Peter and Paul, and on 30 November, Feast of St Andrew, representatives of the Catholic and Orthodox Churches would be present for the celebration in Rome and in St George's Cathedral in the Phanar in Istanbul. The Pope determined that he himself would be present at the Phanar in 1979. Speaking there on the eve of the feast, he recalled for his listeners that "these two sister-Churches had maintained full communion in the first millennium of Christian history." They had "developed their great vital traditions" within the bond of unity. Now they were meeting in "this common apostolic faith . . . to walk toward this full unity which historical circumstances have wounded." Patriarch Demetrios in response described their meeting as "intended for the future – a future which will again see live unity, again common confession, again full communion in the divine Eucharist."[21]

The following day, in the liturgy of St Andrew, the Pope exchanged the kiss of peace with Demetrios, joined him in giving the final blessing of the Mass, and asked if, at the end of the second millennium, "is it not

[19]Weigel, 512, 514.

[20]I got to write myself the chapter "John Paul II and Ecumenism" for Gerard Mannion (ed.), *The Vision of John Paul II: Assessing His Thought and Influence* (Collegeville, MN: The Liturgical Press, 2008), 215–34, and hence became very familiar with this aspect of the Pope's work. References here will be to my own chapter.

[21]Helmick, 217f. John Paul himself described this whole event in a volume titled *Turkey: Ecumenical Pilgrimage* (Boston: St. Paul Editions, 1980), 27.

time to hasten toward perfect brotherly reconciliation" for the sake of evangelization? Formal dialogue was thus brought about between the Roman Catholic Church and Orthodoxy at an international level.[22]

The year 1983 was counted as the 1950th anniversary of the redeeming death of Jesus Christ on the cross. Pope John Paul declared it a Holy Year, as had Pope Pius XI for the 1900th anniversary in 1933. It was also the 500th anniversary of the birth of Martin Luther. On 31 October, the Pope wrote to Cardinal Johannes Willebrands, president of the Secretariat for Promoting Christian Unity, in which he praised the "deep religious feeling manifested by Luther," whom he described as "driven with burning passion by the question of eternal salvation." It was time, he wrote, to heal the Reformation breach, relying on continued historical scholarship "without preconceived ideas," in order to arrive at a true image of the reformer, of the whole period of the Reformation, and of the persons involved in it. Fault, where it exists, must be recognized, wherever it may be."

This was a far cry from the familiar blaming of Protestants for abandoning the Church, and the use of such terms as "the reformer" in a papal document was without precedent. Lutherans and Catholics, the letter continued, would have a "new point of departure" for theological dialogue, beginning with what they have in common." The dialogue should proceed in a spirit of "penitence and readiness to learn from listening."[23]

On the Third Sunday of Advent, following up on this letter about Luther, the Pope visited the Lutheran Christuskirche in Rome, participated in an Ecumenical Service of the Word and preached. The Luther quincentenary, he proclaimed, should be "the daybreak of the advent of the rebuilding of our unity and our community." Such an undertaking would be "the best preparation for the advent of God in our time."[24]

Ecumenical dialogue with the Reformation churches would quickly reach the doctrinal level of the great controversy questions that had torn the churches apart in the sixteenth century. In that era,

---

[22]John Paul II, ibid., 39–48.

[23]The letter to Cardinal Willebrands, "Martin Luther, Witness to Jesus Christ," is printed in the Secretariat for Promoting Christian Unity's *Information Service* 52 (1983/II), 83–92.

[24]An account of this visit can be found in E. M. Jung-Inglessis, *The Holy Year in Rome: Past and Present* (Vatican City: Libreria Editrice Vaticana, 1997), 297–9.

when violence and war was accepted as the way to deal with such matters, either side had sought to find the point on which they could anathematize the other. Now multilateral and bilateral commissions for the discussion of those issues became the normative behavior of the churches, seeking the points of agreement, hearing the perceptions of the others in such a way as to get behind the language of rejection and find how the other truly understood basic matters of the Gospel message. Increasingly, the doctrinal disputes were proving to be issues of another time, not the true problems the different churches had with one another now, and it became more and more evident that the true issues of difference in our time were internal to each of the churches.

The great test of this strategy of dialogue came with the doctrine of justification, which had been the most serious breach between Catholic and Lutheran in the sixteenth century, and which such theological pioneers as Karl Barth and his Catholic student Hans Küng had been exploring already.[25] The Lutheran World Federation and the Pontifical Council for Promoting Christian Unity (the new title for the former Secretariat) worked at the question throughout the '90s, and reached a *Joint Declaration on the Doctrine of Justification*, which was announced by Cardinal Edward Cassidy, the Australian President of the Pontifical Council, on 25 June 1998. The declaration, he told a press conference, represented "a consensus on basic truths concerning the doctrine of justification" and a relation of faith to good works in the scheme of salvation.

Opposition there was, of course, from the usual curial sources. Consultation had gone on as heavily between Cassidy's Pontifical Council on Christian Unity and the Congregation for the Doctrine of the Faith as between Catholic and Lutheran members of the Joint Commission, and on the same day the Holy See published a *Response of the Catholic Church to the Joint Declaration of the Catholic Church and the Lutheran World Federation on the Doctrine of Justification* that called for further clarifications.[26] This document had been

---

[25]Hans Küng, *Justification: The Doctrine of Karl Barth and a Catholic Reflection* (Westminster: John Knox Press, 1964), reissued for its fortieth anniversary, 3 November 2004.

[26]*Origins* 28, no. 17 (16 July 1998) gives the texts of both the *Joint Declaration* and the *Response*. Weigel, 826–8, recounts the whole episode based on interviews he held with Cardinal Cassidy on 10 October 1998, and 7 June 1999, and with Cardinal Ratzinger on 16 December 1998.

prepared jointly by CDF and CU. The Lutherans expressed their acute sense of betrayal, believing the Catholic Church had reneged both on its own and the Lutheran theologians. Cardinal Cassidy then wrote a personal letter on 30 June 1998, to Dr Ismael Noko, Secretary General of the Lutheran World Federation, reiterating, and even underlining in his letter, that "there is a consensus in basic truths on the doctrine of justification," and that "very few" further clarifications were required, which, in fact, "do not negate the consensus. The Catholic Church, he wrote, was ready to "affirm and sign the *Joint Declaration*." No major problems impeded "further study and a more complete presentation."[27]

Undoubtedly, these last-minute maneuvers had damaged trust between the Catholic and Lutheran partners. Some further discussion followed between the two cardinals, Cassidy and Ratzinger, and some Lutheran theologians and officials. The Holy See then suggested that an agreed "Annex" be appended to the *Joint Declaration*, clarifying the points raised but emphasizing that those concerns did not invalidate the consensus on "the basic truths of salvation." This Annex, and "Official Common Statement," clarified the partners' variant understanding of the human propensity to sin, human cooperation with God's grace, and the necessity of locating the doctrine of justification within the broader scheme of Christian belief, concluding: "The teaching of the Lutheran Churches presented in this Declaration does not fall under the condemnations of the Council of Trent. The condemnations in the Lutheran Confessions do not apply to the teachings of the Roman Catholic Church presented in this *Declaration*."

Now the document was ready for the personal approval of Pope John Paul, and on Reformation Sunday, 31 October, the amended document was signed by Lutheran and Catholic representatives in Augsburg.[28] A bloody course, but a major ecumenical accomplishment was achieved.

Ecumenical contact with the Orthodox Churches also moved apace through the Holy Year 1983. On 16 April 1983, John Paul received in the Vatican Karekin Sakissian, Armenian Catolicos of Cilicia; on 13 May, Ignatius IV Kazim, the first Greek Orthodox Patriarch of Antioch to pay a formal ecumenical visit to Rome; on

---

[27]Cardinal Cassidy presented to Weigel a copy of his 30 June letter, as he mentions in *Witness to Hope*, n. 58, 943-f. Dr Noko's lengthy letter of 20 August to the LWF, enclosing Cassidy's letter, appeared in *Origins* 28, no. 17 (16 July 1998), 228–90.
[28]For the entire episode, Helmick, 222–4.

6 June, Moran Mar Basileius Marthoma Matheos I, Catolicos of the Syrian Orthodox Church of India; and on 30 June, Metropolitan Meliton of Chalcedon, representative of the Ecumenical Patriarch Dimitrios for the celebration of the feast of Sts Peter and Paul.[29]

This sampler of the ecumenical activities of Pope John Paul should suffice to illustrate what would be the character of the pontificate through the rest of his time. A climactic moment was in 2001, meeting the Orthodox Church of Greece as the Pope traveled in the footsteps of St Paul from Greece to Syria to Malta. This was the first visit of a Pope to Greece in 1,291 years. No Eastern Orthodox leader came to greet him, and the monks of Athos raged at his coming.[30] He met briefly in private with Archbishop Christodoulos of Athens, after which they both spoke in public, the Archbishop leading off by reading a list of 13 offenses of the Roman Church against the Orthodox Church, including the infamous sack of Constantinople in 1204, for which, he said, "there has not been a single request for pardon" for "the maniacal crusaders of the 13th century." The pope responded at once: "For the occasions, past and present, when sons and daughters of the Catholic Church have sinned by action or omission against their orthodox brothers and sisters, may the Lord grant us forgiveness," and spoke of the sack of Constantinople as a matter of "deep regret" for Catholics.[31]

The Pope's modesty and repentance won the day. Archbishop Christodoulos applauded, and the Pope's demeanor won him great respect throughout Greece. They met again at the Areopagus, where Saint Paul had preached to the Athenians, issuing from there a "common declaration." "We shall do everything in our power, so that the Christian roots of Europe and its Christian soul may be preserved. . . . We condemn all recourse to violence, proselytism and fanaticism in the cause of religion."[32]

---

[29]Weigel, 472.

[30]I reported this entire visit, Helmick, 228-f., in *The Vision of John Paul II*.

[31]Vatican website, "The Address of John Paul II to His Beatitude Christodoulos," Archbishop of Athens and Primate of Greece, Friday, 4 May 2001, Vatican.va/holy_father/John_paul_ii/speeches/2001/documents/hf_jp-ii_spe_20010504_archbishop-athens,en,html. Consulted 10 January 2013.

[32]Vatican website: "Common Declaration of Pope John Paul II and His Beatitude Christodoulos, Archbishop of Athens and All Greece, before the Bema of St. Paul, the Apostle to the Nations," 4 May 2001: vatican.va/holy_father_john_paul_ii/speeches/2001/documents/hf_jp-ii_spe_20010504_joint_declaration_en.html, Consulted 10 January 2013.

No less significant were the Pope's inter-religious activities. The Assisi meeting, much as it had rankled Church conservatives, had been iconic for his entire position. Judaism was always closest to his heart after his personal experience of the Nazi persecution of Jews during his youth in Poland. He had extensive knowledge of the writings of Max Scheler (about whom he had written his *Habitationsschrift*), Franz Rosenzweig, Martin Buber, and Emmanuel Levinas.[33] His visit to the Rome synagogue on 13 April 1986 was the first by a Roman Pontiff since the early days when Peter was a regular visitor to the Temple and doubtless to synagogues, as Jesus had been himself.[34]

A relation to Muslims came next among papal concerns, the occasions often relating to political events. At the invitation of King Hassan II of Morocco, he addressed 80,000 Muslim youths at a stadium in Casablanca on 19 August 1985, the first time a Pope had ever addressed a Muslim audience. During the Iran-Iraq War (1980–88), he sent Cardinal Roger Etchegaraya as his envoy to both countries to help ease the conflict. When Saddam Hussein invaded Kuwait on 2 August 1990 and throughout the Gulf War, he called for a nonviolent solution to the problems of the Middle East, and before the 2003 Iraq War, he did all he could to prevent the war from happening.[35] He visited the Grand Ommayad Mosque in Damascus in 2001 (another first for a Pope), and on 24 January 2002, held another gathering of world religious leaders in Assisi to reject all use of violence in the name of religion.[36]

The crowning achievement in this area was his trip to the Holy Land in the summer of 2000, in which his respect both for the Jewish hopes with regard to Israel and for the Palestinian claims and suffering was equally apparent.[37] His visits to the Yad Vashem and to the Western Wall were transformative events for Jewish

---

[33]I will not attempt to detail all this, but simply refer to the chapter Peter C. Phan, "John Paul II and Interreligious Dialogue: Reality and Promise," in Mannion (ed.), *The Vision of John Paul II* (Collegeville, MN: Liturgical Press, 2008), 235–57.

[34]Phan, 239.

[35]Ibid., 241.

[36]Paul McPartland, chapter "John Paul II and Vatican II," in Mannion (ed.), *The Vision of John Paul II*, 52.

[37]Get back to my own book for page references here.

understanding of Christians' relation to them.[38] For Palestinians, Muslim and Christian, the great event was his visit to the refugee camp at Dheisheh outside Bethlehem.

Tremendously important, too, in the later days of Pope John Paul's reign, as the millennium approached, were his major address, *Tertio Millenio Adveniente*[39] (1994), the Encyclical *Ut Unum Sint*[40] (1995), and the closely related Day of Pardon which the Pope organized for the First Sunday of Lent, 12 March 2000. The *Tertio Millennio* address sounded a first call to the members of the Church to repent of "the acquiescence given, especially in certain centuries, to intolerance and even the use of violence in the service of truth." The Church's whole past would stand under judgment, then, and that in the light of the Second Vatican Council. "From these painful moments of the past a lesson can be drawn for the future, leading all Christians to adhere fully to the sublime principle stated by the Council: 'The truth cannot impose itself except by virtue of its own truth, as it wins over the mind with both gentleness and power.'"[41] Left far behind, therefore, was the concept that "Error has no rights," which had blighted the Church for so many centuries. The Day of Pardon liturgy presided over by the Pope in 2000 would make explicit what was meant, naming the Crusades and the Inquisition as deeds for which Christians must do penance.

The Day of Penance, 12 March 2000, would also address "sins regarding relations with the people of the first Covenant,

---

[38]Rabbi Stephen Cohen, who had been a central figure in the establishment of diplomatic relations between the Vatican State and Israel, commented that Jews had been so beaten about the ears for centuries that they could hardly hear the better things Christians had been saying to them since Vatican II, but that the sight on Israeli television of the Pope at Yad Vashem and his message set between the stones of the Western Wall were visible and convincing proof of his efforts at reconciliation. Eye-witness report.

[39]Vatican website, vatican.va/holy_father/john_paul_ii/apost_letters/documents/hf_jp-ii_apl_10111994_tertio-millennio-adveniente_en.html, Apostolic Letter *Tertio Millennio Adveniente* of His Holiness Pope John Paul II. To Bishops, Clergy, and Lay Faithful on Preparation for the Jubilee of the Year 2000, 10 November 1994.

[40]Vatican website, vatican.va/holy_father/john_paul_ii/encyclicals/documents/hf_jp-ii_enc_25051995_ut-unum-sint_en.html, Ioannes Paulus, pp. II. *Ut Unum Sint*, on Commitment to Ecumenism, 25 May 1995. Consulted 12 January 2013.

[41]*Tertio Millennio Adveniente*, #35, quoting from the Council's Religious Liberty declaration, *Dignitatis Humanae*, #1. Consulted 12 January 2013.

Israel: contempt, hostility, failure to speak out." These were the words read out by a curial cardinal during the service in St Peter's Basilica, but also the subject of intense prayer by the Pope himself that same month when he wrote and signed them on the paper he slipped between the stones of the Western Wall in Jerusalem.[42]

Ut Unum Sint would draw the line of Catholic repentance tighter still, John Paul II placing the spotlight on his own papal ministry itself. Recognizing the fact that the Petrine office and ministry, which was meant to be one of unity in the Church, had itself become a source of division, he called upon the leaders and theologians of all the Christian traditions to engage him in "a patient and fraternal dialogue," to help him exercise his ministry in a way that would be "a service of love."[43] It was in this way, following the decisions of the Council,[44] that "the Catholic Church committed herself *irrevocably*[45] to following the path of the ecumenical venture."

Given these most extraordinary accomplishments of this volcanic Super-Pope, bursting with so much energy and zeal, immensely popular, how is it imaginable that, at the end of his 27 years in the papacy, the Church should be such a wreck of itself, so diminished in numbers, of priests and of faithful practitioners, even his words, which were so often celebrated, largely ignored? Young people, especially, who would be uninterested in joining in service to the Church and would fall away even from regular attendance or use of the sacraments, even of marriage, had flocked to his World Youth Days every second year. Was all that enthusiasm an artificial creation, the result of hype, as at a rock-star concert? He had his fervent personal following, such as those who put up the chorus of "*Santo subito*" at his funeral. We do love to celebrate and even canonize our popes, even those whose careers have been damaging to the Church. That has not always been so, but the tendency has grown ever since the 1869 decrees of the First Vatican Council on papal primacy. Cult of personality it would be called in the different culture of the Soviet Union. Could these developments be blamed on Pope John Paul, or he in some way be held responsible for the general disarray?

---

[42]These events described by Paul McPartland in the chapter "John Paul II and Vatican II" in Mannion (ed.), *The Vision of John Paul II*, 52.
[43]*Ut Unum Sint*, ##95–6.
[44]"*Unitatis Redintegratio*," #1.
[45]*Ut Unum Sint*, #3. Emphasis in the original.

Of course, the sex abuse crisis, which had gone on, in hiding, for so many years (it is still indeterminate how long) but had come to the surface only in 2002 and become the main thing people adverted to or commented on in assessing the Catholic Church, contributed mightily. We will take that up in a separate chapter, but the decay had already been visible for many years, accelerating throughout John Paul's long pontificate.

Surely we cannot load all this disappointment on this Pope's shoulders. A feeling of malaise could already be sensed in the Church, which had so yearned for a "smiling Pope" after the anxious years of that patently good man, Paul VI. The sense was that the opportunity for full, active participation in the life of the Church, what had been promised so alluringly in Vatican II, was disappearing. A solo performance, however brilliant, would not fit the bill. An increasingly educated people turned to things they could affect, in the political sphere, in the promotion of human rights, in the arts and culture. Such things became the goals of serious people's lives. They saw the Pope as a show, like much else.

As Archbishop of Kraków, Karol Woytyla had an influential voice at the Council. His support for the religious liberty proposal and mobilization of Eastern European support for it was a key element in its acceptance in the face of a long history of official intolerance. His was one of the strongest voices in support of a radical revision of the Church's relation with Jews. It is significant that his similar-minded successor as Pope, Benedict XVI, singled out these two, as he thought, peripheral decisions of the Council as the very center of its adaptation of the Church to living in the Modern World, those rather than the Pastoral Constitution on the Church in the Modern World, in his assessment of the Council's work at 50 years.[46] It seems strange now to classify those accomplishments as peripheral to the Council's concerns as they have made such a basic difference in the Church's life. The Pope's assessment becomes more intelligible, however, when we consider that these tremendous accomplishments were, in fact, seen at the time (and in the Pastoral Constitution *Gaudium et Spes*, which Pope Benedict saw as less important or successful) as subordinate to the characteristic major insights of the Council which have been so evaded and neglected since collegial government and the role of the *Populus Dei*.

---

[46]Cf. above, Chapters 9, 11.

Paul VI's decision on birth control decision still remained corrosive to trust in the moral authority of the Church, in sexual matters, and even more widely. The influence of Archbishop Wojtyla, in letters sent from Poland as he was unable to join the deliberations in Rome, confirming that of the tiny minority of the papal commission who had opposed any change from the position of Pius XI's 1930 Encyclical *Casti Connubii*, was of critical importance. Clearly it was Pope Paul himself who was determined to draw that conclusion despite any opposition. Paul VI had stayed personally firm in that decision, whether or not it was, as Cardinal Suenens feared, another Galileo case in the Church. But for Pope John Paul II, conformity to the judgments of *Humanae Vitae* became an essential talisman of loyalty to the Church.

From the time he came into the papacy in 1978 John Paul had a sense that there was dangerous alienation between the people of the Church, even its bishops, and the closed shop of the curial authorities in the Vatican, so separated from *gli stranieri* and dismissive of them. His strategy was to retain decision-making power to himself and let the curia and its power atrophy. For some time, given his heavy travel schedule, this meant long waits for decisions. Eventually, the Pope would replace the old officials with new men more energetic and like himself, but it never ceased to be true that Vatican business could wait a long time.

Officials more like himself! Bishops throughout the Church, during Paul VI's papacy, had differed in their grasp of the new winds of the Council and their enthusiasm for it. Now, with Pope John Paul, there came to be tightly defined litmus tests for the selection of bishops. Papal nuncios around the world were alerted to these as they sent in their recommendations for the appointment of bishops, after receiving the recommendations of the national and local associations of bishops. Primary among these litmus tests was acceptance of *Humanae Vitae*. It was as absolute as is protection of abortion rights as a litmus test in the appointment of American judges.

It was not alone as a litmus test for bishops. Abortion hardly needed to be named as a litmus test. So firm was Catholic opposition to the practice that support for it would convince any Catholic that their standing in the Church was open to question. Yet, equally mandatory for designation as bishops were opposition to the ordination of married men as priests and rejection of the ordination of women.

No one would argue that either the birth-control judgment of Pope Paul VI or the refusal to ordain married men as priests was an essential and infallible matter of faith. The opinions expressed by the vast majority of Paul VI's advisors in 1968, bishops, theologians, and others, and the ordination practices of the other Catholic churches of Eastern rite would never allow that. In the case of the ordination of women, Roman authorities have been asserting that the prohibition is as good as infallible, of "infallible by authority of the ordinary *Magisterium* of the Church."

Nonetheless, this exclusion of women from priestly office, which in effect is their exclusion too from all the positions of decision-making and power that are the hierarchical structure of the Church, has increasingly alienated women from the Church in recent time. Feminism, the assertion of the equal dignity of women and their entitlement to voting, to compensation for their work, access to position, etc., has been a growing movement since some time in the nineteenth century, more and more a cause over the course of the twentieth century and now a critical core demand within the Catholic Church, whose male leadership has heard it with the greatest reluctance. So great has been the dissonance over this issue that, for apparently the first time in the Church's history, women's acceptance of the Church and its terms is seriously at risk. That women's entrance into religious life is at an all-time low has other reasons in the particular ways their participation in the work of the Church has been effectively discouraged by male authority ever since the time of the Council itself. The disappearance of numerous lay women, though, from the Sunday liturgy and other Church activity, even the distancing of themselves from bringing up children in the faith, is a very serious alarm bell, threatening the future. The women, not all of them, of course, but in hugely significant numbers, feel disparaged and held in low value by the Church, not treated with the respect that is their due.

Even before the 1978 election of Pope John Paul II the question of women's ordination had been raised. On 15 October 1976, the Congregation for the Doctrine of the Faith discussed it and issued a *Declaration on the Question of the Admission of Women to the Ministerial Priesthood*.[47] Their conclusion was that, for a variety of reasons—doctrinal, theological, historical—the Church "... does not

---

[47]Vatican website, vatican.va/roman_curia/congregations/cfaith/documents/rc_con_cfaith_doc_19761015_inter-insigniores_en.html, Sacred Congregation for the Doctrine of the Faith, Declaration *Inter Insigniores* on the Question of the Admission of Women to the Ministerial Priesthood. Consulted 13 January 2013.

consider herself authorized to admit women to priestly ordination."
This judgment was not massively definitive. This decision followed
a study in April, 1976, by the Pontifical Biblical Commission, on the
exclusion of women from the priesthood from a biblical point of
view.[48] Its conclusions: "The masculine character of the hierarchical
order which has structured the church since its beginning . . . seems
attested to by scripture in an undeniable way." Yet:

> It does not seem that the New Testament by itself alone will permit
> us to settle in a clear way and once and for all the problem of the
> possible accession of women to the presbyterate. (Approved in
> the Commission by a vote 17-0.)
>
> However, some think that in the scriptures there are sufficient
> indications to exclude this possibility, considering that the
> sacraments of eucharist and reconciliation have a special link
> with the person of Christ and therefore with the male hierarchy,
> as borne out by the New Testament. (Rejected by the Commission
> by a vote 12-5.)
>
> Others, on the contrary, wonder if the church hierarchy,
> entrusted with the sacramental economy, would be able to entrust
> the ministries of eucharist and reconciliation to women in light of
> circumstances, without going against Christ's original intentions.
> (Accepted by the Commission by a vote 12-5.)

Pope John Paul issued an Apostolic Letter in 1988, *Mulieris
Dignatatem*[49] "On the Dignity of Women," in which he cites the
dignity of Mary as *Theotokos*, "Mother of God," the Church as
Bride of Christ, the role of women as in the Bible as first witnesses
to the Resurrection, and a number of women saints, then goes to
the importance of the feminine roles of mother, teacher, daughter,
but concludes, in defense of the all-male clergy: "In calling only
men as his Apostles, Christ acted in a completely free and sovereign

---

[48]womenpriests.org/classic/append2.asp, "Biblical Commission Report Can Women
be Priests?," Appendix II to *Women Priests*, eds. Arlene Swidler and Leonard Swidler
(Rahwah, NJ: Paulist Press, 1977), 338–46. Consulted 13 January 2013.
[49]Vatican website, vatican.va/holy_father/john_paul_ii/apost_letters/documents/hf_jp-
ii_apl_15081988_mulieris-dignitatem_en.html, Apostolic Letter, *Mulieris Dignitatem*,
of the Supreme Pontiff John Paul II On the Dignity and Vocation of Women On the
Occasion of the Marian Year, 15 August 1988. Consulted 13 January 2013.

manner. In doing so, he exercised the same freedom with which, in all his behaviour, he emphasized the dignity and the vocation of women, without conforming to the prevailing customs and to the traditions sanctioned by the legislation of the time."

On 22 May 1994, John Paul issued another Apostolic Letter, this time *Ordinatio sacerdotalis*, "On Priestly Ordination."[50] This time, he presented the Roman Catholic understanding as that the priesthood is a special role specially set out by Jesus when he chose 12 men out of his group of male and female followers. He cited several Scripture passages as confirming this males-only practice: that Jesus chose the Twelve (cf. Mk 3:13–14; Jn 6:70) after a night in prayer (cf. Lk 6:12) and that the Apostles themselves were careful in the choice of their successors. The priesthood therefore is "specifically and intimately associated in the mission of the Incarnate Word himself (cf. Mt 10:1, 7–8; 28:16–20; Mk 3:13–16; 16:14–15)." He quotes Pope Paul VI to the effect: "The Church holds that it is not admissible to ordain women to the priesthood, for very fundamental reasons. These reasons include: the example recorded in the Sacred Scriptures of Christ choosing his Apostles only from among men; the constant practice of the Church, which has imitated Christ in choosing only men; and her living teaching authority which has consistently held that the exclusion of women from the priesthood is in accordance with God's plan for his Church." And he concludes:

Wherefore, in order that all doubt may be removed regarding a matter of great importance, a matter which pertains to the Church's divine constitution itself, in virtue of Our ministry of confirming the brethren. We declare that the Church has no authority whatsoever to confer priestly ordination on women and that this judgment is to be definitively held by all the Church's faithful. (*Declaramus Ecclesiam facultatem nullatenus habere ordinationem sacerdotalem mulieribus conferendi, hancque sententiam ab omnibus Ecclesiae fidelibus esse definitive tenendam.*)[51]

---

[50]Vatican website, vatican.va/holy_father/john_paul_ii/apost_letters/documents/hf_jp-ii_apl_22051994_ordinatio-sacerdotalis_en.html, Apostolic Letter *Ordinatio Sacerdotalis* of John Paul II to the Bishops of the Catholic Church on Reserving Priestly Ordination to Men Alone. Consulted 13 January 2013.

[51]*Ordinatio Sacerdotalis*, #4.

On 28 October 1995, the Congregation for the Doctrine of the Faith issued a clarification, explaining that *Ordinatio Sacerdotalis*, though "itself not infallible, witnesses to the infallibility of the teaching of a doctrine already possessed by the Church. . . . This doctrine belongs to the deposit of the faith of the Church. The definitive and infallible nature of this teaching of the Church did not arise with the publication of the Letter *Ordinatio Sacerdotalis*."[52] Instead, it was "founded on the written Word of God, and from the beginning constantly preserved and applied in the tradition of the Church, it has been set forth infallibly by the ordinary and universal *magisterium*," and for these reasons it "requires definitive assent."

The Vatican's Congregation for the Doctrine of the Faith issued and published on 29 May 2008, in the Vatican newspaper *L'Osservatore Romano*, a decree signed by Cardinal William Levada, on the existing ban on women priests by asserting that women "priests" and the bishops who ordain them would be automatically excommunicated "*lata sententia*."

Not infallible, therefore, but requiring definitive assent. The category is novel. We are thrown back, for all the very lofty assertion, on the theological quality of the argument itself, which is basically scriptural, that Jesus, a man himself, chose only men. How certain is this? The argument avoids reference to the event of the Last Supper itself, traditionally cited as the original ordination of ministers of the Eucharist. One can hardly say with any certainty that no women were present in the Upper Room when Jesus said: "Do this in memory of me" or "As often as you shall do this, you will do it in memory of me." Tradition regularly places Mary there, and most likely the holy women who had accompanied Jesus and his disciples throughout their ministry. Who is to say they were not there and heard these words addressed to themselves?

The New Testament is always vague about who presides at a communal celebration of the Lord's Supper. The Apostles and their associates do not reserve this to themselves. It seems most probable that the presider was the host in whose home the assembly was

---

[52]Letter Concerning the CDF Reply Regarding Ordinatio Sacerdotalis by then-Cardinal Ratzinger. This letter defining the teaching as infallible in a sense was signed by Cardinal Ratzinger, Prefect of the CDF, and not by the Pope, as is required for a definition of infallibility, and is for that reason sometimes contested. The signer, though, has subsequently become Pope himself, but that technically makes no difference.

held, and in several New Testament passages this was a hostess. There is evidence, as well, of certain pictorial representations that include women celebrating the Eucharist.

Why, then, has this matter of women's ordination been made, along with opposition to married priests and acceptance of *Humanae Vitae*, so absolute a litmus test for the selection of bishops, even while opposition to abortion is so acceptedly a Catholic position that it doesn't need to be included among the litmus tests? It bespeaks a certain doubt among those who set the litmus test, and ultimately a defensive position for the preservation of some male prerogatives.

I write this passage shortly after I read, in *The National Catholic Reporter* (10 January 2013), of the expulsion of Father Roy Bourgeois, American Catholic priest social activist and peace advocate, from the priesthood and from his Maryknoll congregation. Bourgeois has made himself conspicuous by his support and frequent argumentation for the ordination of women as priests, even taking part, despite warnings, in such ordination ceremonies. His letter of dismissal was careful not to give a reason, which raises canonical questions, but it looks more than probable that it was this. The decision is irrevocable, without recourse, as made by the present Pope himself.

Some part of the disarray and loss of the Catholic Church must be attributed to this prolonged and acute discomfort on the part of women. The latter part of Chapter 9 gave some statistics of the losses, already very visible in the time of Pope Paul VI but escalating sharply during the pontificate of John Paul II. The statistics cited took us only to 2002, year of the great shock of the sex abuse crisis, topic of the next chapter. They were bad then, but have become devastatingly worse since.

Attention has to be drawn, however, to those great marks of the Council's work for the reform of the Church: collegiality and regard for the entire membership of the Church as People of God. Pope John Paul II did so much to promote and implement other major decisions of the Council, as we have seen: religious liberty and a new attitude toward Jews, as well as Muslims and the other world religions. We have followed the enormous strides he took in the promotion of ecumenism, both with the Orthodox and with Protestants. The warmth of ecumenical relations at the time of the Council has inevitably cooled, though, as the Catholic Church has become so exclusively engrossed in "the Social Issues," predominantly abortion, that it has seemed there was no other important content to

Catholic faith, and there was dissonance with some other churches on these very issues.

Chosen on tightly restrictive grounds, due largely to those litmus tests, the world's bishops became more and more functionaries of the central firm, franchises rather than those holders of the *cura ecclesiae universalis* envisioned by the Council. For the most part, good and holy men if extraordinarily conformist, some few were ferocious in their fury at any breach of the exclusivist agenda of those "Social Issues," ideally qualified to have been Inquisitors in an earlier age of the Church, and twins to the most fundamentalist of the Protestants.

Bishops' Conferences, in the early years after the Council, had become serious bodies for planning to meet the needs of regional churches, as witness the early years of CEPAL. The US bishops, with their meetings twice a year, in Washington each November (later in nearby Baltimore) and elsewhere in the Spring, published superb documents in the early 1980s. Founded right after the Council in 1966 as the joint National Conference of Catholic Bishops (NCCB) and United States Catholic Conference (USCC), it is composed of all active and retired members of the Catholic hierarchy (i.e., diocesan, coadjutor, and auxiliary bishops and the ordinary of the Personal Ordinariate of the Chair of Saint Peter) in the United States and the Territory of the U.S. Virgin Islands. Their *Pastoral Letter on War and Peace* of 3 May 1983,[53] directly challenged the reliance on nuclear deterrence in US policy and had the full, if apprehensive, attention of the Reagan Administration, which went all lengths to influence it and, when that failed, to discredit it.

George Kennan at the time described it as "the most profound and searching inquiry [into nuclear ethics] yet conducted by any responsible collective body." McGeorge Bundy called it a "landmark" and *The Boston Globe* called it "revolutionary." Andrew Greeley went so far as to conclude that the Pastoral Letter "appears to be the most successful intervention to change attitudes ever measured by social science."[54]

---

[53]nuclearfiles.org/menu/key-issues/ethics/issues/religious/us-catholic-bishops-pastoral-letter.htm. Consulted 13 January 2013.
[54]Quotes from Jerry Powers, "Catholic bishops and nuclear policy: the possibilities of a pastoral," *Christianity and Crisis* 49, no. 2 (20 February 1989), 38.

The following year the bishops set to work on social issues, producing by 1986 another major Pastoral Letter, "Economic Justice for All: a Pastoral Letter on Catholic Social Teaching and the U.S, Economy."[55] It carried forward the tradition of social teaching initiated with the *Rerum Novarum* of Leo XIII and pursued by the Church throughout the next century.

After that, the bishops were given to understand, from Rome, that such statements were fine, but it was the business of Rome to issue anything of the sort. The tamed bishops in subsequent years produced mighty documents ordering such things as that the conclusion at the end of a liturgical reading should no longer be "This is the Word of the Lord," but simply "The Word of the Lord."

The main intended engine of collegiality in the Church's governance, the Synod, had been devalued from the start, when Pope Paul VI announced its rules.[56] It was to be an advisory body only, providing more information than advice to the Pope, who would determine the topics for each of its infrequent meeting. It was to decide nothing except in acceptance of papal decrees, and even then subject to the Pope's ratification. In the beginning, the Synod meetings were at least to issue documents summing up their endeavors. However, in the 1974 meeting, the participants could not agree on a synthesis of two divergent drafts about evangelization. They turned the document over to Paul VI, who wrote *Evangelii nuntiandi*,[57] one of his finest efforts, but far later, issued on 8 December 1975. In their failure to reach consensus, the bishops had surrendered what little autonomy the Synods had. They became thenceforth a rubber stamp, submitting the reports to the curial authorities, who would then replace them, always after long delays, with reports of their own. John Paul II himself wrote his *Familiaris consortio*[58] in 1982 as a report on the

---

[55]usccb.org/upload/economic_justice_for_all.pdf. Consulted 13 January 2013.

[56]Cf. above, Chapter 7, p. 2f.

[57]Vatican website, vatican.va/holy_father/paul_vi/apost_exhortations/documents/hf_p-vi_exh_19751208_evangelii-nuntiandi_en.html, Apostolic Exhortation of His Holiness, Pope Paul VI, *Evangelii nuntiandi*, 8 December 1975. Consulted 14 January 2013.

[58]Vatican website, vatican.va/holy_father/john_paul_ii/apost_exhortations/documents/hf_jp-ii_exh_19811122_familiaris-consortio_en.html, Apostolic Exhortation *Familiaris Consortio* of Pope John Paul II to the Episcopate, to the Clergy and to the Faithful of the Whole Catholic Church on the Role of the Christian Family in the Modern World. Consulted 14 January 2013.

1981 Synod on the family, but it was widely observed that he could as well have issued it if the bishops had never met.[59]

Pope John Paul II, the Pope of all those marvelous accomplishments enumerated in this chapter, gave his own reading of the concept of collegiality in his first Encyclical, *Redemptor Hominis* ("Man's Redeemer").[60] He wrote first in praise of Pope Paul VI, acting in "the difficult postconciliar period" when "the church seemed to be shaken from within," affected by "various internal weaknesses." It was in this time "of difficulties and tensions," John Paul wrote, that Vatican II's principle of collegiality "showed itself particularly relevant." For "the shared unanimous position of the college of the bishops, which displayed, chiefly through the synod, its union with Peter's successor, helped to dissipate doubts." Here, then, was the function of collegiality for the new Pope: the bishops act collegially when in chorus they agree with him. He presented as established fact what he intended as his own governing policy.[61] This was to be a top-down Church—ecumenical, friendly to Jews and those of other religions, proponent of human rights and political freedom, but otherwise approximately what the curia of the Council era would have liked to see, the bishops, all obedient recipients of management's directions. Even curial cardinals now would be a long step below a small circle of the Pope's favorites.

Such a spectacle of subservience! The other main principle of the Council's work, the active role of the Church's full membership as People of God, was turned even more in a similar direction. The function of the people was to cheer. Clergy were as much superior to them as the Pope was to them and their bishops. When the further crisis of the sex-abuse tales hit the Church early in 2002, an underline would be drawn under all these assumptions, but that is a tale for another chapter.

---

[59]Website article by John Wilkins, "Bishops or Branch Managers? Collegiality after the Council," *Commonweal*, 12 October 2012.

[60]Vatican website, vatican.va/holy_father/john_paul_ii/encyclicals/documents/hf_jp-ii_enc_04031979_redemptor-hominis_en.html, John Paul II, Supreme Pontiff, Encyclical Letter *Redemptor Hominis*, to his Venerable Brethren in the Episcopate, the Priests, the Religious Families, the Sons and Daughters of the Church and to All People of Good Will, at the Beginning of this Papal Ministry. Consulted 14 January 2013.

[61]*Commonweal*, Wilkins, *op. cit.*

All the time, as this went on, the Pope wandered the earth doing wonders. As a sick old man in his last years he was a model to all the Church of the grace-filled acceptance of suffering and death. One of the last pictures of him is standing shakily at the window of the papal apartment to bestow his blessing on the crowds waiting in the plaza below, yet unable to speak or make any sound. His dying was an inspiration.

We can conclude that he was a most marvelous Pope for the world, but not that much so for the Church. The drastic decline in every measure of Catholic affiliation and practice gives sad witness to that.

11

Sex scandal in the new millennium

Among the too little prized People of God, some of the most precious were children. Little boys often had the privileged experience of being altar boys. (It was only very much later before little girls were also seen as worthy to serve at the altar.) Far more of us were altar boys when I was growing up, a normal part of growing up Catholic, before parents became frightened of ever leaving a child alone in a sacristy with a priest.

Sex abuse of children had been going on for a long time. It is rather hard to determine whether Catholic priests were more inclined to it than others—teachers, sports coaches, fathers of families or who else?—as there are no credible statistics of any of this. Many observers are anxious to believe it started with the sexual-revolution period of the '60s, coinciding therefore with the Council, to the delight of those who would like to blame the Council for everything. But there are cases for the '40s and the '50s, and where are we to find witnesses to what went on before that?

Conventional wisdom is that the sex-abuse scandal in the Catholic Church began with the publication by *The Boston Globe* on the day of the Epiphany, 6 January 2002, of the blockbuster article by Michael Rezendes, backed by the Globe Spotlight Team, reporters Matt Carroll, Sacha Pfeiffer, and editor Walter V. Robinson, headlined "Church allowed abuse by priest for years," on the career of Fr John Geoghan as a serial abuser of children. A second article followed next day, written this time by Sacha Pfeiffer for the same team, "Geoghan preferred preying on poorer children," with a subtitle, "To therapist, priest cited sexual revolution," quoting psychiatrist

Dr Edward Messner of Massachusetts General Hospital, who noted on 30 December 1984, "A priest had admitted abusing minors in the past and has been acting out again recently . . . police and the district attorney are involved. . . . The allegations mirror what has come up before." The case, therefore, was not new on 6 January 2002. A flurry of supplementary articles amplified the bad news, and the grand scandal was out on the table.

The Archdiocese of Boston, in head and members, the Catholic Church in the United States, the Vatican itself went into shock. Despite efforts to explain, nothing would put the toothpaste back in the tube as more and more cases cascaded out into public. Fr Geoghan's astonishing conduct was anything but an isolated instance. Others in Boston, others all over the country would be revealed. Geoghan himself would be tried in civil court, convicted on what was, in fact, slippery evidence, and at last horribly murdered in prison by a fellow inmate.

Due warning had, in fact, been given. A conscientious Dominican priest, Fr Thomas Doyle, O.P., then an official in the Apostolic Nunciatur in Washington, the representation of the Holy See to the United States, with his Doctorate in Canon Law, took up the unpopular issue in 1984, making himself an outspoken advocate for victims of this abuse, building his expertise in the canonical and pastoral dimensions of the problem. What might have been a brilliant diplomatic career in the Church went up in smoke, but Doyle interviewed over 2,000 victims in the United States, gave court testimony as expert witness in over 200 cases, lectured widely, served as an Air Force Major in Germany and in Iraq, earning 16 military awards and decorations for distinguished service, and ranks now as consultant/court expert in clerical abuse cases throughout the United States, Canada, Ireland, Israel, and the United Kingdom. He has been honored repeatedly for his work on behalf of the abused, including, in 2003, by his Dominican order, which commended him for his "prophetic work in drawing attention to clergy sexual abuse and for advocating the rights of victims and abusers."[1]

Reporter Jason Berry surfaced, in two scathing articles for the provincial newspaper, *The Times of Acadiana*,[2] the depredations of

---

[1]Biographical note by Richard Sipe, author of Priests, Celibacy and Sexuality, at richardsipe.com/Doyle/index.html.

[2]*The Times of Acadiana*, "The Tragedy of Philip Gauthe," Part I, 23 May 1985; Part II, 30 May 1985.

Fr Gilbert Gauthe, which went back to 1972, when as a 32-year old new priest he had begun molesting a boy in Broussard and eventually admitted under oath to sexually assaulting 37 youngsters in hundreds of incidents in Southern Louisiana parishes belonging to the Diocese of Lafayette. This eventually cost the diocese many millions of dollars in damages. Berry would become a frequent writer on this theme. The case would achieve some notoriety but failed to produce any national reaction.

On 30 December 1987, Carl Cannon published an article in the *San Jose Mercury News*, "The Church's Secret Child-Abuse Dilemma," citing the Louisiana scandal as one instance during a heightened national awareness of the sexual abuse of children in which the Church still managed to cover its tracks. Catholic parents, he reported, brought charges with little result. He quoted Fr Thomas Doyle as having for 2 years tried to force the U.S. Catholic Conference to address the problem. "The sexual molesting of little boys by priests is the single most serious problem we've had to face in centuries," said Doyle, adding: "I don't say that because of the numbers of priests involved. There are 53,000 priests in this country, and I have concrete knowledge of 200 cases or less. But when people perceive the Church is covering up, condoning and stonewalling, they are doubly scandalized."[3]

A series of three articles in the *Star Tribune* of Minneapolis-St Paul in December 1988, by Bob Ehlert detailed graphically the process of seduction by which Fr Tom Adamson seduced one of several altar boys he held in sexual thrall for a period of years, the concealment, the process of discovery, the reluctance of bishops to recognize, and the ruinous life damage to the child as he grew up.[4] Once again, the revelation stirred some local indignation, but failed to make these episodes a national cause.

Other instances dotted the succeeding years. Santa Barbara was stunned to hear in 1993 that, over the course of at least 23 years, a number of Franciscan Friars, a quarter of the faculty of Saint

---

[3] *San Jose Mercury News*, "The Church's Secret Child-Abuse Dilemma," 30 December 1987.
[4] *Star Tribune*, "Don't Tell Anybody. . . . You'll Get in Trouble, and So Will I," by Bob Ehlert, Part One, 11 December 1988; Part Two, "Lawyer Found Priest Had Abused Other Youths," 12 December 1988; Part Three, "Secrets Finally Become Part of Public Record," 13 December 1988.

Anthony's Seminary, had been systematically abusing dozens of boys, some as young as 7.[5] At no time was the seminary without at least one predator priest. In all, 34 men came forward with charges, but there were no criminal charges, as by the time of the revelation both the Church's 4-year limit on accusations and the state's 6-year statute of limitations had passed. The Franciscans were bracing for a flood of civil suits, of which the first was registered days before the article in the *Santa Barbara News-Press* was published. In 1997, *The Indianapolis Star*, joined by *The Indianapolis News*, published a galaxy of articles analyzing in detail the history of some 16 current and former priests accused of sexual abuse or misconduct over 25 years.[6] The diocese, yet another Diocese of Lafayette, this one in Indiana, forced by the newspaper publicity, admitted to 12 troubled priests and 40 victims over just the previous 12 years. One victim, Ron Voss, had himself become a priest and a priest predator, and had been quietly transferred to Haiti, where he was

---

[5]*Santa Barbara News-Press*, "Shattered Faith: Silence Hid Evil Secret," by Victor Inzunza and Morgan Green, 5 December 1993.

[6]*Indianapolis Star* over several days: 16 February 1997, "Faith Betrayed: The Lafayette Diocese has been home and haven to men of God who shattered lives and walked away," by Linda Graham Caleca and Richard D. Walton; "Trusting Young Victims, All Easy Prey," by Richard D. Walton and Linda Graham Caleca; "Sins of the Fathers," thumbnail sketches of the 16 priests accused; "Chicago Archdiocese Broke the Mold with Open Investigation," by Judith Cebula, describing how Cardinal Joseph Bernardin of Chicago had initiated the process in 1992 after various accusations of sexual misconduct, beginning with himself, who had been accused by a former seminarian that year, his accuser retracting the accusation before his own death of AIDS; "Confessions: A Glimpse into the Minds of Priests Who Preyed," by Linda Graham Caleca and Richard D. Walton; an article "About the Series" and a listing of "Where to Get Help;" 17 February 1997, "The Bishop's Justice," by Linda Graham Caleca and Richard D. Walton, on the highly defensive procedures followed by Bishop William L. Higi and his Vicar General, Rev Robert Sell; "Bishop's Words Reveal Struggle Over Friends Who Abused," about two favorites of Bishop Higi, Msgr Arthur Sego and Rev Ron Voss, whom the bishop was most reluctant to proceed; 18 February 1997, "Abuse of the Collar," by Richard D. Walton and Linda Graham Caleca, about priests who seduced adults; 20 February 1997, "Bishop Will Look to Chicago Archdiocese for Help," by Will Higgins, on Bishop Higi's resentment of the series; 2 March 1997, "Priest Series Stirs Protest, Praise, Calls for Action," by Linda Graham Caleca and Richard D. Walton; "Seminaries Work to Make Celibacy Practical," by Judith Cebula, on the more enlightened ways of teaching celibacy and sexual self-knowledge being introduced at St Meinrad's School of Theology in southern Indiana and elsewhere.

working at the time of the articles. The series had the attention of the Indianapolis area, where some, including the bishop, felt it was quite wicked of the newspapers to write of such things and others praised the papers for raising consciousness of these terrible abuses, one Catholic calling for the bishop's resignation, but the articles made few enough waves elsewhere in the country.

One of the most flagrant cases fell to *The Boston Globe*'s revelation in a series of often daily articles by The Spotlight Team from 1 May 1992 through much of 1993, with Boston radio station WBZ also participating.[7]

Fr. James Porter of the Fall River diocese in Massachusetts, ordained in 1959, had begun molesting children even as he went through the seminary, his first known victim in 1953, just before he entered seminary. Put in charge of altar boys in St Mary's parochial grammar school in North Attleboro, Massachusetts in April 1960, he very soon faced complaints ranging from fondling to rape. No action was taken until 1964, when he was arrested for molesting a 13-year-old boy and sent to a mental institution for 13 months. On release, he was assigned to a different parish, then shuffled to two other parishes as accusation after accusation piled up, until he was again hospitalized in 1967. It was a general belief at that time, among psychiatrists and others, that this derangement was treatable, like alcohol addiction. Released again after a few months, Porter was sent, on a probationary basis, to parishes in other states: Texas, New Mexico, Minnesota, always with access to children. The complaints kept mounting, with no other action taken but to transfer him yet again, until in 1973 he wrote a letter to Pope Paul VI requesting release from the priesthood, admitting his child molestations over all these years and states. The request was granted in 1974. He married, settled in Minnesota, and he and his wife had four children.

In 1990, Frank Fitzpatrick made public accusations that Porter had molested him in the '60s. Over the next 2 years, he contacted state police, the FBI and the media, with the result that more than 200 others came forward and leveled accusations of abuse against Porter. A segment on Diane Sawyer's newsmagazine program, "Primetime

---

[7]*The Boston Globe*'s website, boston.com/globe/spotlight/abuse/extras/porter_archive. htm, gives a list of all the articles, along with a chronology of offender James Porter's priestly career. The articles cover his career with such thoroughness that they are the source for the biographical details that follow.

Live," on ABC-TV in 1992 drew national attention. He was arrested, convicted of abusing his children's baby-sitter in 1984, and served 6 months of a 4-year sentence before his conviction was overturned by the Minnesota Supreme Court. As dozens of law suits accumulated against him in Texas and New Mexico, 200 in Minnesota alone, his lawyer made a plea-bargain and he was sentenced to 18 to 20 years prison.

Boston and especially the Diocese of Fall River were shaken by these events. The Capuchin missionary bishop of St Thomas in the Virgin Islands, Sean O'Malley, was called to take over the Fall River diocese and repair the damage. Working with his chosen lawyer, Tom Hannigan, he proved his solicitude and care for the victims and successfully calmed the situation. This was seen, after all, as a single extreme case of an errant priest, not a general pattern. Yet now the country was alerted. The revelations in *The Boston Globe* of widespread abuse, beginning with the articles of 6 January 2002, 8 years later, then burst upon the public consciousness with enormous impact. The Geoghan case, exposed that day, was only the introduction to a constant drumbeat of new revelations. Rumors flew of patterns of abuse all over the country.

In some panic, the bishops of the United States had their annual summer meeting in Dallas in June. The *Dallas Morning News*, anticipating their arrival, did some rapid research, publishing on the first day of their meeting, 12 June 2002, an article which claimed, on the basis of published reports, court records, interviews, and church records obtained in civil litigation, that two thirds of the American bishops had been covering up the situation, letting accused priests continue working, to the neglect of the safety of children.[8]

The Bishops' Conference (now called the USCCB, U.S. Conference of Catholic Bishops) agreed, at that meeting, on a "Charter for the Protection of Children and Young People," which included among its provisions, a "Zero tolerance policy on abusers: If a credible

---

[8]*The Dallas Morning News*, 12 June 2002, "Special Report: Catholic Bishops and Sex Abuse," by reporters reporters Brooks Egerton and Reese Dunklin. The article, still easily available by internet, (dallasnews.com/cgi-bin/bi/dallas/2002/priests.cgi. Consulted 20 January 2013), included notes on the record of each of 109 bishops whom it accused of this offense, with pictures of most of them, plus reference to a downloadable spreadsheet (available at bishop-accountability.org/resources/resource-files/databases/DallasMorningNewsBishops_status.htm. Consulted 20 January 2013).

accusation is made against a cleric, they are permanently removed from ministry regardless of how long ago the offense occurred."[9]

The provision has incurred some criticism, as it means any priest accused, truly or falsely, is instantly cashiered. For some time, it was assumed that accusations would be basically true, as people had been hesitant for so long ever to bring charges against a priest. With the passing of more time, priests are more vulnerable to accusations that may not be substantiated. Process of investigating these cases take typically many years, and many priests who are eventually cleared of suspicion have been in limbo for life-destroying periods of time.

For bishops, in the meantime, there are no sanctions. Frightful as the sex abuse is in itself, the cover-up by bishops has been even more shocking.

Cardinal Bernard Law, Archbishop of Boston, where the scandal first broke upon the wider public, became a favorite target of opprobrium. As one who saw him familiarly—my brother was his secretary for many years—I was very conscious of the personal toll it took on him, and aware from the start that there was no way he could survive this storm. In the initial *Boston Globe* story of 6 January, he and his five auxiliary bishops were pictured as a kind of rogue's gallery. They too have remained marked men ever since. Television trucks were constantly lined up at his gate. As early as April of 2002, he made a trip to Rome, leaving from another airfield in order not to be seen at Boston's Logan Airport. He offered his resignation but was not permitted to escape his ordeal. Not until December, when some 50 of his own priests had petitioned for him to be removed from office, would the Romans accept his resignation.

Replacing him was a problem. What bishop could take on the burdens of this job? To myself, it was clear from the time of Cardinal Law's resignations that the only possible replacement would be Bishop Sean O'Malley, who had so successfully dealt with the Porter crisis in Fall River, but in the meantime, the Holy See transferred him to the Florida Diocese of Palm Beach, where he faced another catastrophe: his two immediate predecessors as bishop had been sex-abusers themselves. After many months' wait, the Roman officials

---

[9] old.usccb.org/ocyp/charter.shtml, for the basic items of the Charter and links to its many connections.

recognized the inevitable and transferred him again to Boston to face the disaster.

Apart from Cardinal Law, there was no penalty for bishops who had screened the public away from knowledge of the affair and shielded their priests from scrutiny of their crimes. A small proportion of bishops were found over succeeding years, like the two in Palm Beach and another in Springfield, Massachusetts, to have been child abusers themselves, and they had to go. Even the Cardinal Archbishop of Vienna fell into that class and had to be peremptorily removed. Other than for that direct involvement, bishops could not be fired except by the Pope himself. Roman authorities had to fear that, if they once started dismissing bishops, whole hierarchies would go down like a row of dominoes.

Was this out of individual personal malice on the part of these bishops? There is no way the cover-up can be excused, but it was not for individual bishops to decide whether to go along or not. This was high policy, its origin in Rome. Any bishop who let bad news about the Church get out to the public would quickly cease to hold his position. That does not mean the Pope did it. This was a work of bureaucracy, the Roman curial system, much like any other institutional bureaucracy from Enron to the government of the United States. We were all being exposed to a demonstration of the true priorities of Church leadership. Protection of the institution had more importance for them than any talk of care for the People of God.

Defense of the Church has always ranked high among the objectives of the hierarchy, but now we would have some insight into what they understood by the Church: its people as communion of faith or the institution with its ranking and privileged authorities. Such a spectacle could only disappoint and shock the Catholic people. For the many estranged or hostile observers from within or outside the Church, mockery was the only reasonable response.

The world had cooperated willingly with the cover-up. The drunken priest, the vagrant priest, or the priest caught doing the unthinkable with children was brought by police forces to their diocesan authorities who, when necessary, would pay heavy indemnities to keep any process out of the courts. Much as the predator priests would regularly demand secrecy from their victims, the Church authorities who handled the cleaning up after their activities would regularly exact promises of secrecy from the victims as they made their apologies and paid compensation for the crimes.

So extreme was the catastrophic situation that one has to remind oneself that the crisis of confidence in the Church was already long underway and an established fact.

Institutional costs were staggering. The financial cost of settlements with victims would bankrupt several dioceses, some religious orders, many parishes, schools, and other institutions. Seminaries, already starved for candidates, emptied out. Priests were pilloried, suspected of the worst. Many began to dress always in mufti to avoid public insults.

How could all this have happened? Was it that all these priestly gentlemen, sometimes bishops, archbishops, and cardinals, had turned out to be unable to keep their zippers up? That is much too simple-minded an explanation.

Let it be said plainly; the besetting sin within the Catholic establishment is clericalism. The sense of privilege, of being set apart, better than those one dealt with, entitled to deferential treatment and even submission from others has often been inculcated from the start, as part of the seminary training, the expectation built up in priests and practically the air they breathed. It was experienced in the actual life of the priest and so insistently that it had to be consciously and deliberately fought if anyone were to escape it. We have looked at some models of this in the popes we have studied so closely: John XIII, who seems actually to have escaped it, even as Pope; Paul VI, a person of actual humility and all evidence of holiness, who was yet shaped by it; John Paul II, who gloried in it and strove to make it a principal instrument of his influence. We have all known priests who exemplified these varied responses to its nearly inevitable presence. For many, it is a thing to insist upon, a mark of their personal dignity and prerogative of office, any refusal of it an insult to be resented and held against the person who violated the norm. Especially in these troubled times when much of that deference is likely to be refused, it becomes part of priestly formation to expect it, and it is seen as virtue in the layman to concede it unquestioningly.

My own experience as priest in Northern Ireland through the times of upheaval in the 1970s taught me much about this. When I was totally new to the situation and the culture, within the first few days I was among people who were exposed to all the dangers of the conflict, I attended, as guest, a community meeting in which a matter of some small importance had to be decided, whether or not to send representatives to a discussion of "The Troubles." Listening to the proceeding, I had a sense that it was taking much too long to reach a fairly simple decision. It was only after an excessively long time that I realized they were waiting for me, as the one priest present, actually to make the decision for them. I was lucky to tumble to that just shortly before someone turned to me and asked: "What do you think, Father?" That gave me the time to prepare my answer, that it was not a decision for me to make, but for them.

How does a priest resist this, if it is a pattern that repeats itself in all circumstances? The easiest way out is always to give the expected directive: let it be done so! Yet this was not truly a pattern of dependency imposed on the priest, but a pattern imposed on the society by command of the clergy.

That sort of dependence occurs very commonly in deprived societies. In the United States of the nineteenth and early twentieth centuries, Catholic people, immigrants, very poor and without much formal education, had to rely on their clergy as the only educated and accredited persons who could speak for them, and they responded to their clergy with gratitude and utter deference. The Polish church through the Communist period, even more than in the earlier period of domination by the three countries (Russia, Prussia, and Austria) which had divided the territory of Poland among them, relied similarly on their clergy as their only free spokesmen. Once liberated from the Communist regime, the Poles then found themselves obliged to dissolve those dependency ties to their clergy as well. In Ireland, after many centuries of the British hold, the situation was far more extreme, and also resented.

In my own long association with all the parties to the "Troubles" of Northern Ireland, I would discover this and eventually write it up in a 1977 article for the English Jesuit publication, *The Month*, in which I identified it as a principal cause of the conflict between Catholic and Protestant.[10]

The reason for Catholic rebellion in Northern Ireland was evident enough: gross discrimination against the Catholic population by the Protestant (and Unionist) majority. That discrimination showed

---

[10]Raymond G. Helmick, S.J., "Church Structure and Violent in Northern Ireland," *The Month*, August 1977, 273–6.

itself in the areas of employment, in denial of housing and in gerrymandered voting patterns, but the underlying discrimination was in defining the whole Province as *not theirs*, a place where control was to be exercised only by Protestants. It was not so easy to discern what was the grievance of the Protestants that brought them to exercise that sort of domination. My conclusion, after hearing people out for a good 5 years, was that they regarded Catholic Ireland as incapable of living a democratic life.

Democracy was important to Protestants. They regarded themselves as the inventors of such democracy as existed either in Britain or in the United States. They proclaimed their definition of it, first, as "majority rule," but that could not be the meaning of their democracy, as majority rule was the instrument of their domination, and they had even manipulated the borders of the Province to guarantee them that majority. Their true understanding of it went back to Cromwellian times, the seventeenth-century Commonwealth, which had understood the Good Society as one that gave priority to protecting the rights of dissident, nonconformist minorities. The Puritans of the seventeenth-century revolution against the Stuart kings had been that, but Cromwell believed it should apply to all minorities. While his reputation in Ireland has been one of terror because of his putting down rebellion with terrible massacres at Drogheda and elsewhere, in Britain as a whole he attempted to offer the same protection to Catholics as well as all others, frustrated in his efforts by the refusal of Roman authorities to subscribe to the principles of tolerance that he represented.

The Northern Ireland Protestants, however, had a grave problem of conscience, an inner conflict with themselves, because they defined themselves by those Cromwellian principles, but were not willing to extend that protection of their rights to their own dissident, nonconformist minority, who were the Catholics. Scapegoating patterns resulted from this, but the reason they treated Catholics so was fear: that the kinds of clerical domination they saw among Catholics made them incapable of democracy.

For the ordinary Irish Catholic, the worst thing that could happen was a falling out with his/her priest. The Catholic in a "bad" marriage had no place in the community and had better simply leave. Similarly, if a Catholic thought he might build a filling station on a piece of property he owned in the village, but the parish priest didn't want it, or if the priest simply thought a Catholic was not deferential enough to the clergy, that signaled deep trouble. For the public person—doctor, lawyer, teacher, politician—the worst thing that could happen was conflict on any matter with a bishop, or worse, with the bishops. He would receive "a belt of the crozier," and would have lost at once any quarrel he had. That resulted in a kind of politics in the Irish Republic, by both major parties and even by the slim minority of Labor politicians, that was always cravenly conservative, unwilling to risk any possibility of embracing a position that the bishops might disapprove. Even things the bishops might have liked were avoided for fear of that. In the North too, it was taken for granted that Protestant politicians, the only ones who had actual power, would be prejudiced and discriminatory toward Catholics. No Catholic was happy with that, but there was no way to quarrel with it. The Protestant politician, however, who laid unholy hands on one of the issues that were the pillars of the power and privilege position of the Catholic bishops—marriage policy, control of Catholic education, or the provision of caring services such as hospitals—would find that his career had just ended.

Catholics would deny, of course, that they were so clericalized a people, just as the Protestants would deny that they were discriminatory. Defending those denials would provide the occasions of violence between the two communities.

For years I hesitated to write of this, fearing I would only further inflame the passions. Early in 1977, however, I described it to Archbishop Bruno Heims, then Apostolic Delegate of the Holy See to Britain, saying I thought this a matter that the Church should take seriously, and wondering if Church authorities even saw it or had any plan to deal with it. To Archbishop Heims this was a new way of thinking, but he agreed with it and asked me to write a set of notes on our conversation, the first written form it ever took. He sent those notes directly to the Secretariat of State in the Vatican. After some months, authorities there sent word—not in writing but over the telephone from Archbishops Heims—that they too took it very seriously and recommended that I publish something about it, warning me, however, that the Irish bishops would be very angry and suggesting that I speak with four of them before publishing. Those were, of course, bishops with whom I had discussed it already, but I went back to them all the same. The article, when printed by *The Month* in August, opened a deep discussion in Ireland, in which the new Cardinal Archbishop of Armagh, Tomas O Fiaich, Primate of All Ireland, took my point and pressed it with his fellow bishops.

All these years later, when I see the Catholic Church in Ireland so devastated by the sex abuse scandal, I cannot but recognize the same patterns of clerical arrogance and privilege. The crime of rape is essentially not about sex, but about power, an instrument of domination.[11] It is no secret that these sexual abusers of young boys committed to their care or other persons either youthful or weak are the habitual demanders of clerical privilege. Nor is it surprising that many of them rise to actual positions of prominence as bishops or even a Cardinal Primate of Austria, as those extremes of clericalism win approval and are reasons for promotion within a clericalized Church.

From the time the sex scandal broke so definitively on public consciousness with *The Boston Globe*'s publication on the Epiphany Day of 2002, I was convinced that we faced, as a Church, a crisis of Reformation scale, which we could not afford to deal with defensively as we had the Reformation itself without doing once more at least as much damage to the Church by our self-righteousness. It seemed to me that the way the Church deals with major crises is through an Ecumenical Council, and that having had the Second Vatican Council and so grossly ignored its main recommendations, we needed another Council. Others have argued since that, because a corps of such conformist bishops as we see now has been selected worldwide over the long pontificate of John Paul II, a Council could not succeed again in addressing the core problems in the Church's life. I have always argued against that proposition, seeing that it was a similarly conformist episcopate that met in the Vatican in 1962 but was set free to reflect as seriously as it did on the condition of the Church by so great a Pope as John XXIII, it could be done again. The Pope himself would be critical to the task, and at his age and in his condition of health it was clear that Pope John Paul would not be the one. A new election had to intervene, and the electors would need to be very clear about what they were dealing with.

Themes for that Council would need to address directly the clerical culture of the Church and two immediately pressing anomaly situations.

---

[11]Cf. the standard reference on the psychology of rape, A. Nicholas Groth and H. Jean Birnbaum, *Men Who Rape: The Psychology of the Offender* (Cambridge, MA: Da Capo Press, November 2001).

One was the existence among Christians, not Catholics only but as widespread among Protestants as well, of a practically Manichaean concept of human sexuality. Sexuality was seen as the bad thing about people of which they should be ashamed and pretend they didn't have it. The great St Augustine, convert from Manichaeism, had not left that bit behind him. It has no standing at all as Christian teaching but has had a practical hold on Christian imagination. If we begin with that supposition, we should never be surprised by any bizarre results that follow.

The other main theme that a Council should address was its tradition of law. Christianity is not a religion that turns easily to a culture of legalism. St Paul is constant in his warnings that our salvation is not a matter of following precepts of law but of faith, and the later-written Gospel accounts reinforce his teaching. The subtext that runs throughout the Sermon on the Mount[12] is: never be satisfied with fulfilling the precepts of law; always do more. That principle lies behind the rule of life recommended by the sixteenth-century founder of the Jesuits, St Ignatius Loyola, always to do more than anything prescribed. The early Christian Church of the first few centuries strove always to live by that rule, and it cannot be codified. It was only when Constantine, legalizing the practice of Christianity, loaded the Church up with civil responsibilities it had never had before that it found itself in need of a code of order. It then reached for the obvious, Roman Law, with its central principle that the will of the executive is law, and that has remained the basis of Canon Law ever since. Its effect has been that there is no accountability in the Church except upwards, toward the Pope. No superior is accountable to his subjects. This lack of accountability downward shows its effect in the way that bishops, other than those who prove to have been rapists themselves, are subject to no censure (other than from the public). Their habitual covering up of the crime has been more of a shock to the Church than the crime itself.

With that, we have the crisis of confidence in the Church full blown. Clerical sex abuse is less in the headlines now than at the beginning—that story has been told—and we often hear bishops and Vatican officials wondering, hoping, it may all have gone by.

---

[12]Matthew, Chapters 5 through 7.

It has not, nor will it before the fundamental problems have been addressed seriously, and they have not.

Much attention has been given, rightly, to the safety of children, training given to all clergy and Church personnel on how to behave around children, and pledges exacted of correct behavior. One may wonder how much good those pledges are from the actual predators. All this, though, is on the supposition that priests are and will remain a danger to children—and others; in other words, that we should expect there to be something very wrong with them.

At least, it is customary in seminaries now to expect that young men should learn something of their own sexual identities and not remain, as they have long been, discouraged even from attempting such understanding. There is far to go on that front. We have long been familiar, in the recruitment of our Catholic clergy and religious, with the opportunities created for young persons simply to evade or postpone dealing with the issue of their sexuality at all, treating it as something that has nothing to do with them. Surely we know celibates who, even much later in life, have never genuinely faced themselves. This is especially tempting to those with some ambivalence, uncertainty, or fear about their own sexuality. We may try to screen out such persons as candidates, but can expect little success should the screeners themselves still share those attitudes.

Still to be awaited is some attention to the underlying problem of the dangerous clerical culture of privilege and the expectation of deference; more dangerous, in fact, for the upper reaches of clergy and hierarchy, but surely very much a risk for lower-ranking young priests who are still kept in humiliating stages of subordination.

A particular problem, affecting those who are likeliest to rise to higher rank, is the lack of genuine spiritual direction and provision for personal growth among the young *minutanti* who man the Roman bureaucracy. They are put in a situation where their main concerns are career advancement and promotion. Here is the seed-bed of the tyrant churchman, clinging to one rung of a promotion ladder and reaching for the next, wary of all about him, the ultimate fostering of the culture of clericalism.

Clericalism has been the danger of priesthoods other than that of the Catholic Church. In many religious cultures, the central message is that salvation or future well-being, the favor of God, is a function of obedience to the priests. It is submission to them and their power demands, rather than anything seriously to do with faith that is taught. We have had much experience of that through the centuries in the Catholic Church.

Pope John Paul, full of great deeds, giving himself totally in devoted service to the Church, was in his dotage by the time these manifestations of vast trouble in the Church came to full light. He gave us a model of final devotion, bearing up under his many illnesses and remaining at his post. The power of the papacy was exercised effectively by several subordinates. The entire terrifying problem would now be left to a successor.

12

What shall be done?

The crisis facing the Catholic Church has proven so debilitating that we should expect no quick cure. The election, in 2013, of the new Pope Francis, with his radically different style, his proven devotion to the poor, and his deferential way of dealing with the cardinals and others about him as "fellow bishops," has, in fact, filled many of us with a renewed hope Often, during the interval between the popes, we were told how the ills of the Church were too much for one man to change it all, and we should not expect too much from a new Pope, whoever he might be. Yet, a Pope is very important, as we saw with John XXIII, and the transformation we see with Pope Francis is already profound.

We have seen the pontificate of another worthy man of transparent honesty, Pope Benedict XVI, 8 years in which, with regard to the crisis of confidence, nothing changed. At the end of it, as of 28 February 2013, Benedict XVI has resigned his office, choosing not to put the Church through another prolonged period of having an essentially disabled Pope. Instances of papal resignation have been rare in history, the last one nearly 600 years ago, but never before has a Pope laid down his office for this reason, that the ravages of age had left him believing he no longer had the energy to meet his obligations. For that, we should be properly grateful, in this era of longer life spans and disabling diseases of the elderly. It may well be the principal gift to the Church for which he is remembered.

Joseph Aloisius Ratzinger, Cardinal Prefect of the Congregation for the Doctrine of the Faith (CDF), had taken on the daunting task of the papacy on 19 April 2005, elected by the conclave convened after the death of John Paul II. He took the name Benedict XVI. We hear now, as unconfirmable rumor emerging from all the elaborate secrecy of conclaves, that Jorge Mario Bersoglio, now elected to succeed Benedict, had figured prominently in that conclave, and if that were so, he must have wondered often, in the intervening years, what might have been.

In the Council years, Joseph Ratzinger had been counted as one of the liberal theologians. He had been professor of theology at Bonn University, transferring in 1963 to the University of Münster, brought to the Council in 1962 by Cardinal Josef Frings of Köln as his theological consultant (*peritus*). In advance of the Council, Frings had given a path-breaking speech contrasting the needs of the time with those that had obtained at the time of the First Vatican Council. Pope John got hold of the speech and summoned Frings to a meeting. The Cardinal, as he left for Rome, did not know whether the Pope had liked or disliked what he said, and told his secretary, Dr Hubert Luthe, in his *Kölsch* dialect, "*Hängen se m'r doch ens dat ruude Mäntelsche üm, wer weiß ob et nit das letzte Mohl is*," ("Please wrap the little red coat around my shoulders again, who knows if it will not be the last time you do it?" The Pope, however, was delighted with Frings' address, and it heralded a close friendship and long link between them in their thinking. The speech had been drafted by Joseph Ratzinger.[1]

As a theologian, Ratzinger was associated with Hans Küng and Edward Schillebeeckx and, as the Council went on, he cooperated closely with Karl Rahner. At the conclusion of the Council, he took a chair in dogmatic theology at the University of Tübingen, where he was colleague to Hans Küng. His 1968 book, *Introduction to Christianity*, in the year of Paul VI's *Humanae Vitae* decision on birth control, taught that a Pope had the duty to hear differing voices within the Church before making a decision. It was about this time, however, that his own thinking took a rightward turn.[2]

Increasingly disillusioned with the student revolution of the 1960s, which had adopted a Marxist tone over 1967 and 1968, Ratzinger separated himself from the general spirit of Tübingen.[3] Always a most

---

[1]Jared Wicks, "Six texts by Prof. Joseph Ratzinger as *peritus* before and during Vatican Council II," *Gregorianum* 89, no. 2 (2008): 234–5.

[2]Ratzinger himself, however, in an interview given in 1993, when he was Prefect of the Congregation for the Doctrine of the Faith, said: "I see no break in my views as a theologian [over the years]." From Richard N. Ostling, "Keeper of the Straight and Narrow: JOSEPH CARDINAL RATZINGER," *Time Magazine*, 6 December 1993.

[3]Daniel J. Wakin, Richard Bernstein, and Mark Landler, "Turbulance on Campus in the '60s hardened views of future Pope," *The New York Times*, 24 April 2005.

prolific and intelligent theologian, constantly writing, he never ceased to be counted among reformers, but his articles in the reformist theological journal *Continuum*, whose contributors were largely the *periti* of the Council, were of consistently more moderate tone than those of Küng and Schillebeeckx. Transferring to the University of Regensburg in 1969, he founded the rival journal *Communio*, together with Hans Urs von Balthasar, Henri de Lubac and Walter Kaspar, among others. Never illiberal, *Communio* would always represent a more defensive position on traditional teaching. Ratzinger himself, never ceasing to write books and articles, would be a proponent of a number of the most progressive decisions of the Council—the breakthrough about respect for the Jews and other religions, ecumenism, religious liberty— but very little conscious of others—responsibility of all bishops for the universal Church, recognition of the entire faithful membership of the Church as People of God—which had to do with structure and authority in the Church. He would continue contributing frequent articles to *Communio* right up to his election as Pope, and has kept publishing books since.

In 1977, he was made Archbishop of Munich-Freising and quickly raised to a Cardinal. Subsequent complaints have been raised to the effect that, as a bishop, he let his attention be held more by instances of priests whose teaching contained something novel than by cases of sex abuse by priests which came by his office in those days.[4] Those are difficult years to judge, since however much of such behavior was occurring, only a few pioneers were then pursuing these cases.

---

[4]Richard McBrien raised, in an article "Papal resignations" in the 12 April 2010 issue of the National *Catholic Reporter*, the issue of Pope Benedict's actually resigning as Pope over the case of a priest convicted in civil court of sexual abuse, sentenced and fined as a criminal without imprisonment, who was then sent away for therapy and returned to pastoral ministry while Cardinal Ratzinger was Archbishop. His then Vicar General took full responsibility for the decision when it was later raised, saying the future Pope "was too busy with many other administrative responsibilities." That explanation failed to satisfy Hans Küng or the great advocate for the abused, Dominican Father Thomas Doyle. I actually wrote personally to Pope Benedict at the time (26 April 2010), advicing against resignation, as it would be terribly damaging to the Church; that he was "too big to crash," like the grand American corporations which had engulfed their country and the world in financial crisis, but were judged "too big to fail." The Pope could crash, though, other than by resigning if he failed to meet the challenges set before him. And that is the question of this present chapter: Did he address sufficiently the challenge of the present crisis of confidence in the Church?

In 1991, Pope John Paul II called Cardinal Ratzinger to Rome to become Prefect of the CDF, the former "Holy Office," descended from the Roman Inquisition, the Dicastery which, in times of anxiety about possibilities of heretical teaching, becomes the kingpin office of the Roman Curia. It had been that in the time of Cardinal Ottaviani in the years of Pope Pius XII's theological panic during the 1950s. On that basis, Ottaviani had expected and felt entitled to control the Council when it came to town, felt unjustly frustrated when the Council did not bend to his will or cower before him, and celebrated its departure with the recognition that "*gli gente da fuori*" were gone now: "You go home, but we remain."[5] The Holy Office had enjoyed such power in many previous critical times, when it was able to put suspects to the torture and ultimately to "hand them over to the secular arm," for execution by burning at the stake.

The CDF's worries during Cardinal Ratzinger's long period in office, 1981–2005, centered on such topics as birth control, homosexuality, interreligious dialogue and the social teachings of the liberation theologians, basically ethical questions. In the early twentieth-century days of the anti-Modernist campaign, the endangered species among Catholic theologians had been Scripture scholars. Today, it is ethicians or moral theologians.

Liberation Theology had been a particular bug-a-boo to Pope John Paul II, who, along with his strong social conscience, had a made-in-Poland horror for anything that smelt of Marxism. John Paul's inclination was to demand, first, that the socially minded Latin-America priests renounce any idea that a priority concern for the poor meant a license for the use of force against their oppressors, and second that they renounce any reliance on a Marxist analysis of the economy. Granted those two things, he would agree: they were right. Cardinal Ratzinger, in his role as doctrinal enforcer, retained more of a Central European distaste for anything resembling a theology of liberation, which, however, had wide appeal in the Church at large. Franciscan theologian Leonardo Boff, one of the original proponents of the priority option for the poor (along with Gustavo Guttierrez) and a sharp critic of hierarchical cooperation with oppression, was suspended from teaching, first silenced by the CDF in 1985 for a year, for his book *Church: Charism and*

---

[5]Cf. Chapters 9, 2, above, as quoted by Peter Hebblethwaite, *Paul VI: The First Modern Pope* (New York/Marwah: Paulist Press, 1993), 455.

Power.[6] Boff would later accuse Cardinal Ratzinger of "religious terrorism," *terrorismo religiosa*, describing him as a "fundamentalist" and his methods as those of the Inquisition.[7]

Both Pope John Paul and Cardinal Ratzinger professed dedication to interreligious dialogue, but for practitioners it was a rocky path that could bring condemnations and revocations of teaching license. The writings of Indian Father Anthony de Mello, famed Jesuit psychiatrist and spiritual teacher, familiar with many Buddhist and Taoist currents of spirituality, came under posthumous suspicion and had a "notification" placed on them in 1998 for "religious indifferentism," of saying that Jesus was but "one master alongside others," and other positions "incompatible with Catholic faith."[8] This was far from the judgment of others who saw de Mello as a significant teacher of Catholic faith.

Belgian Jesuit Jacques Dupuis, for many years a teacher of theology in India and a student of Hinduism, likewise received a "notification" for his 1997 book *Toward a Christian Theology of Religious Pluralism* (Maryknoll, New York, Orbis Books) which had discussed "the seeds of truth and goodness that exist in other religions," relying on the teaching of Vatican II.[9] After several

---

[6]Harvey Cox, *The silencing of Leonardo Boff: the Vatican and the future of world Christianity* (Indianapolis, IN: Meyer-Stone Books, 1988).

[7]In a November 2001 interview with *Communità Italiana*, available on the internet at comunitaitaliana.com.br/Entrevistas/boff.htm. Consulted 3 February 2013.

[8]Vatican website, vatican.va/roman_curia/congregations/cfaith/documents/rc_con_cfaith_doc_19980624_demello_en.html, Congregation for the Doctrine of the Faith, Notification Concerning the Writings of Father Anthony de Mello, S.J. Consulted 3 February 2013.

[9]The key passage is *Lumen Gentium*, 16: "Finally, those who have not yet received the Gospel are related in various ways to the people of God. (Mk. 1:15; cf. Mt. 4:17) In the first place we must recall the people to whom the testament and the promises were given and from whom Christ was born according to the flesh. (Cf. Rom. 9:4-5) On account of their fathers this people remains most dear to God, for God does not repent of the gifts He makes nor of the calls He issues. (Cf. Rom. 1 l:28-29) But the plan of salvation also includes those who acknowledge the Creator. In the first place amongst these there are the Muslims, who, professing to hold the faith of Abraham, along with us adore the one and merciful God, who on the last day will judge mankind. Nor is God far distant from those who in shadows and images seek the unknown God, for it is He who gives to all men life and breath and all things, (Cf. Acts 17:25-28) and as Saviour wills that all men be saved. (Cf. 1 Tim. 2:4) Those also can attain to salvation who through no fault of their own do not know the Gospel of Christ or His Church, yet sincerely seek God and moved by grace strive by their deeds to do His will as it is known to them through the dictates of conscience. (Mk. 4:14)."

other formulae for the notification were discussed with Dupuis and rejected as misrepresentations, a final formula was chosen: The CDF "found that his book contained notable ambiguities and difficulties on important doctrinal points, which could lead a reader to erroneous or harmful opinions." Dupuis consented to sign this, noting that the same could be said of either the Old Testament or the New Testament.[10]

Always conspicuous to his coworkers in the CDF for his gentleness and kindness, Cardinal Ratzinger had the reputation outside of being "God's Rottweiler," tracking down every whiff of heterodoxy. He has always professed respect for ecumenical dialogue as one of the great fruits of Vatican II. Yet on 6 August 2000, his CDF published the Declaration "*Dominus Iesus*,"[11] asserting of Jesus, almost in the exclusivist language of Leonard Feeney,[12] that "Salvation is found in no one else, for there is no other name under heaven given to men by which we must be saved."[13] Protestants, it declared, did not have churches, but merely "ecclesial communities which are not yet in full communion with the Catholic Church."[14] The ecumenical community, so recently asked by Pope John Paul for its help in his making the Office of Peter a true center of unity in the Church,[15] was shocked.

In the partisan atmosphere of division that had come to characterize the Catholic Church by this time, however, there were

---

[10]William Burroughs, longtime Editor of Orbis Books, who published Dupuis's books, spoke of this in his presentation for the Boston Theological Institute's Costas Consultation, Boston College, 21 March 2013. Cf. William Burroughs, ed., *Jacques Dupuis Faces the Inquisition: Two Essays by Jacques Dupuis on Dominus Iesus and the Roman Investigation of His Work* (Eugene, Oregon: Pickwick Publications, 2013), reviewed by Matthew Ashley, *Commonweal*, 1 June 2013.

[11]Vatican website, vatican.va/roman_curia/congregations/cfaith/documents/rc_con_cfaith_doc_20000806_dominus-iesus_en.html, Congregation for the Doctrine of the Faith, Declaration "Dominus Iesus," on the Unicity and Salvific Universality of Jesus Christ and the Church, 6 August 2000, the Feast of the Transfiguration of the Lord. Consulted 3 February 2013.

[12]Cf. above, Chapter 1, 3.

[13]Dominus Iesus, #13.

[14]Ibid., #16. I received about this time an email from a young Franciscan seminarian friend in Sarajevo asking "what was this terrorist document that had just come out from the Holy See? I responded that I would hesitate to call the document by so extreme a name as "terrorist," but I doubted whether the Lord Jesus would much approve anyone who had attributed to him such a reputation.

[15]Cf. above Chapters 10, 12, on the Encyclical *Ut Unum Sint*.

those who felt that only in such forthright assertion of exclusive right of the Church was true fidelity to the Gospel to be found, while for others this was the substitution of a foreign alternative for true faith in God in Christ. Things stood thus when the venerated Pope John Paul II came so nobly to his death on 2 April 2005.

In his capacity as Prefect of the CDF, Cardinal Ratzinger was responsible for internal Church investigations into accusations made against priests of certain crimes, as defined by the document *Crimen Sollicitationis*, issued by the Holy Office in 1962.[16] The document dealt mainly (70 of its 74 paragraphs) with solicitation during confession, but it would be used to deal with sexual abuse. Paragraph 11 of the document stipulates that such cases are covered by the "secret of the Holy Office," today known as pontifical secrecy, the strictest form of secrecy in Church law. Excommunication was prescribed for anyone who violated this secrecy.

On 18 May 2001, on the eve of the sudden tidal wave of publicity about sexual abuse bursting on the Church, Cardinal Ratzinger wrote a letter, *De delictis gravioribus*, on inquiry into more serious crimes.[17] Envisioned in the document were mostly offenses against faith or the sacraments: many offenses regarding the Eucharist; three concerning the sacrament of Penance: absolving an accomplice in sexual sin, making a sexual advance in, or under the pretense of, confession (the ordinary meaning of "solicitation"), or direct violation of the secrecy of confession. One sin not concerned with faith or a sacrament was included as reserved to the CDF, like the others: the offense of a cleric (a bishop, priest or deacon) who commits a sexual sin with someone under 18 years of age.

This letter had the effect of bringing every instance of sex abuse under the purview of the Prefect of the CDF, and as the scandal and the awareness of this crime escalated, it all landed right on Cardinal Ratzinger's desk.

The document is often accused of prescribing the concealment of the crime and has been used to justify such concealment. It does not

---

[16]Vatican website, vatican.va/resources/resources_crimen-sollicitationis-1962_en.html., Instruction of the Supreme Sacred Congregation of the Holy Office on the Manner of Proceeding in Causes of Solicitation.

[17]Vatican website, vatican.va/roman_curia/congregations/cfaith/documents/rc_con_cfaith_doc_20010518_epistula_graviora%20delicta_lt.html, Congegratio pro Doctrina Fidei, Epistula De Delictis Gravioribus eidem Congegrationi Pro Docrina Fidei Reservatis.

proscribe reporting of such cases to the civil police, nor does it do much to clarify that aspect of the problem. In his own handling of these cases, Ratzinger seems to have been serious as protector of the victims and anxious always to pursue the perpetrators, but he had an obstacle to deal with in the reluctance of many in the upper reaches of the Vatican administration to let the story be told. Ratzinger was especially frustrated by the untouchability of Fr Marcial Maciel, founder in 1941 of a religious movement, the Legion of Christ, the priestly branch of a larger movement, *Regnum Christi*, which acquired the status of a Congregation of Pontifical Right. Its highly conservative character attracted seminarians of that sort in some 22 countries and rich donations from wealthy Catholics who preferred a more conservative Church. Fr Maciel brought about the success of Pope John Paul's first visit to anticlerical Mexico in 1978. He remained a papal favorite, with many visits to the Vatican, and much reluctance to hear anything against him. Cardinal Ratzinger seems to have known that Maciel was a serial and sustained sex abuser, but he was unable to move against him until he became Pope.[18]

As Dean of the College of Cardinals, Cardinal Ratzinger celebrated the funeral Mass for the dead Pope, at which were heard those cries of "*Santo Subito*." As the Conclave opened for the election of a successor, he preached again at a Mass for the assembled Cardinals, warning against what he described as a spirit of doctrinal relativism in the Church.

The election was held under the rules set by Pope Paul VI in 1971 (slightly modified by John Paul II in 1996), according to which only Cardinals under the age of 80 may vote. Of the 183 Cardinals in the April of 2005, only 117 were, thus, eligible. 115 of those were present. Of these, only two had been raised to the office by Pope Paul VI, Cardinal Ratzinger himself and Cardinal William Baum, all the rest by John Paul II, and chosen basically to represent his outlook, including those stringent litmus tests which he used in the

---

[18]This whole painful episode is more than we should try to examine here. Much has been written about it, and accusations have flown about, leading to a wide inquiry by the Vatican, which remains largely perplexed on how to deal with the Legionnaires. A good overview can be found in an article by Elisabetta Povoledo, "Vatican Inquiry Reflects Wider Focus on Legion of Christ," *The New York Times*, 11 May 2012.

selection of bishops. They were predominantly from Europe (58) or the Americas (35), with 11 each from Africa and from Asia and the Middle East, and 2 from Oceania. The obvious candidates from opposite ends of the spectrum were Cardinal Ratzinger, who was taken to represent the most continuity with John Paul, and the strong reformist, Cardinal Carlo Martini, both elderly men, Martini 78 since February, Ratzinger only days short of that age. Either could cast his votes to the other or to some other, but Cardinal Martini had let it be known that, as he was in the early stages of Parkinson's disease, he hesitated to accept the role.[19] Only more recently have we heard, as rumor, that Cardinal Jorge Bergoglio, Archbishop of Buenos Aires and since elected as Pope Francis, also received a significant number of votes.

Early in the afternoon of the second day, the white smoke rose from above the Sistine Chapel, followed by the pealing of bells, and the announcement of Cardinal Ratzinger's election on the fourth ballot. He took the name Benedict XVI.

When, some years later (26 April 2010), I wrote my letter to the Pope, at a time when he seemed under unreasonable pressure, I told him: "I have a strong suspicion that the Cardinals who elected you Pope meant to install the Inquisition in the Chair of Peter, but I have noted with great satisfaction that, as Pope, you have with all deliberation abstained from being that." That letter received a very gracious reply (as with all such letters, through the *Assessore* in the Secretariat of State). Some have felt, in the course of 2012, that the Pope's abstention from the Inquisitor's role has suffered during the investigation visited upon the US nuns, but Pope Benedict had,

---

[19]Martini, a Jesuit Scripture scholar who for some years was a spectacularly successful Archbishop of Milan, attracting disaffected young people in unheard-of numbers to his cathedral, where he would respond to their questions with great openness, had upon his retirement taken up residence in Jerusalem at the Pontifical Biblical Institute, where he was living once more in a Jesuit community. He regularly told the Rector, Fr Tom Fitzpatrick, S.J., that he regarded him as his religious superior. Tom, a bit staggered at the thought that he should be the Cardinal's superior, realized he was responsible for his health among other things. The Cardinal traveled regularly, and when he did, Tom would drive him to the Lod Airport, where El Al would have them wait for his plane in a VIP lounge. As the Cardinal waited there to fly to Rome for the conclave, Tom told him he was about to do something he had never done before, namely, as religious superior, to give him an order under Holy Obedience. The order was: "If you are elected, say yes."

from the start of his pontificate, set it as his standard that he was there to preach faith in Christ, not to pursue miscreants.

What, though, were the needs of the Church, already deeply enmired in what we have been calling a terrible crisis of confidence, when Pope Benedict was elected in 2005? It would have been a deep current of reflection on how we are presenting, as a Church, the Gospel of Jesus Christ, in our teaching and in our conduct in head and members (and in the bureaucratic apparatus, the Curia, by which we are governed), carried out in full coordination with a serious movement of reform. This is what happened when the graced Pope John XXIII called the Second Vatican Council, at a time when the Church was not visibly in such crisis, but Pope John could foresee precisely this sort of crisis forming. As we have been seeing, the principal elements of that reform have met determined resistance from a faction in the Church that has placed its faith on the forms of submission to their own authority rather than on the substance of the Gospel call to faith. That faction has held a controlling influence within the bureaucratic system of the Church.

Possibly those were the gifts that Cardinal Martini would have brought to a papacy. He had great insight, and left a memorable legacy of such reflection to the Church in his last interview before his death,[20] as in his life. A Pope John XXIII, with his personal experience of a life so much in service to the love of Christ, strenuously rescuing so many persecuted Jews of the Holocaust period, and his opportunity, while Nuncio in France, to study in depth the brave recommendations of Yves Congar, is a rare gift of God to the Church.

Pope John XXIII, boldly summoning a Council to consult the Church for the purpose of its *aggiornamento* and *ressourcement*, had the support of heroic bishops, some of them Cardinals such as Leo Suenens of Mechelen-Brussel, Achille Liénart of Lille, Josef Frings of Cologne, for whom Joseph Ratzinger himself had drafted many of his major reformist statements, Bernard Jan Alfrink of

---

[20]ncronline.org/blogs/ncr-today/translated-final-interview-martini, *National Catholic Reporter*, Online, Translated final interview with Martini, John L. Allen, 4 September 2012. Cardinal Martini's view of the Church, first published by *Corriere della Sera*, was so consonant with the outlook represented by this book that I will include a translation of it as an Appendix.

Utrecht, Patriarch Maximos IV Saigh of the Melkite Church, and of course Augustin Bea, who worked so tirelessly for the Declaration on the Jews and other religions. All these had seen the catastrophes of the Nazi tide and had grown into the ecumenical spirit that resulted from the work of Resistance. Where are we to find such men of the Church and the Gospel in the present age of franchise bishops? Yet, the Church of our time had a Martini in it, and surely there must be others hidden somewhere in the mass. The bishops who made up Vatican Council II, with all those giants among them, themselves for the most part knew nothing other than deferential submission to the Curia of their time but learned something different when John XXIII threw open the windows. Teaching in Jamaica at the time the Council ended, I got to know quite well Archbishop John McEleney, S.J., and understood how he had discovered, at the Council, what it meant to be a bishop.

Pope Benedict XVI, a learned and dedicated man, brought as his main gift to the Church a kind of continuity with the pontificate of John Paul II that went before him. He held some of the great decisions of the Second Vatican Council dear, those on the Jews and other non-Christian religions, the breakthroughs in ecumenism, and the great discovery that the Gospel demands liberty of conscience and religious freedom. He has made this clear many times, notably in his speech commemorating the 50th anniversary of the opening of the Council.[21]

Some actions of his have raised questions in exactly these areas. Jews have felt provoked, notably on three occasions: when he restored the old Latin prayers in the Good Friday liturgy, which prayed for their conversion; when he lifted the excommunications from the four bishops of the Society of St Pius X, apparently without realizing that the infamous Bishop Williamson was so unblushingly anti-Semitic; and when he renewed the effort to bring about the canonization of Pope Pius XII. They would probably be comforted if they realized that none of those actions was done with any reference to them, but only as part of a "Restoration" effort within the Catholic Church on behalf of those who wanted to undo the "damage" wrought by Vatican Council II (for some of whom this damage included the new quest for reconciliation with Jews itself). No one was thinking of Jews when those decisions were made.

---

[21] *L'Osservatore Romano*, 19 November 2012, cited above.

Muslims too took offense at an academic address Pope Benedict gave at his old University of Regensburg on 12 September 2006, which opened with a quotation, attributed to one of the last Christian Emperors of Constantinople, Manuel II Palaiologos, speaking in 1391, before the Ottoman conquest of the city, which associated Islam with forced conversion and holy war. The Emperor had asked: "Show me just what Muhammad brought that was new and there you will find things only evil and inhuman, such as his command to spread by the sword the faith he preached." The Pope simply quoted this without comment as the opening of an address on faith and reason. Mass street demonstrations in protest took place in many Islamic cities, and the Pakistani Parliament unanimously called for the Pope to retract "this objectionable statement,"[22] The ultimate Muslim response, however, was the extraordinary statement, an invitation to dialogue, issued by 138 prominent Islamic scholars, addressed to Christians and to the Pope in particular, the following year on 13 October 2007. The document quoted in parallel the many places in the New Testament and the Qur'an which set the identical standards of love of God and love of neighbor as criterion for both religions.[23]

Protestants too take umbrage at the *Dominus Iesus* statement of 2000, issued while Cardinal Ratzinger was still Prefect of the CDF, which denied them the status of churches and reduced them to "ecclesial communities not yet in full communion with the Catholic Church."[24]

Nonetheless, Pope Benedict should be credited with treasuring these outcomes of the Second Vatican Council, which, he says, were regarded as side issues in "minor documents" at the time but now stand out as the important ways the Council put the Church in true contact with the Modern World in which it lives.[25] What he has not credited are those two main transformative benchmarks of the Council's teaching, collegiality and recognition of the Church as the

---

[22]*The Telegraph*, 16 September 2006, Melanie McDonagh, "The Pope's message of greater dialogue achieves the opposite."
[23]This important statement is now the subject of a website, acommonword.com/, which gives the original text and a compilation of the many Christian responses that have been made to it.
[24]See above, n. 3.
[25]Where is my earlier reference in this book to the 50th anniversary celebrations?

People of God, the very things the neglect and practical abrogation of which, in this author's view, are the substantial cause of the crisis in confidence which the Church now so drastically suffers. The Pope saw these, and the "Schema XIII" which grew into the great Pastoral Constitution on the Church in the Modern World, *Gaudium et Spes*, as not really having achieved their purpose of relating the Church to the modern world. That they have been brought, thus far in our history, to failure we can only agree.

The Pope placed great value, too, on the liturgy and sacraments as the font of Catholic life,[26] yet it becomes increasingly clear that the liturgy he most favored is the one the Second Vatican Council set out to reform. His restoration to use of the Latin liturgy of Pope John XXIII's very lightly reformed preconciliar Missal of 1962, generally known as the "Tridentine Mass," has been the index to that preference. The "reform" he either instigated or permitted in more recent years to the earlier reform of the '60s and '70s, demanding in vernacular translations the most rigorous conformity with the Latin text, has had the malign effect of making the liturgy of the Eucharist once again remote and unintelligible to the ordinary person, encased in an artificial language that relates rather to its Latin cognates than to the language people actually speak. As one of the actual translators of the English version that was approved for use in 1972, I have a particular awareness of the principle we all then understood: that to address God in a language that is either archaic or artificial is to say, in effect, that He is not real.[27] We have

---

[26]We have taught our people too long to think of the Sunday Mass as a matter of fulfilling an obligation, simply to be there in obedience to a "law of the Church." The idea that the Eucharist is the thing people actually live by, the enactment of the faith that is the shaping of their lives, is far from the catechesis they receive. This places the action altogether in the realm of obedience to ecclesiastical authority, not a direct relation to the living of our faith. The Sunday obligation is, thus, reduced to something far less than "the primary and indispensable source from which the faithful are to derive the true Christian spirit (*Sacrosanctum Concilium*, #14)."

[27]Raymond G. Helmick, "'Opaque and Clumsy,' English translation of the Missal," *The Tablet*, 30 October 2010. See also John Wilkins, "Lost in Translation: The Bishops, The Vatican and the English Liturgy," *Commonweal*, 2 December 2005; Philip Endean, "Worship and Power," *The Tablet*, 28 August 2010, on the top-down procedure which produced the new translations; Paul Philibert, "For you and who else?" *America*, 3 January 2011; Philip Endean, "Sense and Sensibilities: New Missal Translation," *The Tablet*, 19 February 2011; Anthony Ruff, OSB, "Liturgy Under Benedict XVI" (GIA Quarterly, Vol. 22, No. 1 (2010)), judging the new translation and the procedure of its

to fear that, with an unintelligible liturgy, we will lose more people than we have already.[28]

Pope John Paul II throughout his pontificate, by reason of his immensely charismatic personality, affected the Church volcanically, molding it to his understanding of its nature. Pope Benedict has commanded great respect, but he is no such personality. The continuity he offered, for which he was elected, was to hold the line with the John Paul model of a massively centralized hierarchical Church. Given the crisis of confidence we have been studying, already manifest as John Paul was still Pope, that would not seem to be what the Church has most needed at this time. Whether Pope Benedict was able to sustain

---

implementation by the norms of the 1963 Constitution on the Liturgy, *Sacrosanctum Concilium*; Anthony Ruff, "An Open Letter to the U.S. Bishops on the Forthcoming Missal," *America*, 14 February 2011: the Chairman of the music committee of the International Commission on English in the Liturgy (ICEL) withdrawing all cooperation with the project of the new translations; Robert Mickens, "Unlocking the door of the vernacular," *The Tablet*, 18 June 2011; Robert Mickens, "How Rome moved the goal posts," 25 June 2011; Robert Mickens, "A war of words," *The Tablet*, 2 July 2011; John R. Donohue, "Cup or Chalice? The Large Implications of a Small Change," *Commonweal*, 1 June 2012; Fr Nonomen (sic), "Up against the Wall: The Liturgical Wars Heat Up," *Commonweal*, 15 July 2011; Rita Ferrone, "It Doesn't Sing: The Trouble with the New Roman Missal," *Commonweal*, 15 July 2011.

[28]John Baldovin, in his article, "An Active Presence: The liturgical vision of Vatican II 50 years later" (*America magazine*, 27 May 2013), discusses Pope Benedict's championship of "the reform of the reform" encouraging both a return to the practice of the priest turning his back to the people and a revival of the pre-Vatican-II Latin liturgy. One could see this as simply accommodating that minority in the Church who yearned for the old form, seemingly a growing trend, with some seminaries actively training future priests to celebrate the older rite and some groups actively encouraging its spread. "It is very difficult," he comments, "not to regard this development as somewhat divisive," acknowledging that some of the dissidence arises from shoddy implementation of the original liturgical reform, external reform that was not accompanied by an interior renewal. Nonetheless, he continues: "On the other hand, the older liturgy is clearly symbolic of a vision of church, theology and the world that the Second Vatican Council consciously moved away from in some very important ways. It is not for nothing that the most recalcitrant followers of Archbishop Marcel Lefebvre, founder of the St Pius X Society, join their love of the Latin liturgy to a profound suspicion, if not denial, of the council's declaration on religious freedom and its general mood of welcoming conversation with the modern world. In other words, opting for the older liturgy often bespeaks a rejection of Vatican II and all that the council brought with it. As Massimo Faggioli has convincingly pointed out, to reject the liturgy that resulted from the Vatican II constitution is to reject the council itself."

it in that condition to the end of his reign without further decimation was always the question.

The new Pope, taking the name of the great Saint Francis, servant of the poor, living as poor as they, the man who risked his life willingly to bring the message of Christ's peace even directly to the Sultan of Egypt, the first time any Pope has taken to himself this so revered a name, awakens hope in many of us for genuine restoration in our Church.

His first appearance, Jorge Mario Bergoglio of Argentina, the stark white figure on the balcony blinking into the klieg lights without any of the gold, scarlet and ermine we are accustomed to, announced something quite different. His opening "*Buona sera*," refusing the elaborate papal stole for the blessing until he had first asked the blessing of the 150,000 people before him, and all we heard subsequently of his sharing his elevator with his cardinal companions, returning to the electors' quarters in the Santa Marta with them on the bus, refusing the papal limousine, his greeting Mass-goers out in the street, his announcing that he would celebrate the Holy Thursday liturgy in the prison, all went to confirm that man-of-the-people image.

No sooner was his election announced than we heard charges that, as Jesuit Provincial in the time of Argentina's Dirty War, (1976 to 1983) he had betrayed Jesuits working with the poor in a slum into kidnap and torture by the regime. The accusation disintegrated as we learned that it was the targeted assault of a single journalist, Horacio Verbitsky, who had circulated it before, in 2005, and had now returned to the attack after his charges were long dismissed through heavy judicial review.[29] That, as Cardinal-Archbishop, he had lived in a small slum apartment, traveling to his office by bus or subway, open to talk to anyone who approached him, revealed him as himself living much as had those two Jesuit victims of the junta.

---

[29]I found I had to take the Verbitsky charges seriously enough to refer them at once to my own students and subject them to close analysis. My friend Jerome Maryon, a distinguished lawyer who regularly helped with my classes, prepared a very exact dossier on the Verbitsky attack which I include at the end of this volume as Appendix II. Verbitsky, a consistent human rights defender in the Argentinian press, is a professed atheist who is convinced that the Catholic Church is the ultimate enemy of those rights. He had an easy target in the great majority of the Argentinian hierarchy, who were, in fact, so closely attached to the military junta.

How, as Pope, Francis will respond to the series of issues which interest reform advocates in the Church, responses surely to be built on his own Latin American cultural background rather than European or North American perceptions, we have yet to see. On the two central marks of the Vatican II reforms to which we have kept returning throughout this book, collegiality and recognition of the Church as consisting of the entire People of God, the things the Church's leadership since the Council has so repudiated, his actions as Archbishop and Cardinal give good promise. On the basis of what we have seen so far, we can pronounce him innocent of the besetting ecclesiastical sin of clericalism.

When Angelo Roncalli emerged from the conclave of 1958 as Pope, neither we nor the cardinal electors had any idea what to expect of him. That he would be transformative, recalling the Church, through his twin insistences on *aggiornamento* and *ressourcement*, to its deepest root convictions, the most basic Gospel values, as the way to bring her into the world of twentieth-century reality, was beyond anyone's expectations. We should not expect to duplicate what happened then, but we find ourselves with a man of deep humility, calling the whole Church leadership, as his brother bishops, to share his commitment to the needs of the poor and the suffering.

We end, then, with a question: Have we a man who understands the needs of the Church? We had to recognize precisely that question when the sex abuse scandal first scarred everyone's impression of the Church. It was clear then that John Paul II, already burdened with advanced Parkinson's disease, would not make the moves that it would take to address the deep problems of the Church. Pope Benedict's health held up well for most of the 8 years of his pontificate, but his age and his established habits always argued against expecting real innovation or reform. Chosen for continuity, he faithfully provided what he was elected for. Pope Francis' age of 76 might be expected to limit his effectiveness too, but the same might have been said of John XXIII himself.

Will the administrators he appoints understand any better than the current scandal-tainted Curia the situation they are living in? The most intolerable symptom we find in the Church is the inclination to believe that all the trouble is merely the machinations of enemies, people who would like to see the destruction of the Church, rather than the despairing cry of people who love the

Church but have been profoundly scandalized and disappointed. In 2010, when a hue and cry arose for the resignation of the Pope, his Secretary of State, Cardinal Bertone, and the preceding Secretary of State, Cardinal Sodano, both loudly proclaimed that thesis. It is a favorite claim from bishops and in rectories. Benedict himself was innocent of that dodge, but those around him had their own opinions.

In the conclave of 2005, the choice of the Cardinals was to stand pat. Of Pope Benedict XVI, devoted servant of the Church, one may judge that he did no further harm, even if things continued to deteriorate around him, but that he came to represent stasis, no change in its manner of operation.

Cardinal Martini visited us at Boston College in 1998 while he was still Archbishop of Milan and 4 years before the full drama of the sex abuse crisis broke upon us.[30] He had traveled widely in Europe, he said, taking the pulse of bishops on how they viewed the already drastic shortage of priests and what solution they would look for. This, along with the disappearance of lay Catholics from the pews, provided the index to the gathering crisis of confidence in the Church.

We were then deep in the age of those litmus tests for the election of bishops, among which the refusal to accept the ordination of married men was prominent. Martini found, though, that the bishops were generally quite clear that they needed to make a breakthrough by ordaining some "*viri probati*," men who had shown themselves solidly committed and responsible in their marriages. That, of course, was before the enormous fright bishops were given when sexual abuse became the instant theme when people spoke of the Catholic Church.

On the most central of the litmus test issues, the *Humanae Vitae* decision of 1968, bishops throughout the Church had sensed, at the time, a grievous violation of the collegiality they had decided on at the Council. For the lay members who make up the bulk of the People of God that is the Church, this clerical decision was a back-breaker, an initial reason for the break of so many of them with Catholic practice.

---

[30]Mark Sullivan, "Cardinal Says Faith rows with Questions," *Boston College Chronicle*, 12 March 1998.

We do find ourselves now scrutinizing the past positions of Cardinal Bergoglio, especially over the period when he headed the Council of Bishops in Argentina, to see whether, on this and other of the litmus-test questions, the new Pope has shown himself, in the past, at least open to reflection. It would be unfair, though, to make these questions a prior test of the new Pope, from whom we should instead most earnestly expect a fundamental respect for the role of other bishops and of the Church as a whole, the things Pope John tested by calling Vatican Council II.

John XXIII, seeing the Church in perilous dissonance over much of its history from the Gospel it professed, had learned from the thinking of Yves Congar the lessons that reform of the Church must come from within, from those who love it, who see it as the means to reveal to the world the presence within it of God in Christ; that it cannot be something done *to* the Church, even by its Pope, but must be done *in* the Church by its entire membership, the Body of Christ. The task of leadership, he understood, was to free the Church of all that would prevent it from undertaking that task.

APPENDIX

The final interview with Cardinal Carlo Martini

Cardinal Carlo Maria Martini died in Varese, northern Italy, on 31 August at the age of 85. Two weeks earlier, on 8 August, Martini gave a final interview to his fellow Jesuit Fr George Sporschill, with whom Martini had collaborated on a book titled Nocturnal Conversations in Jerusalem, *and an Italian friend named Federica Radice Fossati Confalonieri. Radice has told Italian media outlets that Martini read and approved the text of the interview, intending it as a sort of "spiritual testament" to be published after his death.*

The following is a National Catholic Reporter *translation, by John L. Allen, Jr, published 4 September 2012, of the interview published in Italian by the newspaper* Corriere della Sera. *Reproduced with permissions.*

How do you see the situation of the Church?

The Church is tired, in the Europe of well-being and in America. Our culture has become old, our churches and our religious houses are big and empty, the bureaucratic apparatus of the church grows, our rites and our dress are pompous. Do these things, however, express what we are today? . . . Well-being weighs on us. We find ourselves like the rich young man who went away sad when Jesus called him to be his disciple. I know that we can't let everything go easily. At least, however, we can seek people who are free and closest to their neighbor, like Archbishop Romero and the Jesuit martyrs of El Salvador. Where are the heroes among us who can inspire us? By no means do we have to limit them by the boundaries of the institution.

Who can help the Church today?

Father Karl Rahner often used the image of the embers hidden under the ash. I see in the Church today so much ash under the embers that often I'm hit with a sense of impotence. How can we liberate the embers from the ash, to reinvigorate the fires of love? For the first thing, we have to seek out these embers. Where are the individuals full of generosity, like the Good Samaritan? Who have faith like the Roman centurion? Who are enthusiastic like John the Baptist? Who dare the new, like Paul? Who are faithful like Mary Magdalene? I advice the Pope and the bishops to seek out 12 people outside the lines for administrative positions, people who are close to the poorest, who are surrounded by young people, and who try new things. We need to be with people who burn in such a way that the Spirit can spread itself everywhere.

What tools do you recommend against the exhaustion of the Church?

I recommend three very strong ones. The first is conversion: the Church must recognize its errors and follow a radical path of change, beginning with the pope and the bishops. The pedophilia scandals compel us to take up a path of conversion. Questions about sexuality, and all the themes involving the body, are an example. These are important to everyone, sometimes perhaps too important. We have to ask ourselves if people still listen to the advice of the Church on sexual matters. Is the Church still an authoritative reference in this field, or simply a caricature in the media?

The second is the Word of God. Vatican II gave the Bible back to Catholics. Only those who perceive this Word in their heart can be part of those who will help achieve renewal of the Church, and who will know how to respond to personal questions with the right choice. The Word of God is simple, and seeks out as its companion a heart that listens. . . . Neither the clergy nor ecclesiastical law can substitute for the inner life of the human person. All the external rules, the laws, the dogmas, are there to clarify this internal voice and for the discernment of spirits.

Who are the sacraments for? These are the third tool of healing. The sacraments are not an instrument of discipline, but a help for people in their journey and in the weaknesses of their life. Are we carrying the sacraments to the people who need new strength? I think of all the divorced and remarried couples, to extended families. They need special protection. The Church upholds the indissolubility of matrimony. It's a grace when a marriage and a family succeed . . .

The attitude we hold toward extended families determines the ability of the Church to be close to their children. A woman, for instance, is abandoned by her husband and finds a new companion, who takes care of her and her three children. This second love succeeds. If this family is discriminated against, not only is the mother cut out [from the Church] but also her children. If the parents feel like they're outside the Church, and don't feel its support, the Church will lose the future generation.

Before communion, we pray: "Lord, I am not worthy . . ." We know we're not worthy. . . . Love is a grace. Love is a gift. The question of whether the divorced can receive communion ought to be turned around. How can the Church reach people who have complicated family situations, bringing them help with the power of the sacraments?

What do you do personally?

The Church is 200 years behind the times. Why doesn't it stir? Are we afraid? Is it fear rather than courage? In any event, the faith is the foundation of the Church. Faith, trust, courage. I'm old and sick, and I depend on the help of others. Good people around me make me feel their love. This love is stronger than the sentiment of distrust that I feel every now and then with regard to the Church in Europe. Only love defeats exhaustion. God is love. Now I have a question for you: What can you do for the Church?

ABBREVIATIONS

AS
Acta Synodalia Sacrosancti Concilii Vaticani II.
32 volumes, Vatican City: Typis Polyglottis Vaticanis,
1970–1999.

AAS
Acta Apostolicae Sedis: Commentarium officiale,
Vatican City: Typis Polygottis Vaticanis, 1909–.

ADP
*Acta et Documenta Concilio oecumenico Vaticano
II Apparando. Series secunda (Praeparatioria).* 7
volumes, Vatican City: Typis Polyglottois Vaticanis,
1964–1969.

Caprile,
Cronache
Giovanni Caprile, ed., *Il Concilio Vaticano II: Cronache
del Concilio Vaticano II.* 5 volumes in 6, Rome:
Edizioni "La Civiltà Cattolica", 1966–1969.

INDEX